Organization Theory and Project Management

Administering
Uncertainty in
Norwegian
Offshore Oil

Organization Theory and Project Management

Administering
Uncertainty in
Norwegian
Offshore Oil

Arthur L. Stinchcombe
and
Carol A. Heimer

Norwegian
University Press

Norwegian University Press (Universitetsforlaget AS), 0608 Oslo 6
Distributed world-wide excluding Scandinavia by
Oxford University Press, Walton Street, Oxford OX2 6DP

London New York Toronto
Delhi Bombay Calcutta Madras Karachi
Kuala Lumpur Singapore Hong Kong Tokyo
Nairobi Dar es Salaam Cape Town
Melbourne Auckland

and associated companies in
Beirut Berlin Ibadan Mexico City Nicosia

The book is published in cooperation with Industriøkonomisk Institutt/Institute of
Industrial Economics, Bergen, Norway.

ISBN 82-00-07600-8

Printed in Norway
by Reklametrykk Grafisk A/S

CONTENTS

PREFACE

Since it began in the early seventies, Norwegian petroleum production has risen considerably. And despite its youth, it has for several years played an important role in the Norwegian economy, currently accounting for almost 20 percent of gross domestic product, 20 percent of government revenues, and 40 percent of total exports. In fact, for the last fifteen years the petroleum economy has compensated for the effects of the recession in traditional Norwegian export industries.

The growing importance of petroleum production to the Norwegian economy is partly due to increases in the real price of oil and natural gas during this period, though these have fallen recently. But substantial investment has also made it possible to steadily increase the volume of Norwegian production. This investment, currently amounting to some 3–4 billion US dollars per year, consists mainly of the construction and installation of platforms for offshore petroleum production, pipeline systems, landing plants, and the like. In other words, offshore petroleum investment involves a series of large, complex and challenging projects.

In order to carry these projects through, a whole range of important and challenging tasks have to be mastered. This is not only a question of new technical challenges for engineers, but of how to create practical arrangements to deal with these complex tasks in an efficient manner.

In the late Seventies after the completion of several large scale petroleum production projects, the question of how to manage these tasks gained a lot of public attention in Norway. This was mainly due to delays and to significant discrepancies between budgeted and actual costs. In response the government appointed an expert group (the Moe Committee) with a mandate to look into the costs of developing North Sea petroleum fields.

This committee completed its work in 1980. In its report organizational questions were identified as important factors in delays and cost overruns. The report raised questions about coordinating jobs carried on at different sites and by different contractors and about the incentive implications of various contractual arrangements for the operators, owners, engineering companies, and construction crews.

Organizational challenges of this kind were by no means new. The international oil companies had been engaged in large petroleum development projects for many years. Similar organizational challenges had been faced by companies involved in constructing nuclear plants, hydroelectric power plants, steel plants, large chemical plants, oil tankers, and the like. And since such projects had been carried out in Norway, there were people and organizations with experience on large scale projects in construction companies and shipyards.

Nevertheless, the program of investment on the Norwegian continental shelf led to increasing attention to administrative and organizational arrangements. One question was how several organizations, with different cultures, experiences, and career systems, could be united in a common administrative arrangement to carry out a project. A second was how to facilitate the interaction, communication, and cooperation between people with different professional backgrounds. In looking for answers to these questions, such concepts as "coordination" and "motivation" were repeatedly mentioned. In short, a whole series of questions about how to organize relations between the temporally, spatially, and organizationally separate but interdependent parts of a project, were put on the public agenda as well as on the agenda for scientific work.

By that time the Institute of Industrial Economics had already undertaken several projects on offshore petroleum activities. In the beginning, the main concern was the industrial impact of petroleum investment, with special interest in regional impacts. But soon questions about the organization and governance of the petroleum business were added to the program of the Institute.

This expansion of the research program at the Institute coincided with Arthur Stinchcombe's first visit to Norway. And, as he happened to be located in Bergen, he was asked to conduct a project at the Institute. He accepted, and his report from this work, "Delays and Project Administration in the North Sea" (see Chapter 1 of this book), was published in 1979. This work introduced our cooperation, which not only continued, but was also extended when Carol Heimer, fortunately, was willing to join it.

During the last couple of years, research on the different aspects of offshore petroleum activites has been organized in one unit at the Institute of Industrial Economics. Eight researchers are currently engaged on a permanent basis to work on different but substantively related projects in this field. The common theme in their research is the internal and external governance of the petroleum sector, with special attention to the interplay between economic and organizational aspects, between micro and macro, between local and national. More concretely, these questions are analyzed by looking at the way government bodies, oil companies, suppliers, and companies in other industries make their strategic choices and organize their business, as well as by studying how the relationships between these parties are arranged.

The fundamental ideas behind these projects are being developed in a research program titled "Industrial Impacts of Offshore Petroleum Activities", scheduled to last through the Eighties. Basically we want to explore the nature and development of PetroNorway. In other words, we will try to elucidate the economic and political processes taking place in a small open economy with a single dominant economic sector.

This work currently involves studies in five empirical areas:

– The first more or less captures the core of the Norwegian petroleum economy by investigating decision making processes and power relations within the domestic petroleum sector.

- The second covers the strategies of companies and public authorities in the market generated by the petroleum activities' demand on domestic industries.
- The third covers the indirect industrial impacts transmitted to the national economy through the huge petroleum revenues earned in foreign currencies.
- The fourth focuses on public growth policies – how they are formulated and implemented, and how firms adapt to such governmental attempts to stimulate the national business life. It is our opinion that studies in this area should pay attention to the fact that the Norwegian economy and social welfare have become increasingly vulnerable with the rising importance of petroleum production. Thus our research here is intended to broaden and strengthen the international competitiveness of Norwegian industries.
- And finally, the fifth deals with the institutional setting and current trends of international oil and natural gas markets. While these markets have extremely important effects on economic and political processes in PetroNorway, they are not really subject to Norwegian control.

In this work we must pay special attention to two types of relations that hold a central position in the social sciences. These are:

- micro-macro relations. For instance we must pay attention to the aggregate effects of decisions made at the micro level, such as the supply capacity in a market, or changes in national economic variables caused by deciding whether or not to develop a petroleum field. But macro causes also have micro effects, and we can see companies adjusting to changing macro condition. And
- governing principles that are put to work in relations between institutions operating according to different decision making criteria. We can see such governing principles in interactions between public bodies and private companies.

Obviously this research has to draw on different schools and disciplines within the social sciences. Thus in our empirical work, we make use of sociology, organizational theory, economics, business administration, and public policy analysis. We hope that this orientation to the social sciences will help us to formulate our applied research questions in such a way that we will be able to shed light on issues of general theoretical interest. In particular, our aspiration is to use Norwegian petroleum activities as a case where we can develop and test more general theories about how the mixed economies of small capitalist countries function.

The work of Arthur Stinchcombe and Carol Heimer, presented in this book, plays a crucial role in this program. And though most of these papers are empirically grounded in Norwegian offshore petroleum activities, we think they quite nicely illustrate our policy of conducting applied research which also has a scientific purpose and adds to our shared theoretical knowledge. But in addition these essays are problem oriented in a way that strengthens the reputation of social science as able to advise and make recommendations to those grappling with complex decisions about administrative and economic policy.

Beyond doubt, this work is fully in accordance with the goals of the Institute of Industrial Economics, as formulated in the Institute rules. These rules specify that the Institute be a problem-oriented research institute dealing with issues of current interest on the border between basic and applied research.

We are grateful to Arthur Stinchcombe and Carol Heimer for the work they have accomplished at our Institute. Nevertheless (and fortunately for us as social scientists), the field of organization theory and project administration still contains a series of questions that need to be studied in more detail, and more questions will certainly be generated. The empirical work on these matters could well be undertaken in Norway. Thus we hope to continue our cooperation with Arthur Stinchcombe and Carol Heimer. Most likely we will have privilege of hosting them again as early as the spring of 1986.

Bergen, August 1985

Ole Berrefjord and Per Heum

INTRODUCTION

The overall thrust of the studies in this book is that often the most important part of administration deals with uncertainty and its reduction, that in many cases, especially in project administration, such uncertainty reduction requires the cooperation of a number of organizations, and finally that such uncertainty reduction is never merely a technical and economic matter, but is instead a matter of how social arrangements shape the flow of information, authority, and risk bearing within and among organizations. These observations are not new, of course; they have been the core of many of the contributions of the Simon-March fashion of analyzing organizations. Instead the contribution of this book is to study these matters at a research site in which the inherent uncertainties are extreme. Here almost every important matter is dealt with by a number of organizations held together by contracts, and the social arrangements for resolving the uncertainty are just being created because the business we are studying is new in the social setting where we studied it. Consequently the sociologically humdrum observations that one only needs management when there is uncertainty to be resolved, that contracts among organizations allocate risks among them, and that there is a precontractual setting that shapes such contracts, are highlighted because they are the main thing going on.

We started these studies at a time when basic theoretical work on the sociology of administration of the oil business in Norway could be considered "applied" work. When everyone knows what they are doing because they have all done it before, presenting a coherent picture of what is mainly going on in the structure as a whole is not usually considered applied; it does not help people do their job. Many of the people in the oil business in Norway have to form political opinions or administrative policies, decide on their career plans, and the like, but do not have an overall picture. One can present general work which tells them what they are doing and where their troubles are coming from, and have the applied function of providing many people with a language for talking about it. At least that is what we believed, and it was an idea convincing (or if not convincing an acceptable hypothesis) to our employer, the Institute of Industrial Economics in Bergen, Norway. The purposes of the Institute of Industrial Economics in supporting our work are suggested in the Preface above by Ole Berrefjord and Per Heum.

But when we set this work in the larger intellectual picture that we were working on simultaneously (especially Heimer's book *Reactive Risk and Rational Action* (1985) on moral hazard in different lines of insurance and Stinchcombe's work partially represented in Chapter 2 below and his ongoing research into interorganizational relations in computer and software industries), it seemed to us that the phenomena we observed in the North Sea, and the ideas that were useful in understanding them, were of more general significance. We believe that these studies, heterogeneous as they are in subject matter and approach and tied as they are to empirical material that is a lot more interesting to Norwegians than to other people, constitute a sort of theoretical monograph on uncertainty in management and its relation to the social structures of industry. This Introduction then outlines the argument that unifies our studies. The economic and technical uncertainties dealt with by formal organizations shape the sociology of political life, managerial life, and work life on large scale capital projects. We hope our observations will be useful in analyzing situations similar to that in the North Sea.

The first essay, "Project Administration in the North Sea," gives a general introduction to the system by which large scale construction projects are managed in the Norwegian North Sea. In the course of this discussion, it introduces a number of important theoretical ideas for looking at the administration of projects, which help us understand what is distinctive of this sort of administration. In particular, one distinctive feature of the technical job to be done, that one starts off with almost complete technical uncertainty about what ought to be done (and certainly cannot do what one did yesterday even if that made money then), sets the parameters of the rest of the administrative process.

In resolving this uncertainty, the crucial process is *engineering decision making*. In the link between starting off not knowing how much gas or oil is in the reservoir and having to know eventually exactly what should be welded to what before a skilled craftsman can be instructed to weld it, engineering decisions add information about what ought to be done, and provide the basis for the economic decision about whether doing that will be worth the while.

In the actual arrangement of engineering and construction, the crucial problem is that many organizations have to cooperate, and in the design of such complexes of many organizations the crucial considerations are summarized in the *decoupling principle*, namely that if two activities are very dependent on each other, they should be carried out by the same organization under the same authority, and that if one wants to separate activities in different organizations one must *decouple* them, reduce their detailed interdependence.

Finally, in the information and control system in project management we distinguish the different parts by the concept of the *resolution* of the system, so that for instance the cost-engineer's progress curve or S-curve can tell that one is delayed, but it probably will take a construction superintendent's observations to tell why. The work supervisory system has higher resolution and can show more detail, but cannot give an overall picture to higher management. The connection between information systems of different levels of resolution is therefore the master concept for understanding the information and control system of project management.

What this essay does for the book, then, is to show how the basic features of project administration in the North Sea relate to the fundamental uncertainty that one starts with, that one does not know what to build or what has to be done to build it except in a vague and general way. The interrelation between the flow of information about the uncertainties, the decisions resolving the uncertainties, and the feedback of information about whether the resolution worked, are the guts of project administration. We start the book then with the descriptive facts about the uncertainties and about the basic arrangements that resolve them in the North Sea.

The second essay, "Contracts as Hierarchical Documents," explores available information on other systems similar to that in North Sea construction, made up of multiple organizations connected together by contracts, to locate the distinctive features of such contractual links. The basic argument is that we can find deep analogies to the administrative problems of offshore oil project management in such areas of the economy as weapons Research and Development, software development and the computer manufacturing industry generally, building construction, and some sorts of sales organizations (such as franchise car dealerships). What is common to them is uncertainty at the beginning of the project (and at the start of the contract) about what ought to be done and how much it will cost, and the consequent necessity to build devices into the contracts to change course in midstream, and to adjust the commercial terms of contracts to respond to an ever-changing situation. The intention of this essay then is to set offshore project administration in the context of other administration that is a lot like it, so that we can learn more about what to expect and where to look for principles of successful administration.

Chapter 3, "Substitutes for Experience-Based Information: The Case of Offshore Oil Insurance in the North Sea," deals primarily with the formation of policy to deal with uncertainty. Insurance companies (or networks of marine insurers) have to make estimates of risks in order to set insurance rates, and have to set conditions in their insurance contracts so that risks are minimized. The fact that some of the objects insured in the North Sea are so valuable means that insurers have to share the risks, which means that they have to agree on the information to be used.

For very large risks such as the oil platforms that rest on the bottom, the London insurance market is the only one that can organize coverage, so the information has to be acceptable in that market in particular. However smaller risks, such as those for floating drilling rigs, can be managed within the Norwegian insurance market.

What has to be created, in order to negotiate the spreading of the risks among insurers, is a *negotiated information order*, and the conditions of the negotiation are different for fixed platforms than for floating rigs. Consequently the terms under which fixed platforms are insured are set in London, while those for covering smaller floating rigs are often set in Norway. In order to know what to do about insurance, then, uncertainty has to be resolved by information. But in this case it is not only the *technical* acceptability of that information, but its *social* acceptability as well, its acceptability in London in one case and its acceptability in Norway in the other, that makes it able to resolve the uncertainty about how large the risk is and what conditions will minimize it. What information will be acceptable (e.g. whose certification that a steel jacket can be towed will make the insurance valid) is a formal part of the contract, and one which varies with the social arrangements among the multiple organizations involved.

This chapter shows that it is not only the flow of information which might help resolve the uncertainty that counts, but also *the negotiation of the social validity of the information*. Different conditions of negotiation of validity produce differences in what information can reduce uncertainty, because information cannot reduce uncertainty about what to do unless it is accepted as valid by all the people who have to base their decisions on it.

Chapter 4, "Authority and the Management of Engineering on Large Projects," is focused specifically on the production of engineering decisions. The way most investment is done in the North Sea, the resolutions of technical problems proposed by the consulting engineers have to be acceptable to their client, the "operator" of the oil field (the operator acts as an agent for the owner group of the field, who hold the concession, arrange the investment financing, manage the construction and production of the field, and are responsible to the government for adequately meeting Norwegian objectives and regulations in the field).

Arranging authority over professional level workers like engineers is always problematic, and in the North Sea this is further complicated by the fact that the professionals are employed by one or more consulting organizations which are not themselves responsible for the decisions to be taken on the basis of engineering information. The core of the authority system for engineering is then a system of proposals by the engineering consulting firm and approvals by the project organization of the operator as client. That system has to be adapted to the different amounts and kinds of uncertainty in different kinds of engineering, to the different engineering decision tasks that need to be done at different stages of the project, and to various normal malfunctions of engineers and of large complex organizations.

This chapter then enters into the microsociology of uncertainty reduction. Besides deciding the large questions of uncertainty about, say, whether to build a steel or a concrete platform, one has to decide also the detailed questions of uncertainty such as whether the specifications for steel tubes are ready to go out to bid, or later whether the welds that hold them together satisfy the safety standards so that the "client" can accept delivery of the platform from the "builder." Variations in the character of the uncertainty at different points in this flow of detailed decisions shape the temporal variations and the variations between engineering specialties in how the approvals process and authority system actually works.

The uncertainty of the oil construction business generally produces uncertainty in the careers of employees of the contractors. Chapter 5, "Organizational and Individual Control of Career Development in Engineering Project Work," looks at the reactions of engineers, managers, and clerical workers working for engineering consulting firms to the problems of developing their competences, and of convincing their employer and potential competing employers that they indeed have these competences. The employers in their turn have to try to hold the loyalty of their valuable employees (partly valuable because of the employer's training investments in them), in the face of the fact that they do not know for sure what work they will have next year, or whether their client at that time will be convinced that a particular engineer is, say, an appropriate manager for a task force on platform safety.

So the employers have to make their policies on personnel, on investment in competences and promotions, in an environment in which the payoffs to them are very uncertain even if the employee stays; and of course the employee is developing contacts in the oil business and establishing a reputation by working with people from other companies, and may not choose to stay. The problem of who benefits from the investment in competences and from adequate reward levels for employees is thus complicated by the uncertainty of the oil business in Norway as a whole.

Chapter 5 then shows how uncertainties at the macroeconomic level in the flow of work, in who gets the contracts, and in who ends up making personnel assignment and training decisions, affect the way individuals develop their competences. Macroeconomic and administrative uncertainties, here as everywhere, end up creating uncertainties in the lives of individual workers. This chapter previously appeared in *Acta Sociologica*, vol. 27, No. 4, 1984, and is reprinted here by permission.

The Norwegian government is also exposed to the uncertainty of the oil business generally, but it has been exposed to additional uncertainty because it did not know much about oil when it started, and because the objectives of the Norwegian government have been changing. As explained in Chapter 6, "Delays in Government Approvals in Norwegian Offshore Development," part of the policy changes have been deliberate: the Norwegians wanted to buy competence abroad and use that to develop the first oil fields, but they also wanted to use it to develop their own competence to manage their own oil business. But that means that from the first they wanted to run later fields under a different policy (in particular, with less ownership interest and less technical participation by foreign firms) than earlier fields. And they wanted to feel their way into the development of an oil policy.

Many of the delays we observe in Norwegian government approvals (for instance, in the Frigg field, half British and half Norwegian, the British approved an exploitation plan about a year ahead of the approval by the Norwegians) are due to this fact that the administration is developing policy as it goes along – in particular it is often developing policy between the time of an application for an approval of a particular plan and the government decision that it is all right.

The delays of feeling one's way are, of course, a complication of facing an uncertain situation with developing, and hence uncertain, policy objectives and guidelines. This chapter then shows some aspects of the difficulties that government policy faces when it has to manage societal exploitation of an inherently uncertain business, with the additional uncertainty that comes from one's own changing competence (and the changing preferences that may come from increasing competence) to manage that policy.

The final chapter, "Three Origins of Red Tape," places the problem of delays in approvals (which comes up not only in Chapter 6, but also in Chapters 1 and 4) in a wider context. It argues that the first step in analyzing any delay is to determine which general kind it is, for the causes and remedies of different kinds of delay and red tape are different. The three kinds we identify are those due to a given piece of work standing sequentially in multiple queues waiting to be worked on, those due to the lack of incentives of bureaucratic workers who are doing the approvals to work fast and to take priority approvals first, and those due to policy uncertainty.

We have argued in Chapter 6 that policy uncertainty is central to delays in government approvals of large and important project plans. But much evidence indicates that North Sea administration, like other administration, is plagued with all sorts of impediments to expeditious decision-making. This paper tries to provide a practical guide for investigating the causes of bureaucratic or paperwork tangles, and to remedy them differently, depending on their origins. Organizations produce uncertainty by internal mechanisms, as well as responding to uncertainties inherent in the world.

This work could not have been produced without the cooperation of many people and organizations. Gudmund Hernes put us into contact with the Institute of Industrial Economics and with its head, Arne Selvik, as well as introducing us to the intellectual environment in which the sociology of economic life is investigated in Norway. He has been a constant intellectual stimulus and a guide to Norwegian economic, political, and social life. He is only partly and distantly responsible for any of the foolish or uncomprehending things we may say about Norwegian life in this book.

Arne Selvik is an amazing administrator. It is extremely difficult to arrange a contract across international boundaries to hire someone to do research; this is a particular application of the analysis of the administrative difficulties created by multiple uncertainties developed in this book, besides being a common plaint of foreign scholars in all countries. Arne Selvik often untangled tangled relationships, took risks in order to back up contracts with clients for applied research, paid up out of the Institute's resources when the contracts got off track, and is taking part of the risk again in helping produce this book. We hope the work is sufficiently valuable to repay him for his effort and his support.

Our immediate supervisors in Norway for much of this work have been Ole Berrefjord and Per Heum. One of the great difficulties of arranging international scholarly cooperation is the question of whether anyone will be there in the cooperating institution to receive messages and to do something about their contents; the converse difficulty is that the person who does that kind of communication work, the translation of a foreign scholar's requests into bureaucratic and contractual arrangements in a different system, quite often thinks that naturally that should result in their having detailed authority over what should be done, which undermines research, especially research in a new field. Berrefjord and Heum have been reliable and sympathetic counterparts, as well as intellectual colleagues and good friends. Nicolas Wilmot provided many of the same services in the management of our access to people in the Norwegian insurance industry, as well as criticism, discussion, friendship, and a magnificent venison roast.

We have many debts to people who have made those mixed contributions that make a professional tie to a foreign country both manageable and personally bearable, by mixing generosity and a dose of friendship with intellectual and administrative relations. We would like to mention especially Tom Colbjørnsen, Leif Eriksen, Øistein Eriksen, Natalie Rogoff Ramsøy, Bjørn Svendsen, Gunn Tystad, and Anne Vatten.

Some of the work that went into this book was done in the United States. We wish to thank especially the Stanford Graduate School of Business's Public Management Program, James March as its Director and major creator of its intellectual vibrancy, and the Mellon Foundation for providing us both with a year's research fellowship in one of the most exciting intellectual environments we have experienced. Chapter 2 was written during our stay there. The University of Chicago, Universitetet i Bergen, the University of Arizona, Stanford University, and Northwestern University, have tolerated the inconveniences associated with our scheduling this research, and have at various times provided typing, secretarial, and computer resources. The final manuscript was produced at Northwestern with the skilled, patient, and intelligent contributions of Robert Sterbank, Nancy Klein, Elizabeth Pereyra, and Barbara Williamson.

We hope this work stimulates others to show its faults. We do not want those faults to entail any blame for our friends and colleagues who have made producing it often great fun.

CHAPTER 1

PROJECT ADMINISTRATION IN THE NORTH SEA

Arthur L. Stinchcombe

PART 1: ORGANIZATION THEORY AND PROJECT ADMINISTRATION

To understand delays and cost overruns in North Sea oil construction, I will argue, requires us to understand project administration. Project administration is a very different subject than the administration of repetitive operations, such as producing steel pipe in a tube mill (Stinchcombe, 1974). Of course physicians or lawyers or researchers also deal with new and unique problems in each case, and this makes them also different from routine factory workers. But to get a situation comparable to a North Sea oil project, we must take the problems of a physician confronting a new case on the basis of his experience and knowledge, then multiply the 10-15 hours of work invested in a case by a million, and then ask how to administer it.

Organization theory is not very well prepared to deal with project administration, because the important parts of what happens in project administration cannot be written on an organization chart. An organization chart describes those features of an administration which are stable: positions and authority relations. When one is administering a stable repetitive process, the stable features of administration describe much of what is going on. But when an organization at one time is pouring a complex cement structure, at another outfitting a platform on land, at another lifting and connecting up modules at the platform at sea, and at another drilling production wells, the stable features of the administration are the least important part.

The central difference between project administration and administration of repetitive processes is the role of *uncertainty about what to do* in projects, which must be *resolved by decisions*. In a repetitive process most of what one has to do is known – one did it yesterday – and uncertainty only applies to innovations or unusual happenings. This means that most decisions take the form of standing orders: *whenever* we are producing x, do y_1, y_2, . . .,y_n. Standing orders, production routines, a catalogue of numbered products which can be ordered from inventory, and workers and foremen who cannot read engineering drawings and adapt their work to them, all characterize repetitive production. Change orders, forced production to meet a schedule, prototype production, and workers and foremen who must read the drawings, characterize North Sea projects. Every part of the project must be administered as if it were an innovation or a response to an unusual happening. And this means that no one, from top to bottom, can come in tomorrow and do what he or she did yesterday.

This uncertainty from day to day about what each worker will be doing means that the administrative system must produce a decision about what each worker will do each day, and cannot substitute standing orders for decision making. Project administration is active administration. If, on a certain day, a welder must connect a tube to a cast joint at a certain angle, the angle has to have been decided long before so the tube can be manufactured at the right measurements, the joint can be cast at the right angle, the metals specified so that a rolled tube and a cast joint can be safely and effectively welded, and all those decisions have to have got to the right place at the right time so that work in two factories and work at the platform are coordinated.

The reason for using cast joints, rather than welding the tubes directly together at the joint, is that it is uncertain whether the direct welding process (used in the Gulf of Mexico) would stand fatigue from the higher and stronger waves in the North Sea. (Welds are the weak parts of metal structures, and joints are the locus of high stresses, so welds at joints should be avoided if possible. However cast steel tends not to be as flexible as rolled steel, and so breaks under high stress instead of bending, which is why the solution mentioned here is not obvious, maybe not the right one.) That is, the reason we are confronted with a prototype welding process is that the engineering uncertainty of how to deal with North Sea conditions results in a high rate of change in design between one platform and the next.

It is this transmission of uncertainty about the engineering and scientific basis of North Sea construction to the uncertainty of the details of what each worker should do at what time, and the corresponding necessity to produce a series of progressively more specific decisions so that ultimately we can tell both factories and the welder exactly what to do, and the requirement that we do all this on time and in the proper order, that makes project administration difficult, expensive, frustrating, and exciting.

But for the administrative analyst, this produces a requirement for a different sort of organization theory, one oriented to process of *uncertainty reduction through decision*, rather than to the human aspects of standing orders, as in analysis of manufacturing of repetitive products.

Most of this paper is about specific difficulties in the administration of oil exploitation projects in the North Sea. We will start with the *uncertainties in nature and in technical knowledge* in Part 2, and drive through to a last part on *keeping track of the cost implications of detailed decisions and activities* (Part 5). Part 3 will address the problems of *organizing engineering work*, since that is the core of the process of reducing the uncertainties of nature to a reasonably certain description of what a pipe mill, a foundry for casting joints, and a welder on a platform should actually do. (This is also treated in more detail, and from an administrative perspective rather than a decision-making perspective, in Stinchcombe, 1984.) Part 4 will address the problem of *approvals, that is, turning engineering information and proposals into a decision about what will actually be done*.

But before we go into these specific aspects of project management in the North Sea, we need to make some comments about modifying standard organization theory so that we can handle the problems. Most problems become much simpler if we spend a bit of time choosing a strategic intellectual approach to them, and the principles of intellectual strategy so developed can help approach new problems beyond the North Sea.

The Activities Approach to Organization

We can start by taking a clue from a central practical tool of project administration, the network diagram. Activities that have to be completed are graphed against calendar time, and activities that feed into each other are connected at nodes or milestones. These are sometimes called PERT diagrams.

The unit of a network diagram is an activity-and-objective combination. For example, an activity may be "draw isometrics for piping," and the objective is "ready to order piping." The objective then is either the completion of some part of the final structure, or a step on the way which is required before some other activity can be done.

The "activity" is actually *a set of integrated activities needed to achieve the objective*. "Draw isometrics" involves many detailed activities, such as taking measurements off manufacturers' drawings of equipment, relating piping drawings to drawings of structures to support the piping, using the limitations on lengths, weights, diameters of the pipe mills from which the tubes will be ordered, integrating the drawings with specifications for the steel, checking pressure limits to secure safety factors, approving the drawings for final procurement, and the like. There may be a detailed network diagram which specifies each of these activities. The general strategy, however, is to pick sets of activities whose outcomes are important, which are administered together in the light of attempting to reach the objective, and whose quantitative aspects can be estimated.

The key reason that practical people describe the project as a network of activities is that the activities provide a link between three major project resources. On the input side of each activity there are the resources of *hours of work* and *calendar project time*. On the output side the central resource is *administrative readiness to go ahead to the next stage*, whether this is production or further construction. The man or woman hour is the central thing that has to be paid for. Henrik Ager-Hanssen, Executive President of Statoil, estimates that only 15 percent of the costs of realized North Sea projects are material costs, and 65 percent are construction working hour costs (Ager-Hanssen, n.d.). Gulf publishes a book entitled simply *Estimator's Manhour Manual* (Page, n.d.) covering "Piping," "Electrical," "Heating, air conditioning, ventilation, and plumbing," and "General construction," which translates engineering quantities into activities quantities.

Since it is the central cost element, the translation of activities into hours of work forms the basis of the building contractor's estimate of costs, then of the bid and the contract price, and finally of the cost control or followup system. (Note: In general throughout this report I will assume that projects are run by contracting rather than by the owner's direct hire, since this has been common in Norway and is likely to continue to be the main form of administration of North Sea projects.)

The central subject of this report is calendar project time, the calendar time used by an activity before the next stage of the project can start. If it is longer than planned, it constitutes a delay. Calendar time is a resource both in the sense that one needs it to complete the project, and in the sense that if it is wasted in a delay, it costs money. It costs money because hurrying later stages ("forcing the project") lowers productivity and delays returns.

Readiness to go on to the next stage on time, at the estimated costs or below, is the central thing that project administration is supposed to achieve. Administrative attention itself is a scarce resource which needs to be applied whenever activities take more hours of work than planned or take more calendar time than planned.

The network organization of planned activities helps direct administrative attention, and is perhaps the functional equivalent for directing attention and allocating authority of the organization chart in administration of repetitive production.

If practical men and women in project administration find it strategic to organize their thinking around activities, and around series of activities connected in networks, it seems likely that organization theory ought to organize its thinking the same way. Our argument will be that project organization is made up of activities and sequences of activities, rather than positions and lines of authority on an organization chart (Thompson, 1967).

The central theoretical approach of this paper, then, is that in order to reduce the great uncertainty about what should be done so as to produce detailed directions about individual activities, project management has to produce a large mass of decisions, and has to do this so that the system of activities as a whole stays within reasonable limits on hours of work used, on calendar time used, and on achieving objectives on time so as to be ready to go on to the next stage on schedule. The core of project administration, then, is a system for producing decisions under conditions of uncertainty to guide activities on schedule. It is the effectiveness of the existing system, and any future system that might be created by Statoil as operator, in accomplishing these core tasks, which must be studied to analyze management problems in the North Sea.

I will now argue that the consequence of this approach results in the divisions of this paper into parts about (1) *nature and technology*, the sources of uncertainty, (2) the *information*, especially engineering information, used to reduce the uncertainty and form the basis for decisions, (3) the system of *approvals for making commitments*, or decisions to use the information to determine what is to be done, and (4) the *feedback and control* system for measuring the outcome of all the previous stages and locating problems, to govern the allocation of administrative attention.

Nature, Technology, and Project Management

An organizational sociologist might not be supposed to spend a quarter of the substantive parts of a paper telling why oil deposits are of different sizes (and how hard it is to tell how big they are), or why the gas-to-oil ratio is a crucial technical parameter, or why semi-submersible lifting barges are more stable, or how one can maximize the amount of construction built on land and floated out on the platform itself. Aside from the elementary reason that he might not do this, that he is likely to get it wrong or appear ridiculous, it is not obvious why an administrative analyst must be concerned with geology, oil-gas separation, barge stability, or the fine points of exactly where construction should be done. But this amateur concern with the science and technology of the matter follows directly from the activities approach.

The formal reason for this is obvious. If one is to talk of uncertainty and its reduction, the size of the oil deposits, the gas-to-oil ratio, whether a lifting barge can operate in somewhat windy weather, or whether one will have to pay three times as much for an hour's labor (at sea) than one had planned, are obvious uncertainties about what should be done. The scope of these uncertainties depends on two main factors – what is known about nature, and what are the technical possibilities of dealing with the problems that nature poses.

For example the stability of a lifting barge may determine when the next stage of work – hookup – can be done. But that stability depends first on what is known about wave height (a product of storms) and hence depends on the science of meteorology of the North Sea, and depends secondly on the use of the semi-submersible principle, that wave action is much less deeper in the ocean, in the design of the barge. Hence decisions about what to do, how to design the platform, depend on both nature and technology. This dependence affects the planning quantities associated with the activities: calendar time until ready for the next stage and the cost of hours of work spent on shore building modules (that must be lifted) rather than at sea assembling on the platform.

The key is not this formal definitional connection, that if one is going to analyze the reduction of uncertainty one has to know what uncertainty there is. Instead it is that nature and technology jointly determine what it is that has to be, and can be, optimized, and what has to be done to optimize it. It is because as a practical matter one wants to optimize by reducing hours of work at sea that one wants to build modules, and because one wants to minimize delays that one wants to lift those modules with a barge that can work in a bit of wind, that one juggles technical possibilities, and that one pays an enormous fee per day for a barge that can help one minimize building at sea and minimize delays in lifting.

Engineering work has to solve the problems posed by nature, and it has to produce those solutions out of those things we know how to do, that is, out of the known technical possibilities in the "state of the art." The purpose of the section on nature and technology, then, is to suggest which part of engineering difficulties are inevitable, given the nature of the North Sea and the state of the art, and which are produced by organizational troubles.

Producing Engineering Information

By "engineering information" I mean the knowledge that a given structure *can* be built, by activities whose cost and schedule can be (at least roughly) *estimated*, and that this structure will deal with certain events and conditions in nature that may be expected to hold, in order *to produce* (in our case) *gas and oil*. That is, engineering information is a *proposed technical solution, with attached cost and output estimates*.

The proposed technical solution may be described in different degrees of detail. At the very first stage, say of deciding whether a deposit is commercial, a few simple adjustments on the cost of a previous platform may be used to get a rough idea of costs. At the very last stage, the contractor will be paid for having built exactly (well, very nearly exactly) what was in the final drawings, for the price he bid for that part. Then the thing is commissioned, and we find out what it actually produces. In between all parts of engineering information – plans, costs, schedule, estimated output – become more and more definite. Producing that definiteness in the outline of the technical possibilities, so that decisions on what to be built can be taken, is the function of engineering work.

We will argue that many of the central difficulties in administering North Sea projects center around the engineering work. More specifically, it is the late and irregular delivery of engineering decisions to the owner, and through the owner to the builder, which creates much of the cost and schedule difficulties.

We will argue that this is because the present organization of engineering work violates what we call the *decoupling principle*. This says that one should either make activities independent (decouple activities) or else one should administer them under one authority.

The decoupling principle, then, is that if one wants to separate the administration of two activities, such as engineering and construction, one must *decouple* them, make them independent so that one can go on regardless of the progress of the other. Otherwise one gets into troubles in information flow, in decision making, and in schedule and cost control. Or conversely, if one wants to run two activities that depend on each other tight together on a taut schedule, one ought to place them under a single authority. The failure of the present system of engineering organization to satisfy this decoupling principle is, we argue, the central source of cost and schedule troubles, and of bad tempered mutual recriminations among organizations involved in projects in the North Sea.

Approvals and Decisions

Anyone who examines the first part of the network diagram for a project will be struck by the large amount of time allocated to activities described with names like "Review . . ." "Approval of . . ." "Finalize bid packages," "Evaluate . . ." "Certify welders," and the like. Although one may know from the engineering department that a certain plan is one technical possibility, the system as a whole has to decide that this is *the* plan, to put money behind it, to ask for offers, and to sign contracts committing everyone to carry the plan through. Or one has engineering information that welds of a given quality will (probably) hold up under the beating they take from North Sea waves, but needs to decide for sure that these particular welders can produce welds of that quality. That is, in general a proposal has to be turned into a decision before anyone can act on it.

This is difficult enough in any organizational setup, but it is greatly complicated by the organizational situation in the North Sea. The owners, the operator, the engineering contractor, various regulatory agencies concerned with safety, working conditions, or "Buy Norwegian" principles, and finally the organization that agrees to build a specific structure for a specific bid price, all have to agree to the specific plan.

We can illustrate this by the bid of the building contractor. In the United States oil companies often build their projects by a "direct hire" organization, hiring construction labor as it is needed and laying it off afterward. This means that no other building contractor organization has to commit itself to get the necessary labor, to take legal and financial responsibility for using that labor to get a specific task done, to get the safety and other certifications required, to deliver documentation satisfactory to the oil company to show that the work was done up to standard, and so on.

Suppose for example that in submitting an estimate internally in an American oil company, someone forgets that it costs money to get approvals from the authorities and to produce the final documentation in the required number of copies (Semb, 1976).

This will cause a cost overrun for the oil company (it cost Semb's organization 25 percent of the cost of the order), but it is a reasonable cost for documentation that the oil company needs for its own purpose, and nobody's head will roll.

But if a contractor who is legally responsible for the delivery has not calculated in this cost, somebody will be unhappy. O. Usterud gives an example from "a larger project," which includes as "technical final documentation": (1) Equipment manuals, 31 thick A4 volumes, (2) Manufacturing record books (tanks, heat exchangers, steel structure, etc.), 22 thick A4 volumes, (3) Quality control documentation, 10,000 to 20,000 detailed reports, consolidated reports, and films, and (4) As-built drawings (original, paper copy and microfilm, 3,000 to 6,000 drawings) (Usterud, 1976). Thus before making a bid, the contractor must be sure what activities are included in the required work, including, in this case, a good deal of administrative and engineering work after the construction is finished, before it commits itself to deliver that work for a specified price.

What this means is that before making a bid, someone in the building contractor's organization with authority to commit the organization must approve the bid. Note that someone in the owner's organization had to approve the tender before it went out to bid, for all the same reasons that require caution before one legally commits one's organization to a contract.

The general reason that approvals take so much time and create such complications in North Sea projects, is that different organizations have different responsibilities. Or to put it another way, different organizations are trying to maximize (or minimize) different things with the same engineering drawings. The operator (and owner group) is trying to maximize the profitability of the investment in the field. The tax authorities and the Department of Oil and Energy are trying to maximize the benefit to Norwegian society. The building contractor is trying to minimize construction expense. Regulatory authorities are trying to minimize damage to wildlife or fisheries, or to minimize violations of the law on working conditions, or to minimize hazards to navigation in the area of platforms, or what not. It is hard enough to specify tradeoffs between different objectives when setting up a linear programming solution to such a multiple-objective problem within a single organization – it is extremely cumbersome when many authorities have different evaluations of (or different responsibilities for) different objectives.

The cumbersome approvals system is required because each organization has to certify that this particular plan, or this plan with modifications as suggested, is satisfactory with regard to objectives for which they are responsible, and that they are willing to commit themselves to it on that basis (perhaps at a specified cost, in the case of the investors and contractors).

The reason approvals stand in a central place in the administration of North Sea projects then derives from the complex way that a complex objective function – a complex description of all the goals and standards the project has to meet – is represented in the complex of organizations involved. Many delays, as we shall see in Part 4, can be attributed to this approvals process.

The inherent complexity of the approvals process in a multi-organization project administration creates problems in large measure because *the incentives to produce an approval on schedule do not correspond to the importance of that approval for progress of the project.* Briefly, the problem is that the engineers and the contractor are in a great hurry, but the approving authorities take their own sweet time. So while the contractor is working two shifts and weekends to keep to the schedule, the approving office takes off for the weekend, and then has its regular Monday morning staff meeting before getting around to looking at the plans that just came in. The approving officers do not pay, either financially or in getting in bad with the authorities who are in charge of their performance ratings and promotions, for the costly delays they cause in project administration.

This violates a general principle of administration, which we will call the "incentive-consequence-correspondence principle." Briefly the incentive-consequence-correspondence principle is that *a rational administrative system will be arranged so that good performances that are especially important to the overall progress of the enterprise should be highly rewarded, important bad performances highly punished.* In general, approving authorities, when they are in different organizations from those responsible for performance, are subject to their own incentive systems rather than to an incentive system which is rational for project administrative efficiency. This produces inefficiency in *turning engineering information into decisions, and produces delays in getting approvals.*

Followup and Feedback

If all one had to do were to produce the correct decisions about what to do, on time, project administration would be difficult enough but reasonably peaceful. In fact plans and decisions are not enough, because as Ecclesiastes tells us, "time and chance happeneth to them all." One has to collect information on what is actually happening, to compare it to the plan, and when there are deviations, to set in motion corrective action.

There are two main feedback systems, one of which involves angry Texan voices and the other the cost engineer's S-curve. The direct supervisors of a process either see that something is going wrong, or are told they have a problem by the general cost and schedule control mechanism, and they try to correct the activity system and bring things back into line by oral orders in Texan accents.

The cost control engineers translate the physical plans into measures of progress in achieving the plans, then compare these "ideal" figures of planned progress with actual progress. For example, if one calculates the estimated hours of work that have to be accomplished by April 30, in order to achieve the completion of the project on schedule, and compares this to the actual accomplishments up to April 30, one can estimate completion delays shortly after April 30.

If these delays are too serious, the S-curve will not usually tell very much about what is wrong. To find out what is wrong, one needs to go consult the construction manager. To set it right, one has to set a lot of Texan voices to speaking authoritatively.

We will actually analyze the problems of the written, S-curve-cost-engineer, part of the control system. It is beyond our capacities to enter into field construction supervision in any competent fashion. But it is important to realize that the measurements of progress of a cost and schedule engineer are abstractions about the activity of the construction managers and workers, and that the remedies set in motion by cost engineers will have no effect unless they convince design engineers, construction managers, and ultimately construction workers, that problems have to be solved.

This brings up the central problems in this part of the administrative apparatus, the problems of *correct abstraction and access to authority*. When one sets up a control system alongside the regular line system of supervision, a cost accounting system in repetitive production or a cost engineering system in project administration, one is trying to set up a higher level control loop, a measurement and feedback system, to supplement the regular interpersonal supervisory hierarchy. In order for such a loop to work, it has to be able to abstract correctly from the activities to be carried out, so that it is working with accurate cost and schedule information. For example, if the field reports of change orders' authorizations and change orders' execution come in late, then the cost and schedule engineer is working with *both* wrong plans *and* wrong measures of accomplishment. Hence their estimates of deviations will be off, and the overarching feedback loop will be controlling a fictional process, a process that might have gone on if the change orders were not in force. If the true plan is now 120 percent of the original plan, and one has accomplished 110 percent of the original plan, a cost engineer comparing 110 percent with 100 percent (the original plan) thinks we are 10 percent ahead, while we are actually 10 percent behind.

But suppose that the abstraction is done right, and the cost engineer knows something is amiss. Given what we have previously said about decoupling, at this level of abstraction the cost engineer probably does not know whether it is late engineering drawings, late construction activity, or late deliveries. The people who can find out what exactly is the matter, and who can correct it, are construction managers of one rank or another out in the field. Unless *the general indications of difficulty are turned into authoritative searches for the difficulty*, the cost and schedule control system is a loop without an outlet, a control system without operative parts. Thus we will argue that the central problems in the cost and schedule control systems are deficiencies in the abstraction and authority systems connected to them.

Summary

Our difficulties in the North Sea come ultimately from the disproportion between what nature can do to us and what we can do to nature with our technology. The size of this disproportion leads to the projects in the North Sea being unique, engineering intensive, and faced with great uncertainties.

Our first job in what follows is therefore to analyze those uncertainties, to see what is inevitable, what will decrease with time, and what then is left over to be explained by human and organizational failures. That is, the first job in an activities approach is to see what activities are demanded by nature, what activities are possible in the technology.

The system for producing information on what we might do to control nature, and at what cost and schedule, is engineering work. Consequently in project administration engineering is not "staff" work, but is on the direct time line between investments and payoff. Organizing engineering work to produce the information needed on time, and in the form in which it can be acted on on time, is perhaps the core source of difficulties in the North Sea. We will argue that this is because the present organization violates the decoupling principle, that closely interdependent activities should be administered together under the same authority. The second job in the activities approach is to describe the system for reducing the uncertainty about what is to be done to definite decisions to do specific activities. This reduction is done by engineers in North Sea Projects.

Supposing now that engineering is done right, engineering information has to be approved, in order to produce final decisions about how to go ahead. Because in the complex objective function of North Sea oil exploitation, different authorities and organizations are trying to maximize different things on the same drawings, every commitment to go ahead tends to involve multiple approvals. This results in extraordinary growth of bureaucratic paperwork, the ten-copies-of-all-trivia syndrome, and produces long periods of waiting for approvals and decisions on the time line between investment and payoff. We will argue that this is due to distortions in the incentive system, a failure of incentive-consequence-correspondence. Because an approving authority is often not rewarded more if the project is finished on time, nor punished more if it is delayed, delays that are very costly for the society as a whole are produced because speed would cause minor disruption in the offices of approving authorities. The third job in the activities approach is to study how proposed activities become decided activities, activities that will be authorized to be carried out.

And finally many difficulties are caused by not knowing that one is in difficulty, so that one can do something about it. The cost and schedule control system requires that both the plans and the activities carried out be correctly abstracted, shorn of their technical detail so as to provide accurate measures of progress. And it requires that failures in progress should set in motion authoritative correction action. We will argue that many difficulties in project administration are due to inaccurate abstraction of data for control purposes, and inadequate authority behind the control system's corrective actions. The fourth job in the activities approach is to describe the system for correcting activities when they do not give the planned-for result.

Briefly on Formal Structure

Fields in the North Sea are originally owned by the Norwegian government, which makes regulations for exploiting them by giving concessions. The group to which concessions are given for a particular field is ordinarily made up of a number of oil companies, and is called the "owner" or the "owner group."

Historically the first concessions were to groups made up almost entirely of private companies, especially American ones. More recently a larger share of the owner interests have been reserved for the state oil company (Statoil). For example Statoil owns half of that part of the Statfjord field in the Norwegian sector. The concessions involve separate arrangements for exploration of an area and for exploitation of any resulting oil finds. The incentive for private companies to participate in exploration is the chance thereby to get owner interests in any resulting oil or gas fields.

The owner group appoints a sort of "board of directors" for the field, made up of representatives of each ownership interest. This board takes major investment decisions and evaluates the administration of the field.

In addition to its ownership interests, the Norwegian state takes revenues out of the field both in the form of a royalty on oil extracted and in the form of taxes on the profits of the companies.

Part of the concession agreement will be the appointment of an "operator," that is an administrative and business agent for the owner group. This is usually one of the owner group, and typically one of the rewards of being willing to be operator is the chance to get a larger owner interest. It is fairly typical that the operator operates on cost reimbursement basis, making no profit on its administrative work directly, but instead taking profits through the oil ownership interest itself. The ownership interest of the operator is set higher than that of other owners at the time of the concession. Quite often in what follows I will talk of "the owner" or "the client," and this usually means in fact the operator, acting as agent for the owner group. For big contracts, however, the owner group itself will decide.

Some operators supply nearly all engineering and management for a field, while some employ engineering and management consultant firms. In turn these may or may not also take responsibility as prime contractor for actually building the field. A typical arrangement is that for Statfjord, in which engineering and management services are hired from an engineering firm (this one a joint venture created for the purpose between American and Norwegian interests), but the operator (on behalf of the owners) contracts for the construction and retains ultimate economic and managerial control.

In Norway the actual building is typically broken up into several subcontracts, sometimes entered into by the prime contractor, sometimes entered into directly by the operator on behalf of the owners. The prime contract and major subcontracts are always reviewed by the owner group rather than left entirely to the discretion of the operator.

The operator and/or the engineering consultant firm ordinarily enter deeply into the administration of the actual work of construction, supplying the detailed drawings, changing the specifications and drawings after work has started, checking on quality standards and regulating major purchases (quite often making major purchases themselves). Thus there is much more administrative communication (more "documentation") between the construction contractor and the owner than there typically is, for example, in shipbuilding.

Certain functions that are ordinarily part of the administration of a field are reserved to Statoil, rather than the operator. The most striking of these is public relations and the release of information, which in the Statfjord field is the monopoly of Statoil.

PART 2: AN INTRODUCTION TO THE TECHNOLOGY OF OIL PRODUCTION IN THE NORTH SEA

In order to understand the delays in the construction of platforms in the North Sea, it is necessary first to understand something of the technological problems that have to be solved. Our general problem is, how do human and organizational inadequacies in solving the problems of getting ready for oil production cause expensive delays? But in order to judge what is inadequate, one has to have some idea of what is adequate, and what is more or less inevitable inadequacy under the technical circumstances. To understand these things, one needs an amateur's introduction to the technical situation. (For a general introduction, see Cooper and Gaskell, 1976; also Bent, 1979.)

This introduction to the technology of oil production in the North Sea has four major sections. The first deals with the natural setting and its implications for the production problems that have to be solved. This in turn has two major subparts, an analysis of the nature of oil and gas deposits and their size and productivity, and the nature of the North Sea marine environment, especially the weather conditions, in which building and production have to go forward.

The second major section deals with the gross characteristics of the technology of the production platforms themselves and the construction process by which they are put up. The two major subsections here deal with the broad features of the construction of process facilities like oil production platforms and the way they are exaggerated or modified in the case of production platforms in particular, and then a section on the marine technology by which the problems of working at sea, and the problems of maximizing the amount of work that can be done on land, are solved.

The third major section deals with the technical and engineering uncertainties, which determine at any particular stage of the project how much is known about what will have to be done on the project. Uncertainty about the characteristics of the field, about new technologies, about weather, about what the exact features of equipment to be supplied by subcontractors and suppliers will be and about what safety regulations will have to be met as the governments improve their own knowledge, requires constant adaptations of the work in progress as the project develops. This creates administrative problems. The sources of this uncertainty in the technical situation itself therefore help explain the administrative troubles.

Finally we will outline the construction sequence itself, with attention to what parts of the sequence of activities are critical for delays – which parts of the construction have to be completed before other parts can be started, and of these which are the ones that take the longest and therefore can be sources of delays.

Gas and Oil, Rocks, and the Sea – the Natural Environment

Oil and gas deposits are found in deposits of rock that used to be ancient sea bottoms, especially bottoms of shallow seas near continents which provided sediments. They are evidently formed from the decomposition of animals and plants which were buried with the sediments. The oil and gas deposits occur in porous sandstone or limestone rocks which have a cap over them formed of some impervious rock, such as shale formed from sedimentary clay, or rock salt. The oil and gas tend to rise as they are formed, and the cap has kept them from rising all the way to the surface. Geologists search for the impervious domes by studying the echoes these hard surfaces give off when explosions are set off above them, and oil and gas are found in a well when the drill penetrates the impervious cap and enters the porous rock whose empty spaces are filled with oil and gas.

Unfortunately not all impervious domes covering porous sedimentary rock have oil and gas under them; many have only water or simply rock. Consequently the only way to find out whether there is oil under the cap is to drill an exploratory well through it. Further, one cannot tell how big the deposit is from the size of the cap (though that sets an upper limit), and one must drill other exploratory or production wells before the size of the deposit can be estimated accurately.

The occurrence of the domes, the presence of oil or gas under them, the size of the fields, the depths of the deposits, and the production rate of each well, all are determined by geological variations which are more or less random. Areas which have had longer periods of being shallow seas, such as the Middle East, the Texas-Oklahoma-Gulf of Mexico-Venezuela area, the North Sea, or the Arctic shelf, can be generally rich areas for prospecting for oil, but within them the size and location of oil and gas deposits is essentially unpredictable, without a great deal of expensive seismic exploration, and much drilling for confirmation of promising seismic finds.

The size of fields and the productivity of wells determines the economic productivity of a field. Then, when combined with the price of oil and the price of risk capital in the oil industry, the geological variation determines which fields are profitable to exploit and which are "marginal" or "non-commercial." As the price of oil increases, smaller reservoirs and reservoirs in more hostile conditions become economically viable. The lowest cost reservoirs are the Middle Eastern ones, especially in Saudi Arabia and Kuwait, which are large, lie near the surface, and can be drilled on land and shipped short distances to tanker loading facilities. The larger fields in the North Sea are competitive at the price which obtained on the world market before the OPEC price rises, though they are not as low-cost as the Arabian fields. The smaller fields depend for economic viability, at present interest and profit rates, on the price being maintained above its competitive level by OPEC cartel pricing. The general decision about whether a field is "commercial" therefore depends on estimating the geological situation from seismic exploration and exploratory drilling, estimating the cost of capital for development of the field, and estimating the future price development of oil and gas over the period of production of the field, usually roughly 20 years after the start of production.

Hydrocarbons, that is, gas and oil, are of many different weights, with weight determined primarily by the number of carbon atoms in a molecule. Under normal conditions hydrocarbons with up to six carbon atoms in a molecule are gases, those with more than six are liquids. The heavier of the gases (those with more carbon atoms) can be cooled and compressed into liquids, and can then be economically shipped in special tank ships or dissolved in the oil going to shore in an oil pipeline. The lighter gas (fewer carbon atoms per molecule, generally called "dry gas") can be transported to shore only in separate pipes, or can be flared off (burned and wasted at the field), used for energy requirements at the field itself, or reinjected into the reservoir to be recovered again later.

The gas-to-oil ratio of a field is a crucial technical parameter. Generally speaking the fields of the Southern part of the North Sea are more likely to be gas fields – perhaps a result of the decay of vegetable matter rather than animal matter – while those further North tend to be oil fields with some gas dissolved in the oil. Since the oil at the great depths below the North Sea is quite hot and under high pressure, a good deal of gas can be dissolved in the oil. The Frigg field, however, is situated in among oil fields, but is dominantly a gas field.

The main process equipment that is installed in an oil field, such as Statfjord, is separation equipment to eliminate the gas from the oil before the oil is shipped to shore, and sometimes equipment to process the gas for shipment by tanker or by gas pipeline. The technical features of this equipment are determined by estimates of the gas-to-oil ratio of the reservoir. Further, the reinjection strategy, the strategy of landing the product from the field, and the petrochemical and refining industry that it is feasible to build on the basis of the product of the field, are all determined by the gas-to-oil ratio. After the size of the field and the technical cost of developing the field, the next most crucial geological parameter is probably the gas-to-oil ratio.

A final geological parameter of importance is the presence of pollutants in the oil, especially sulfur. This determines the price of the oil, with the low sulfur oil of the North Sea having a slightly higher price than most Middle Eastern high sulfur oils. The mixture of heavier liquids versus lighter liquids (more versus fewer carbon atoms) also affects price, with light crudes like those of the North Sea being somewhat preferable. The lighter atoms are more volatile, and are therefore more useful for applications in which the petroleum product is evaporated at ordinary or slightly elevated temperatures before combustion, as in internal combustion engines.

On the borderline between geology and technology, there are a series of determinants of the percentage of the oil and gas in the reservoir which can be recovered, and the rate of production. These include the porosity of the rock in which the oil and gas are collected, the reservoir pressure (which can be affected by pressure reinjection, either of water which is better for production or of gas which is better for saving the gas which otherwise would have to be flared off until the installations for its shipment can be made), by the depth of the deposit which determines how much length and hence surface area of the bore hole yields oil and gas, and by features of the internal surface of the bore hole, which can be affected by explosive and chemical treatments.

This subsurface geological variation however unfortunately

takes place on the bottom of the North Sea, which is generally speaking a hostile environment for construction and marine work. Generally the Northern part of the North Sea is more hostile than the Southern part, primarily because of differences in the height of the waves. The total energy in the wave action on the open ocean comes ultimately from the wind, though near the shore tides can also affect the energy of waves. The total amount of energy in the wave action is determined by the speed of the wind and the length of open sea over which that wind has had a chance to operate on the wave action. The surface of the sea, so to speak, serves as an *accumulator* of wind energy.

The longer the "fetch," the distance of open sea over which the wind blows continuously for a long period of time, the larger the distance between one crest and the next. Waves break when their height exceeds one seventh of their length, so the height of the wave is determined by the total energy and the length between crest and crest, which in turn are determined by the fetch. In a gale the waves on a small puddle are close together and not very high, while after the gale has blown across the unbroken North Atlantic for hundreds of miles the waves have long distances between crest and more distance between crest and trough. In relatively protected waters like the Persian Gulf or the Gulf of Mexico, wave heights even during hurricanes do not reach the heights observed in the Northern part of the North Sea, where the normal direction of high winds takes them across large expanses of unbroken ocean before reaching the North Sea. The Southern part of the North Sea is protected from this accumulator effect by being shielded from several directions by land masses.

Because the energy in wave action comes from wind on the surface, wave action decreases rapidly with increasing depth. If one can construct a floating object so that it exposes very little surface to the waves at sea level, but has a large mass, large surface, and a large part of its bouyancy far below the surface, it will be much less affected by the waves, and much more stable in bad weather. This is the principle of the "semi-submersible" construction which is used in drilling rigs, in the concrete production platforms such as Statfjord A and B, and in the large floating lifting barges and pipe laying barges used in the construction process in the North Sea. Below the surface, the North Sea is not such a hostile environment, at least as far as storms are concerned.

The depth of the North Sea varies a good deal, at least relative to human construction capabilities and diving capabilities, generally being deeper in the North than in the South. This determines how large production platforms that are going to rest on the bottom have to be, and how deep the diving for inspection, hookup, etc., will be. This in turn determines how important it will be to minimize the number of platforms, to construct integrated platforms for drilling, production, separation, shipping, and accommodation of personnel as is planned for Statfjord, rather than separate platforms as were used in Ekofisk. Ekofisk was developed earlier, is in the more hospitable southern part of the North Sea, and is in shallower water, than Statfjord.

Gross Features of the Construction Process and Marine Problems for Platforms

Most of the engineering work and most of the construction work in all continuous-process plants for the treatment of oil and gas consists of the mechanical installations – pipes, compressors, heating vessels and heat sources, cooling equipment, valves and other controls for the processing of the oil and gas itself, and "utilities" such as electricity, air conditioning, heating, living quarters and office equipment, and so on.

In an ordinary continuous process plant on land, only 5-10 percent of the total cost of a project will be "structures" which house the people and processes, while over 90 percent will be process equipment, piping, and other mechanical engineering. The platforms in the North Sea have to solve more difficult structural problems than, for instance, oil refineries on land, so the structural part may make up 20 percent of the total engineering and construction, instead of 5 percent. Roughly speaking, then, the problem of building in 300 meters of water is about 4 times as difficult as building on dry land, as far as the structure itself is concerned. But most of the work is still mechanical engineering and installation of equipment and its piping connections, controls, power, heating and cooling, pressure, and the like.

Because the oil and gas finds, the sea conditions, the character of the bottom, and the strategic choices of operators and governments, differ from one field to another, the engineering for each field is not very repetitive of the engineering that went into the last previous field. Because "each platform is on the leading edge of offshore technology," the engineering has to be done anew for each platform, though the engineering itself is not particularly difficult or original.

In particular, a number of strategic choices are made early in the planning of development of particular fields which determine the course of engineering work. One is whether the development will use cement structures (which are ordinarily towed out as semi-submersibles and carry much of their equipment already installed, see below) or steel structures (ordinarily towed out on barges). Another is whether the production platform will have accommodations for workers, storage for oil, etc., or whether there will be separate platforms. Another is how far the platform will be an integrated structure assembled in place on the structure, versus modules constructed elsewhere and only hooked up on the platform; another is the level of safety from exceptionally high waves that will be designed into the structure; another is the equipment for shipping the oil to shore, by pipe or tanker; another is what to do with the gas.

Since there have been many different strategic choices made at various times in the North Sea, and since these choices often have to be different from those made in the Gulf of Mexico or in the Persian Gulf, past engineering *experience* helps in the design, but past engineering *plans* cannot be used again. This in turn implies that there is roughly one hour of engineering work done for each three hours of construction work, or that about 25 percent of the total work to be done on a project is engineering work. And this means that delays can happen in the engineering part of the work just as well as in the construction part, and that one wants to start construction before all the engineering is done. We will see later some of the implications of this *engineering intensity* of the projects.

A central determinant of the efficiency of the construction process, both from a cost and a delay point of view, is whether the construction is done on land and then towed out to the platform site (either on the platform or on barges of other kinds). In out-of-pocket costs, an hour of work on the platforms at sea costs about three times as much as an hour with the same skills on land, and depending on what is included in the costs (e.g., inefficiencies of working at sea in bad weather, extra transport costs of materials, etc.) estimates of the true cost difference range up to a factor of six or seven times. This makes the marine technology that is available, which will be discussed below, a crucial determinant of the overall construction efficiency. This has resulted in very large investments in large semi-submersible lifting barges and pipe laying barges, and has resulted in the extensive use in the North Sea of platforms which are, so to speak, their own barges, those that are semi-submersible for towout and then are sunk in place to make a permanent platform.

Another crucial determinant of the efficiency of construction is the amount of space for each worker. An estimate by Mobil starts with a norm of 19 square meters per man. If the builder increases the number of workers in the same space by 33 percent, so that each worker has 14 square meters, the estimate is that *each added* worker will be only about three quarters as efficient as a worker with enough room.

Of course the added workers are just about as efficient as those already hired. But the crowding makes all the workers less efficient. So by adding workers to an amount of 133 percent one only brings total production to 125 percent, because *all* the workers lose 6 to 7 percent in efficiency. So the added production per worker added amounts to about three quarters of the original productivity level.

If instead of adding 33 percent more workers, we had added 60 percent, so that each person has about 12 square meters, then the *added workers* between 33 and 60 percent are only about five eighths as efficient, after subtracting the crowding effect they have on everyone's productivity. As we go to 100 percent of added workers, or about 9 square meters per person, *in total* one adds only about 47 percent more production to the project. Each worker between 60 percent extra and 100 percent extra only adds about an eighth as much net productivity as a worker who has enough room.

Since each square meter on a production platform is very expensive, this constitutes a limitation on the speed with which the project can be completed. This crowding can be reduced considerably by working on land, where nearby areas can be used for pre-assembly, and by using modules assembled on land and then hooked up all at once in the crowded conditions on the platform. Each module has to have enough structural integrity to be shipped out to the platform, lifted on, hooked up, and this adds considerably to the weight and slightly to the space used.

Both using a structure which can serve as its own barge, and the use of modules and heavy lifting equipment, can therefore save money in two ways. In the first place they use the cheapness of labor on land for more of the construction, and in the second they reduce the crowding (and/or slowed up construction) caused by the small space on the platform.

In the choice between concrete and steel for the construction process (the Norwegian platforms are generally concrete), the choice between semi-submersible towout and barge towout, and consequently how much of the total installation can be done already on land, is crucial. Concrete is very heavy and is only practical if the structure can be towed out. Considerable weight has to be added to a tubular steel structure to make it into a thing that will float and be stable, so steel jackets are towed out on barges. Generally speaking, steel is lighter for the same strength (the difference is especially great in tensile strength, and consequently the shape of the concrete – how far stresses can be turned into crushing rather than tensile stresses – is a strong determinant of relative strengths), but more expensive to install. The Aker productivity figure was about 12 man hours per cubic meter of concrete, or roughly 4 man hours per ton, for slip forming the cells on Statfjord A. To outfit a utility shaft there were 500 tons of steel and metal equipment which took about a million man hours, or about 2000 man hours per ton. Of course the utility shaft is a more complex mechanical construction than the jacket of a jackup platform, but this gives some idea of the relative complexity of the metal mechanical versus the concrete structural part of the construction; the metal parts are up to 50 times as complex as the concrete structural parts.

According to Jamie Bent (Bent, 1979), the productivity of Norwegian labor in slipforming the concrete structure of Statfjord A was about the same as American labor doing the same work, while on the mechanical welding work, pipe fitting, and the like, Norwegian labor was about three-quarters as efficient as American labor. (Note that there would also be comparisons of productivity on similar work available from the price of tankers delivered by Norwegian shipyards and American shipyards, discounted by relative wage rates.)

One part of the advantage of a fixed production platform, rather than drilling as one does for exploratory wells from floating drilling rigs, is that the drilling of production wells can be done in all weather. It is possible to drill wells in a curve. While the drilling train that turns and guides the drill bit is made of steel, over the very long distances (up to three kilometers) involved in deep North Sea wells it is quite flexible. Many wells can therefore be drilled from the same platform, looking something like the spines of an umbrella meeting at the top at the platform. The timing of the drilling as compared to the timing of the finishing of the oil-gas separation equipment and the shipping installations on the platform is therefore crucial to bringing the platform into production.

The marine technology of the construction process is organized around two main problems: the *stability* of floating structures, and *weather prediction*. The reason one must have stability in loading goods and especially modules onto the platforms, in drilling wells, in laying pipes, is that the tolerances involved in the construction are small compared with the movements of a freely floating object. The more the action of the waves can be damped down so that large movements of the waves result in small movements in the drilling platform, the pipe laying barge, or the lifting barge, the heavier the weather can be and still have the motion of the working construction vessels be within the tolerable limits.

But then given those limits on the weather one can work in, one cannot start long jobs which cannot be interrupted unless there will be a period of weather within the necessary limits, and one must know somewhat ahead of time how bad the weather is going to be when it takes some time to disconnect and reconnect to drilling or pipe-laying work. If one has not disconnected from drilling or pipelaying when the weather gets really bad, the pipe or the drill train can be broken or twisted. On the other hand one can *keep* a connection to a drill train or a pipe in weather in which it is impossible to *reconnect* to it, so that one does not want to break off the connection unless absolutely necessary.

There are two main principles involved in obtaining stability in drilling rigs, lifting barges, diving mother ships, or platforms during towouts: the *semi-submersible principle* and the *dynamic positioning principle*.

The *semi-submersible* principle has already been described briefly above. Since the wave action is most intense at the surface of the sea and decreases rapidly with depth, the ideal structure for stability in all sorts of weather would be one with most of its weight and bouyancy in large tanks or cells, far below the surface, with narrow legs passing through the agitated waters near the surface, and with a platform in the air far above the tops of the highest waves. Of course the usual conditions for the stability of ships also have to be secured, that the center of gravity of the structure is below the center of bouyancy, and remains below it during the expectable amount of tilting of the structure. Ordinarily the semi-submersible structure doing delicate work such as drilling in a single place is also anchored in several directions for added stability. In addition if the ballast (which determines how deep the structure floats) is contained in cells so that it cannot move freely, and if the movement between cells is controlled by computers which work to compensate for movements during the work (such a system is for example used on the Narwahl self-propelled lifting barge), added stability can be obtained. The flotation structures at the bottom of Condeep type platforms and drilling rigs are therefore made out of cells, with water (or later oil) used as ballast.

The other main system for achieving stability for working in rough weather is dynamic positioning. The basic principle is that some "sensory system" tells which way the structure is moving.

This system of sensors is hooked up, through computers, to multiple motors which can provide thrust in any direction. The thrust compensates, as exactly as possible, for the movement induced by the waves.

One type of "sensory system" for example is a sonar system, in which sound waves are sent toward echo reflectors placed on the bottom; when the sound takes longer to get back to the receiver on board the ship or other structure, it indicates that the distance between the ship and the reflector has increased, and the amount of that increase measures the speed with which the ship is moving away from the sounder and consequently determines the amount of compensating thrust needed. The computer is needed to calculate rapidly the direction and speed of movement induced by the waves from differences in the distances between the ship and the echo reflectors at two different pings, and to translate this into commands to the thrusters about the direction and quantity of thrust. Usually there are at least two "sensory systems," so that when one goes bad (e.g., by a school of fish passing between the source of the ping and the echo reflector) the other can take over.

Clearly the maximum of stability would be achieved by combining the semi-submersible principle with dynamic positions, but either by itself is expensive, so they have not been combined very often.

The marine engineering of the structure and the degree of stability required for a given construction or drilling operation, then, determine the roughness of the seas in which a given operation can go on. Perhaps the most delicate operation is the floating of jackup rigs which have been resting on the bottom, or settling them again in a new place. The towout of the huge concrete semi-submersible platforms, or the tipping and sinking of jackets for steel platforms (which are towed out on their sides on barges and tipped down into place by careful control of the ballast tanks attached for controlled flotation and sinking), is also reasonably delicate, if only because the structures are so valuable that even a small risk of losing them involves great insurance costs. The delicacy of loading modules or equipment onto the platforms at sea varies a great deal with the stability of the lifting barges, being quite restrictive with the ordinary floating barges and quite unrestrictive with the enormous semi-submersible Dutch lifting barges which have recently come into service. The advertisements suggest for example that the Narwahl can work 80 percent of the time in the North Sea.

Weather prediction in the North Sea is quite good, partly because weather prediction was first developed as an exact science in the North Sea region (specifically in Bergen) so there is longer experience, and partly because the dependency of small fishing boats on the prediction of bad weather (even with larger fishing boats and better prediction, fishing is one of the most dangerous industries in Norway) had led to large investments in collecting weather data on the North Sea. If one collects additional weather data in the immediate region of the work, one can achieve near certainty in the prediction of weather for about 12 hours ahead. Forecasts have increasing degrees of uncertainty with longer periods.

Generally speaking the weather in the North Sea is less stormy in summer than in winter. Delicate operations, such as towouts of platforms, drilling from semi-submersible rigs, placement of modules, pipelaying, are therefore usually only carried out during the summer months. A delay in a towout past the so-called "weather window" in the summer therefore generally means that the structure cannot be towed out until the following summer, resulting in about 9 months delay.

Sources of Engineering Uncertainty

There are a number of indications that a central difficulty in North Sea projects is the organization of engineering work, and that engineering *uncertainty* is at the core of it. The central task of engineering is to translate the technical and economic objectives, of obtaining, processing, and shipping oil and gas cheaply, into specifications for work to be done. By engineering uncertainty, we mean then lack of timeliness, clarity, and specificity about what ought to be done.

There are really three rather separate problems, or kinds of engineering uncertainty, here. The first kind might be called *scientific or technical uncertainty*. One may be scientifically wrong about, for example, the gas-to-oil ratio in a given field, and so design the equipment so that some of the gas has to be flared off. Or one may have technical disagreements between the firm that classifies a platform (as a barge to be towed out) to determine the risk as a seagoing vessel for insurance purposes, and the designers of the platform, about the weight it is safe to tow out on top.

A second kind of engineering uncertainty might be called *uncertainty of objectives*, uncertainty about what to maximize or minimize in the design. For example, putting the living accommodations on the production platform may minimize helicopter accidents in transferring personnel from an accommodation structure to the platform or minimize the costs of settling two platforms on the bottom, but it increases risk of fire or explosion injuring personnel in a disaster, and a choice of which to minimize (or maximize) has to be made. Or water reinjection to maintain pressure in a field may maximize production, but (unless shipping facilities for gas are ready) wastes the gas which could be saved if it were reinjected. Or during construction one choice (e.g., leaving a given completed structure as it is) may minimize construction costs and delays, while another (e.g., introducing a "change order" to rip part of the structure out and do it over, do it right this time) may maximize long run productivity. Or concrete may minimize maintenance costs at the price of heavier structures.

Especially when organizations whose responsibility is to achieve different objectives all have to approve of engineering plans, uncertainty of objectives (or uncertainty of the trade-offs between objectives) can be a real administrative headache for engineering management. Changing safety standards are a leading example of uncertainty of objectives, since the standards that will have to be met are not always known at the time basic design decisions are made.

A third kind of uncertainty might be called *uncertain engineering responsibility*, and involves final approval of plans. Quite often for example a contractor has to go ahead with work for which the change order has not been formally approved (see Tovshus, 1976:13-14). That is, presumably the technical uncertainties and the uncertainty of objectives have been resolved at the practical level, or the contractor would not dare go ahead on the basis of the engineer's say so. But the clearance process for final approval of the change order is so cumbersome that the responsible people do not have the formal authority to make decisions for which they have the real authority.

To put this all another way, a solution to some kinds of uncertainty is to find out more about the world and about technical possibilities, scientific and technical uncertainty. A solution to other kinds of uncertainty is to make up one's mind what one really wants, so one can sacrifice low priority goals when necessary to higher priority goals. And finally any uncertainty that is left about what shall really be done has to be resolved by responsible decision making.

All three kinds of uncertainty create problems for the management of engineering work. And they create special problems when the construction project is working right up tight against the engineering completion, when the projects are not familiar so all engineering decisions are somewhat uncertain, when the engineering is part of the critical path which can delay the project as a whole, and when the division of responsibilities in a new enterprise form create difficulties.

With this background, we want to sort out as far as we can, in this section, the uncertainties in engineering work that are truly technical and scientific, in the sense of inevitable, so as to be able to judge better in Part 3, the part which is organizational. This is an inherently difficult task, because the basic organizational problem of the Norwegian government is the same as the administrative analyst's problem, namely, how can one judge whether work was well and efficiently done when one could not have done it oneself?

For convenience we can sort the scientific and the technical engineering uncertainties into the following groups: (1) true scientific uncertainty, in which adequate scientific understanding for resolving the uncertainty does not exist and for which the fund of engineering experience is not adequate to substitute for scientific understanding; (2) uncertainty due to the high cost of knowledge; (3) uncertainty due to the fact that some other person or organization has to provide the knowledge or information; (4) uncertainty which will be cleared up over time with the normal development of the project.

(1) The basic science which underlies petroleum exploration, geology, is a very uncertain and problematic science. One never really knows how much oil and gas can be obtained from a given area like the North Sea until it has been completely extracted from the ground. Of course various investments in exploration (seismic exploration and exploratory well drilling), then the actual experience of exploiting the field, give more and more accurate information as time goes on. But the reason that estimates of reserves in a given field go up over time is that in the face of great geological uncertainties, the geologists and the oil companies bet conservatively. They would not have to bet at all if geology were an exact science.

Similarly the science which deals with the central uncertainty in the construction process itself, the weather and its effect on the sea, is also very uncertain. Because meteorology has neither sufficiently detailed observations nor sufficiently well developed theories to predict weather exactly, there is a good deal in the movement of air masses and winds which appears to us as chance.

Both of these sources of uncertainty mean that moderately often central technical parameters are misestimated. Not only overall magnitudes of deposits, but also gas-to-oil ratios, pressures which blowout valves will have to contain, the consistency and pressure of drilling mud needed to control gas pressure or to maintain the stability of the sides of the drill hole, the weather which will be encountered during towout of a jacket or a concrete platform, whether a particular storm will be bad enough to break the drill train, or to put a kink in the pipe while it is being laid, all are technical judgements which have to be made and judgements which are, moderately often, mistaken.

In addition there are technical questions for which there exists adequate scientific knowledge, but for which there is not sufficient practical experience about the particular applications in the North Sea. For example, the chemical process of erosion of steel is fairly well understood, as is the physical-chemical problem of metal "fatigue" in steel structures. But the exact conditions during welding, the exact exposures, the exact system of strains on a structure exposed to high waves in the North Sea, all are sufficiently badly known so that unexpectedly bad corrosion is found. The collapse of the *Sea Gem* was attributed by the Ministry enquiry to "brittle fracture of the hangers holding the deck" (Cooper and Gaskell, 1976:130-132).

(2) Geological uncertainty can be substantially reduced by drilling exploratory wells. But drilling rigs cannot work on the North Sea during the winter, require a crew of somewhere around 50 on the rig itself (or with a two-week rotation about 100 full-time employees just to run the rig), plus supply ships. The result is that an exploratory well at the depths usually involved in the North Sea cost, in 1979, around 5 million dollars or 25 million crowns. Obviously there will come a point at which the added information that would be obtained from another exploratory well in a given field is judged to be worth less than 25 million crowns, and there will be areas where seismic exploration is sufficiently discouraging so that no exploratory well will be drilled at all.

The result is that design of the production platform and production wells will be guided by imperfect information about the reservoir, not only because of true scientific limitations on knowledge, but because the knowledge is so expensive. Similarly the information about the currents and seabed conditions along the whole length of a pipeline might be had, to predict for instance how deeply it would have to be buried to keep the current from uncovering it, but such investigations might be more expensive than dealing with the problem of an exposed pipeline after laying it.

Sometimes what makes information expensive is the engineering or construction delay that would be involved in obtaining the exact knowledge. Obviously, for example, if one wants to predict "the largest waves that we can expect in a century" to decide the safety parameters of a platform, one would hardly want to wait a century to find out how tall the biggest waves were in fact. More reasonable examples, however, shade off into the fourth kind of technical and scientific uncertainty, so will be dealt with in more detail below.

(3) One principal case of uncertainty due to the necessity to get information from other organizations occurs early in the engineer-

ing process, with the buying of equipment. One has to sketch out the process plant and decide on major equipment specifications, then buy this equipment from the manufacturers, and do this rapidly. The reason is that the exact features of the equipment which are required for detailed drawings of the pipe and power hookups have to be obtained from the manufacturer. For example, one cannot specify in advance that one wants a pump, the center of whose outlet is 19 inches off the foundation, without excluding pump manufacturers whose pumps are 18 and 20 inches off the foundation. But if one designs the pipes to connect at 19 inches, and this turns out to be an inch too high or too low, one will have to do the drawings all over again. So one has to buy the pump first, find out its measurements, and then do the pipe drawings.

Many such specifications from outside bodies come in the form of regulations or standards, from yet another organization which is required to secure some other objective. The features of the lights and sirens on platforms to warn ships that might sail too close in bad weather must be specified by the coastal authorities, so that there is constancy in the meaning of different warning and navigational signals, and so that the signal can be entered on navigational maps. The certifying (or "classifying") organizations, which provide authorization for towout and an estimate of risks for insurance companies, develop standards of seaworthiness (Heimer, 1980). The designer of a construction barge or a platform which will be towed out as a semi-submersible must take these standards into account.

That is, many of the uncertainties of objectives which involve different authorities are resolved by one of the authorities issuing regulations which the engineers of platforms or construction barges or whatnot must conform to. We will deal with the problem of approvals in Part 4. For the present we want to emphasize that it is an uncertainty that has a social source when design criteria come from regulations or standards for approvals, rather than from nature.

When the government is inexperienced in a technical field, as the Norwegian government is in the oil business, or when the strength of political forces change (as does the strength of environmental conservation forces in Norway), these regulations will be in a constant state of flux, and will be additional causes of uncertainty in engineering.

(4) A typical example of an uncertainty which will be resolved with time has to do with the estimate of the quantity of work (e.g., the quantity of earth moving, the quantity of welding) involved in a given project. There are two main times one can "take the quantities off" by analyzing what will be required to build the design in each drawing. One is in the main engineering office, before the drawings go out to the field for construction. Another is in the construction office in the field, near the time when one is about to do the jobs. The one which determines the amount paid, of course, is measured at the time the work is done.

The early estimates in the main engineering office tend to be bad for two reasons. The first is that the engineers there are design engineers, and usually not experienced in construction. So, for example, they will compute the amount of earth to be moved by the amount of space which the subsurface structure takes, without allowing enough for working space for the construction workers, for construction roads to get the concrete in, etc. The second is that either they or the construction supervising engineers will change their minds about what is the most sensible way to build the thing, and the quantities will be different when they finally make up their minds.

One wants to know ahead of time how much a project is going to cost, and to have the quantities input into the cost-and-schedule monitoring process as soon as possible. One wants to know how big the project is, both to be sure to borrow enough money and to predict when the project will be done. So for planning and monitoring purposes, one wants to have the quantities taken off early in the main office.

But the true cost or the true schedule will be much better estimated if one waits until the final change orders have been decided on, and the construction engineers and managers have determined what is actually needed to accomplish the work.

So for monitoring and cost planning purposes, one has the choice of timely inaccurate information or late accurate information.

On a smaller scale the drilling of wells, especially exploratory wells, has the same character. One only really finds out where the walls of the hole will cave in when they cave in, and which layers of hard rock will wear out a bit every few inches when the bit wears out, requiring the crew to pull the whole drill train to replace the bit.

Generally speaking we can distinguish four stages of increasing certainty over time in the engineering process. The first stage we might call the "strategic decisions" stage. This involves such questions as estimating the size of a reservoir and deciding whether it is commercially exploitable or not, estimating the gas-to-oil ratio, deciding whether to build steel or concrete platforms, deciding how many platforms, deciding how the oil or gas is to be transported to shore, deciding the broad degree of integrated platform versus modular construction that will be used, and the like. The choice of broad alternatives generally involves a decisive interplay between the engineering consultants and the investing parties, with accounting standards being as important as engineering standards in the decisions.

These strategic choices then determine which kinds of further uncertainties the whole process will be subject to. For example, more modules means more delicate lifting by larger lifting barges, and so both the availability of heavy lifting barges and the weather conditions in which they can work become crucial uncertainties. But an integrated deck, while it may mean that more of the deck can be constructed on land before the structure is towed out, also means that delays in deck construction either delay the towout or force a higher proportion of construction at sea, which is much more expensive. The broad strategic choices are also choices of what kinds of later uncertainty one has to live with.

When the broad strategic choices are made, the next stage is the broad process design, which determines both the specifications for the major pieces of equipment which can then be put out to bid, and the specifications for the structure which can bear the process equipment. The uncertainties that are resolved, then, are those about specifications of equipment and overall requirements of the structures, so that the bidders for equipment and the engineers for the structures can go ahead.

When detailed specifications for the equipment have been received from the successful bidder, then the detailed drawings for foundations for the equipment and the connections for the equipment can be made. The final uncertainties about detailed design are supposed to be resolved by this stage, so that the work can be described to the construction managers and construction engineers.

The final stage in resolving the uncertainties is the engineering part of the construction process itself. What concrete actions have to be taken on the site to achieve the objectives specified in the design has to be decided, any bugs in the design that develop and can be detected at this stage have to be changed, and the like. The uncertainties that are resolved at this stage are those of what is actually involved in the construction process to achieve the design.

One might also specify a final inspection, hookup, and check-out stage, in which mistakes in all previous stages are found and remedied.

These different levels of uncertainty reduction (or successive stages of the design decision process, if you like) are very generally made by different groups of people, differently organized. The first stage, as we have already mentioned, tends to involve the ownership interests and accountants, as well as engineers, in the decision process. The broad design parameters in the process sketch tend to require widely experienced and talented engineers, and the process sketch often done by a relatively small group of senior engineers with a few assistants. The detailed drawings are relatively straightforward beginning engineer and draftsman work, and, except for keeping track and quality control, usually need not involve senior engineers at all. The construction engineering work requires not only engineering talents and experience, but perhaps more crucially, managerial experience and expertise. Since the job now is to translate plans into managed action, managing the action is as important as getting the plans right. And they were supposed to be right already, anyway.

Stages of the Construction Process

Somewhere around two-thirds of all work that goes into making a production platform goes into constructing the continuous system of well holes, pipes, equipment to separate gas and oil, drying or compression equipment for gas and stabilization equipment for oil to ready the product for shipment. Consequently in the engineering, the construction, and the drilling phases, it is ordinarily this integrated flow technical system which, at any of the stages, takes the most work and the most time. This is the part of the system which has to be designed to fit the characteristics of the field if there is to be productive efficiency, so while the engineering principles are well understood, the exact engineering specifications vary from one platform to another, and the construction process usually involves specially ordered equipment and piping, rather than equipment that can be bought from inventories. Consequently the stages of the construction process are mostly organized around this central system, since the smaller amounts of work on the other systems usually fit in rather well. The biggest exception is the towout and sinking of platforms, which is constrained by the weather to be done in the summer months, and so could hold up the project for about a year.

The first stage of the project as a whole is the general strategic choice stage, involving collecting information through seismic exploration and drilling exploratory wells, negotiating the organizational structure which will exploit the field and the division of ownership and responsibilities, making the major technical choices about what kind of platform(s) to have, and the like.

Since we have discussed this above, we need only add that delays in this part of the process are generally speaking of a "political" nature, having to do with the politics of granting exploratory concessions, ownership regulations of the Norwegian state as they change over time, and the like. We are not concerned with these delays here, and have not made an investigation of this stage of the process (see however Stinchcombe, 1980). The causes of delays are not primarily technical, and probably cannot usefully be analyzed by the devices of "project planning" we will mainly use in this analysis.

The second major stage is mechanical engineering, especially of the major continuous process equipment (the "engineering" of the well drilling is done separately, and is not apparently a cause of delays). It involves three main substages, and the engineering work must be well into the last stage before construction can get into full swing. The first substage is the general layout of the process equipment, so that the specifications of equipment to be bought can be decided. The next substage involves putting the equipment to be bought out to bid and receiving the bids back, in order to get the exact detailed drawings from the equipment manufacturers. This substage involves final approvals of the specifications, preparing commercial documents which make the contract legally and commercially satisfactory, review by the regulating authorities to check whether every effort has been made to make it possible for Norwegian firms to compete, reviewing the bids as they come in, and negotiating the final contract. It therefore takes quite a bit of time, about 5-6 months. Of this, roughly 3-4 months is the very minimum required by an oil company working in the United States with a low level of regulation and no cross-national negotiations to get through, and the other two or so months is added complication due to provisions for special reviews in Norway.

The general point here is that before one can go ahead with the design, one needs the engineering information from the supplier of equipment. But one cannot have the required degree of certainty in that information until the bidding process is complete and the contract is signed, because what makes this information certain is not science, but commercial and legal guarantees.

The third substage of the early mechanical engineering phase is to produce the detailed drawings for the mechanical structures, especially detailed drawings for the foundations, hookups through the foundations, pipe lengths and sizes, and structural steel supports for the piping and ancillary equipment. This is because for the construction process to get into full swing, these are the crucial pieces of the engineering that have to be done, on which all else depends. In the meanwhile, because the design of the structure does not usually involve buying much of anything from manufacturers, the part which is called "civil engineering" in English can go forward, so that the structure is engineered sufficiently well to have some place to put the foundations for the equipment and for the structural steel. It is not usually a cause of delays.

The next major stage is characterized by construction of the foundations and structural steel, and ordering the pipe (to detailed measurements specified in the design) for the major process equipment. This is because the foundations, structural steel, and pipe manufactured to measure, all have to be there for the next stage. Any one of these three processes may turn out to be causes of delays.

The fourth stage comes when the equipment and pipe are delivered, installed and the mechanical hookups are made. Somewhere in the third and fourth stages a cement semi-submersible type platform will be towed out and sunk in place. From the point of view of expense and delays in mechanical engineering, the later in these two stages it can be done (and the more of the "utilities" that can be finished on land) the better.

The fifth stage, drilling production wells, can come only after the platform is fixed in place, and so depending on what is done on shore and what is done at sea, it may go on simultaneously with the last stages of construction of the equipment for separating gas from oil and processing for shipment.

When the wells (or at least some of them) are finished, the testing, final hookup, and commissioning of the platform can take place.

Since there is some part of the engineering which is not on the critical path, along which any delay will delay the next stage, there is some slack in the timing of engineering and construction. Roughly speaking about 80 percent of the engineering work has to be finished before construction can go into full swing. Similarly there is a bit of slack in the relation between construction of the platform and the drilling of production wells, as noted above. And there is some slack at the end of the construction process, and some details can be finished after the platform is in production.

PART 3: ORGANIZING ENGINEERING WORK

Evidence of Difficulty in Engineering

Many signs, small and large, indicate that engineering performance is at the core of the administrative problems in North Sea construction. Perhaps the most elementary sign of this is the complaint by contractors that drawings for construction are not delivered on time. For example, the Director of Victor A/S says:

> Specifications, drawings, materials, and equipment are very often the client's responsibility. As a rule all these things are very much delayed, and the comprehensiveness of changes and additions very large. A doubling of the labor force in relation to that planned is more a rule than an exception. . . . An important reason for delays is also deficient use of modern planning and project management on the side of the construction client. (Storvik, 1976)

Similarly suppliers complain that the drawings when they come often do not contain sufficient information, as for example this statement of the Administrative Director of Høsveis A/S:

> The client used the time to send his "first draft" drawings, where there were suddenly new specifications and details to be seen. Clearing up these details by telex or letter takes time . . . (Semb, 1976:4)

In a discussion of the "Administrative procedures and routines in relation to the contractor's and client's cooperation during the building period," an executive from Akergruppen gives an example of the contents of the monthly meeting, of which point F is *"OVERDUE DECISIONS:* Lists of decisions, drawings, bid tabulations, etc., of which the Client is overdue" (Usterud, 1976:Sect. 3).

Aside from these kinds of evidence at the level of administrative detail, there is also evidence at the gross level of overall engineering performance on specific projects. Halvor Elvik has given figures in *Dagbladet* for example, which seem to show that the amount of engineering man hours has been increasing steadily in recent platforms of a Condeep type built for the North Sea in

the Norwegian sector, that engineering man hours used on Statfjord B were substantially more than projected, and that engineering work was delayed (Elvik, n.d.). E.J. Medley of Mobil
Exploration said that the systems for managerial control of the
Engineering Main Contractor on Statfjord B had taken some time
to develop to a satisfactory standard resulting, in his opinion, in
lowered engineering productivity in the project (Medley, 1979).
Evidence that the engineering work is difficult, or at least difficult
to evaluate, is that the English engineering consulting company,
Matthew Hall, was replaced during the Statfjord A project.
Difficulties with the replacement company, a joint venture
between Brown and Root and Norwegian Petroleum Consultants,
are indicated by the fact that on Statfjord B certain managerial
jobs, specifically scheduling and cost-control, were taken back out
of the engineering contractor's responsibility by Mobil and the
other owners.

The fact that engineering is a core difficulty is also indicated by
various proposals to reorganize the engineering process in order
to render it more efficient. For example, K. Tovshus urges that if
the building contractor does the engineering work, both construction costs and construction time can be minimized, while the
development of detailed specifications and regulations by the
client, the state, or classifying agencies reduces the capacity of the
constructor to work efficiently (Tovshus, 1976.1). See also the
statement by Vice Director Ian H. Miller, Akers Mek. Verksted.

> The oil companies' main philosophy is that the oil company is
> responsible for the technical solutions. . . . For the builder
> this can often result in the fact that the structures are not
> optimal with respect to manufacture and that changes are
> continually introduced that can be difficult for the builder to
> administer. (Miller, 1978:11-12)

One of the consequences of this difficulty with the engineering
work is increased difficulty of Norwegian contractors in becoming
suppliers to the oil industry, because besides adjusting to what the
American companies want, they have to adjust as well to the fact
that the American companies do not know what they want.

Aside from the delays and the increased costs of the projects this creates, it produces disputes about bad performance and possible bad faith; accusations range from the major level of hints that perhaps the Brown and Root company was chosen as engineering contractor because of interlocking ownership in multi-national corporations (since it couldn't possibly be on the ground of their superior performance – just look at their performance), to small bitter details of who should pay the cost of changes: "Apparently small changes that are called 'changes that any experienced pressure vessel manufacturer has included in his quotation,' cost in reality more than the satisfaction you get out of it." (This is a pretty free translation: Semb, 1976:5)

Further it puts the contractor quite often in difficult position, as when he has to go ahead building according to drawings for a changed design, when the "change order" has not been approved (see Tovshus, 1976:13-14) "We insisted that they had to take a decision in order for the work to go forward. Nothing helped." (Semb, 1978:6). In this case there were also disputes about whether the extra charges were justified by the engineering contractor.

There are then multiple pieces of evidence that the delivery of engineering decisions, and the performance of engineering contractors, is a central organizational problem in the administration of projects in the North Sea. Note that the evidence given above involved several different engineering contractors, several different operators, and data from several different building or manufacturing contractors. That is, the problem of organizing engineering work is not simply one of happening to get a bad engineering contractor in a particular case. It is clearly a general problem with this sort of project. The general purpose of this part is to analyze where these problems of engineering organization come from, in order to suggest what might be done about them.

The Decoupling Principle in Project Administration

The overall argument of these sections on organizing engineering work is that the arrangements that have been in use in the North Sea violate a central principle of efficient organizational design, which I shall call *the decoupling principle* (the argument that follows is partly derived from Thompson, 1967). Briefly the principle states that activities that depend on each other (are "closely coupled") should be administered together under the same responsibility, and that *only when activities are decoupled* should they be divided between different firms, or done under different contracts, or be done by different departments within a firm. This implies that *if* one wants to divide responsibility, *one ought to* decouple the activities. Conversely *if* there are practically irreducible interdependencies among activities (if they are closely coupled), *one ought to* administer them under the same responsibility. But first let me elaborate the decoupling principle:

1. The more two activities (or two sets of activities, such as engineering and construction) are interdependent, so that the details of what one does in one activity depend on what the results of the other activity are, the more *information* has to flow from the one activity to the other, so that the activities can be coordinated.

1a. The more two interdependent activities have to be executed *quickly in series*, the greater the quantity and urgency of requirements for *fast communication* between those activities, with the scheduling of the communications then being almost as important as the scheduling of the activities.

2. The more two activities are interdependent in detail, the more combined authority for making adjustments in both activities (so as to adjust one to facilitate the other one) will save time, cost, and administrative headaches.

2a. The more quickly adjustments of activities to each other have been made, because of quick series dependence, *the more important it is for combined authority to adjust both activities to be concentrated at the lowest possible level* above the people who carry out the activities.

3. The more two activities depend on each other in detail, the more deficient performance of either will affect the productivity of the other, and consequently the more difficult it will be to allocate responsibility for costs, delays, inferior quality, or other difficulties, between the activities. To put it more briefly, the productivity of interdependent activities cannot easily be measured separately. Consequently *responsibility for costs and pro-*

ductivity of two interdependent activities should be located in the same place.

3a. When two interdependent activities can be separated in time, the cost, delays, or inferior quality of the first can be assessed before the second activity is done (though often with difficulty). But *when interdependent activities must be done quickly in series, responsibility for poor performance (or for exceptionally good performance) cannot be allocated clearly between them.*

From a practical organizational point of view, all three of these principles lead to the same conclusion, that information, authority, and responsibility for two interdependent activities should be concentrated in the same person, the same firm, or the same decision-making procedure; and that this is more important when one wants to do the interdependent activities quickly in series. The converse of that principle is that if one wants to allocate two interdependent activities to two different firms, one ought to decouple the activities, and that one will pay great costs for being in a hurry.

Of course people do not choose freely what troubles to get themselves into. Engineering intensity caused by each platform being a prototype in the Norwegian North Sea has made it very difficult to decouple engineering and construction activities. The great sensitivity of costs and rates of return on North Sea projects to delays has meant that one could not afford *not* to be in a hurry. The Norwegian engineering firms' lack of experience with oil process equipment and with complete platforms, combined with the Norwegian government's desire to get some of the construction business for unemployed shipyards, made it virtually impossible to put the engineering and construction work under one firm. Both of the administratively rational strategies were therefore more or less excluded (because of higher rationalities of profitability and Norwegian public policy).

The next few sections are an elaboration of this argument into details of various kinds, to show how specific aspects of the difficulties of administration are related to the violation (more or less inevitable under the circumstances) of the decoupling principle.

Because tightly interdependent activities have not been decoupled before they were divided between the operator, the engineering consultant, and the construction contractor, difficulties in information flow (e.g. late drawings), in adjustments of activities (e.g. design for construction efficiency), and in measurement of performance (e.g. "changes any experienced pressure vessel manufacturer has included in his quotation") have plagued the construction process.

The Engineers and the Owners

The owners (and more especially the operator as a representative for the owners) have four major responsibilities for which they need engineering information. (1) They must choose between the main technical and economic alternatives in developing a field, such as concrete semisubmersible gravity structure versus piled steel jackets, pipelines versus loading at sea into tankers, etc., must decide generally whether, given such choices, development is economically profitable, and must arrange for the corresponding amount of investment money. (2) They must supply the technical details, specifying materials to be supplied and the activities which the building contractors and the suppliers of equipment must perform, and take legal responsibility for the contracts entered into with these suppliers and contractors, and to do this they must *authorize*, or make final decisions about the engineering work. (3) They must maintain overall cost and scheduling control to ensure the profitability originally estimated. And (4) they must inspect and accept the work of the suppliers and building contractors and authorize payment.

For the major strategic technical and investment decisions, the owners need (1) fairly accurate early estimates of costs, which depend on engineering quantities. For entering into contracts with suppliers and contractors, they need (2) engineering specifications. For maintaining cost and schedule control they need (3) an engineering plan restated in terms of physical quantities, so that it can be compared to the physical quantities delivered by contractors or suppliers, and some sort of engineering network schedule, so that completed accomplishments of milestones can be compared with scheduled completions. And for acceptance and authorization for payment, they need (4) inspection and certification of the technical adequacy of the delivered product, together with a supply of the necessary technical information so that the owner can actually operate and maintain the completed structure.

Clearly when a fifth to a quarter of the cost of a production platform is likely to be engineering work, the owner does not want to commission all the detailed drawings before deciding whether the project is economically defensible. The best estimates of the cost will come after engineering has been almost completed, when the contracts are let for the construction and outfitting. Even at that time experience indicates that the cost will be underestimated by about 15 to 20 percent. At least 80 percent of the engineering work, or roughly a fifth of the cost of the project, will have been paid out already before such accurate estimates are available. Before that time the estimates are much more uncertain.

The key to earlier estimates, needed for the investment decision by the Norwegian government and by the other owners, is "comparable experience." The question, for instance, of how far experiences in the Gulf of Mexico or the Persian Gulf are relevant to the North Sea applies in large measure to this stage of development of a project. It is true that one has to engineer *all* the projects for the particular site and conditions, and the North Sea is generally more hostile. But in making early decisions on whether a field is commercial, one might (for example) take the cost of a platform of comparable size in the Gulf of Mexico, and multiply it by a factor which corresponds to how much more difficult it is to work in the North Sea (estimated perhaps, by the excess cost of drilling exploratory wells). No doubt the actual procedure is more complex than this, but this gives an idea of what is involved.

If it turns out that the projects are in fact quite different (as it has turned out), these early estimates based on non-comparable comparisons will be shown to be wildly off. In the North Sea, this has meant wildly underestimated.

In contrast, if one wants to estimate what a concrete platform very similar to Statfjord B would cost, as an alternative structure for Statfjord C, the cost of B will provide much relevant information.

Thus the differences between the early estimates and the final costs can be expected to decrease, as the experience of building in the North Sea provides a fund of comparable instances. It appears, for example, that the other owners in the Statfjord field (other than Mobil and Statoil) had access to cost experience in the North Sea which led them to estimate the Statfjord A costs much better than the Norwegian authorities did.

The engineering information required for such early "investment estimates" then consists in two parts – enough engineering information to tell which other projects are comparable, and to tell what aspects of the new project are likely to make it more (or perhaps, someday, less) expensive. This early engineering information is provided by an early decision on strategic questions and the relevant major engineering quantities, and a fund of historical experience (together with costs) on comparable instances, so that these crude engineering quantities can be turned into preliminary cost estimates. It appears that most of this work is done in the normal case by the operator, though they may buy accumulated engineering experience from a consultant.

One general point of great importance here is that the departure of later estimates from these early crude estimates is not to be blamed on the engineering contractor. That is like executing the messenger who brings news of a defeat in battle – the messenger did not lose the battle.

The problem of accumulating historical engineering experience in a form useful for estimates, of validating that information, and of correcting it in the light of further experience, rather falls between the responsibilities of the different specialties or disciplines. Neither engineers, nor experienced managers, nor economists, are specialized historians accumulating experience so as to provide the parameters to translate engineering quantities into cost estimates. By default, then, the responsibility for this tends to fall on the experience of chief executives. In general one needs experienced responsible executives to resolve those uncertainties that, at the present time, one cannot resolve any other way.

Further, much of this historical experience is based on information which is a business secret, squirreled away in the files or experience of the various oil companies and engineering consultants rather than publicly available. Insufficient experience to form sensible early estimates for a variety of engineering alternatives may turn out to be a central deficiency of Statoil as an operator (though what experience they have, will at least apply specifically to the Norwegian shelf).

The central difficulty for the owner does not, however, come from poor engineering information at the estimating stage, at least up to the present time. The fields have turned out to be profitable enough so that mistakes in early estimates merely decrease profits from fabulous to rich. And much of the decrease is in tax returns to the Norwegian state, which may worry the state, but is not directly the owners' problem. Instead the central trouble is in the delivery of specifications for purchasing and letting contracts. We will view this from the point of view of contractors and suppliers below, but a few comments on the owners' problem are appropriate here.

There are really four main forms of contract for construction work with increasing degrees of engineering certainty. The most uncertain engineering information, where the work to be done cannot be described except in most general terms, results in a contract on an hourly basis. Quite generally major pieces of equipment (drilling rigs, lifting barges, pipelaying barges, etc.) are contracted for on a time basis, because it is difficult to predict exactly how long they will be used. But at the extreme, the whole project can be let on a charge-per-working-hour-plus-overhead basis.

The second stage of specificity occurs when the project can be described by the component activities (earth moving, concrete pouring, pipe welding, etc.) but the quantities are not yet known in detail. Then contracts can be let on a price per quantity basis, providing much better incentives for efficiency, providing also a better basis for cost estimates (because the owner does not have to estimate productivity), and providing a better basis for award of contracts to the most efficient builder.

When the construction work can be described in considerable

detail, but there are still final changes expected, one can let fixed-price contracts for specified work, together with agreements about how the costs of changes and additions will be calculated.

And finally (this last stage applies in the North Sea mainly to supplies and equipment rather than construction) one can specify completely what the technical requirements of equipment as installed must be, and expect that these will remain fixed, and enter into a pure fixed price contract.

Obviously from the point of view of estimating costs and maximizing incentives for efficient performance by the contractor, the last type is preferable. But it requires virtual certainty in the engineering information before entering into a contract for construction.

Generally speaking the less the rush to finish (or the lower the returns for finishing early), and the more similar a project is to projects previously built, the easier it is to move toward the contracts that are more preferable from an incentive and cost-prediction point of view. But note that this requires two organizations to perform their respective roles on time – the engineering contractor to provide the final drawings and specifications, and the owner to approve these and translate them into legal specifications for the contractor.

We will analyze the general problem of approvals in Part 4 but a relevant order of magnitude is provided on an "ideal schedule for preparing subcontracts" (Bent, 1979) – preparation of the drawings and specifications is projected to take four weeks, while review and finalizing the contract packages (i.e. the owner's responsibility when engineering and ownership are separated) are projected to take 3 weeks. The time for the actual engineering work then has to be supplemented with approximately three quarters as much time to turn that engineering information into a final decision about what to require in the actual contracts. Obviously this approval work depends in detail on the engineering work itself, and cannot be done before the engineering work is done. And if the overall schedule is to be maintained it must be done quickly in series.

In general, as a consequence, the contract specifications go out late to bid, have imperfections and incomplete descriptions in them, and in other ways are imperfect. And this in its turn creates pressure to cut down the time the contractors and suppliers have to reply to the bids, and to cut down the time allowed (in the specifications) for construction. This in turn increases the costs for bidding and increases construction costs. These consequences of organizational separation between closely coupled activities should be the focus of future studies of inefficiencies in North Sea construction.

We will devote a separate part to the cost control system, and will take up the relation of engineering information to cost control there. The main dependence is that costs and schedules both depend on what actual activities have to be done, so that the whole basis of schedule and cost control is engineering information, broken down in a new way. Engineering specifications have to be reanalyzed into components of costs, and components of time (especially time along the "critical path" of activities which depend on each other). This gives a (supposedly) realistic *ideal* progress of the project as a whole, with which actual physical progress can be compared.

For example, the "S-curve" of person-hours of construction time "expended" and "earned" is a central control device. The "earned" person-hours are computed as follows: the physical quantities to be delivered are taken off the engineering drawings and specifications; the estimated total person-hours to accomplish the specified work is broken down into the work required to accomplish each of the physical quantities, either on the basis of historical experience or on the basis of the contractor's pricing of the components of the contract; the physical quantities of work *actually* accomplished are then translated into the *hours it should have taken* to accomplish that work.

This quantity is then compared with two other quantities, with the number of hours actually expended, giving indication of problems in productivity (and of cost control), and with the amount of work accomplished that was projected to be complete at the time, giving an indication of problems in schedule.

From our point of view here, it is important to note that both the translation of physical accomplishments into person-hours earned, and the comparison of this to the ideal S-curve, depend on translating engineering information into estimates of person-hours required. Thus owner control over costs and schedule depends on the quality of engineering information, and when there is a (typical) 20 percent margin for additions and changes (engineering uncertainty), it necessarily means a 20 percent margin for cost and schedule control (managerial uncertainty) as well as the 20 percent margin for investment decisions (economic uncertainty).

A particular difficulty in this area is that information from the field about changes in construction plans reaches the cost and schedule control centers fairly late, presumably because people out on the site of construction want to get the welders to work first, then correct the cost engineers' projections later. Because the field personnel of the owner and of the engineering contractor, and more especially the personnel of the building contractor, give low priority to change information for the owner's control purposes, the overall quality of cost and schedule control is lower on contracts of the types that involve high engineering uncertainty.

Engineering uncertainty should be pretty well resolved by the time inspection and acceptance is in question. But it should be noted that the people who will repair, or who will plan improvements, do need the information about what was actually built rather than what was once planned to be built. Consequently all the previous engineering decisions have to be incorporated into "as built" drawings. Manuals of procedure and maintenance for the equipment actually installed, organized according to the operating systems rather than according to supplier, are needed. The guarantees against defects in materials and workmanship have to be executed as of the date when the work is accepted, rather than as of the date when it was hoped it would be complete. And the costs of construction have to be added up in a new way to give a total cost for each capital asset which the accountants want to treat separately for depreciation purposes. While the reorganization of engineering information for acceptance, commissioning and accounting is not really resolution of engineering uncertainty, there is more such last minute engineering work when the "as built" plans are quite different from the original draft plans, when the schedule is markedly different, and when the equipment that makes up a given system has been modified and functions differently than planned.

Overall, then, while the owner's responsibilities use engineering information throughout, the principle of decoupling applies especially for the delivery of detailed drawings and specifications prior to putting the contract out to bid. This should presumably be the focus of further studies of delays and cost overruns in the relationship of the owner to the engineering consultant.

Engineering and Purchasing

The general reason one purchases equipment, rather than constructing it to order, is that the manufacturer has his systems, engineering, and tools, all set up to produce a high quality product more efficiently than it can be made to order. But this in its turn means that the technical features of the equipment will be constrained by the systems in the *manufacturer's* plant, and that it will be costly to require variations. When the buyer (and the buyer's engineering consultant) have grown up in the same technical culture as the manufacturer, the specifications will tend to be designed so that they will fit with manufacturers' systems and the manufacturers will be producing to the specifications generally required in their market. To take the simplest example, both equipment and pipes will be oriented to inches in the United States, to centimeters in Europe.

A large part of the technical culture which is required for manufacturers and clients to understand each other, and to design their respective systems so that they fit together, are specified and formalized in "standards" developed by engineering societies. For example the "standards" for pressure vessels may specify thicknesses and qualities of steel, features of welds, testing procedures, and the like. The steel in turn will be described in a pressure vessel standard according to other standards for describing steels in that technical culture. So the set of standards forms an integrated information system which serves to coordinate, in this case, the steel manufacturer, the pressure vessel manufacturer, engineer who designs a system involving pressure vessels, and ultimately the construction contractor.

A principal problem in this area has been that the American oil companies use the technical standards in common use in the United States, which differ in details from those in use in Europe. This makes for several kinds of difficulties. Perhaps the most important is that a "buy Norwegian" policy requires that all specifications be reviewed to see whether they are described, as much as possible, in such a way that Norwegian manufacturers can compete for them, and this review may add as much as a couple of months to the procurement process. Since the procurement process is on the critical path, this adds a couple of months to the project completion time.

A second difficulty is that communication between the manufacturer and the engineers becomes difficult, producing the sort of problems of what the content of specifications described as by Semb (1976:3): "and some lines here and there which were supposed to indicate 'known' details for any experienced 'pressure vessel manufacturer,' as it was said." Obviously guessing what the "known details" would be depends on sharing the technical culture of the engineers who draw up the incomplete specifications.

Planning Engineering Work

The problem with planning engineering work is that if one knew what design one wanted to build, one could describe exactly how much drawing and approving and other engineering work had to go into it. But if one knew the design, one would not need any more engineering work. Precisely because engineering work is reducing technical uncertainties to drawings and specifications, it is uncertain exactly what is involved. This is one of the reasons why engineering services tend to be contracted for on an hourly basis, cost plus overhead. It is also one of the reasons why optimistic predictions about when the engineering work will be done tend to go astray.

The complaint we quoted above from a builder, that the engineering contractors themselves did not use the management techniques that they required of the building contractors, is partly explained by the greater uncertainty of engineering work, and for that reason is unlikely ever to be overcome entirely.

But there are two sources of lack of planning in engineering work which might conceivably be remedied. The first is simply lack of investment in the planning function, that is, in the early formulation of network schedules for the engineering work itself, and in the measurement of "outputs" of engineering work (comparable to the physical measures in construction work) which are required for formal planning and schedule control systems. The second is the accumulation of historical experience about time lags and person-hours required, so that the basic parameters required for rational planning of engineering work would be available.

Perhaps another source of difficulty is that engineers are professionals, proud of the dignity of being the people who use their superior knowledge to help others resolve uncertainties about what should be done. Since it is knowledge rather than activity or "labor" which is their stock in trade, measuring the output of an engineer as if he were merely a laborer might be insulting. Insulting highly skilled labor on whom your schedule depends is a central mistake of labor relations on projects of this kind – Mobil for example has invested considerable time and effort in training their supervisors not to mistreat Norwegian welders or cement masons, and the British have had consistent difficulties in keeping skilled workers at sea rather than on strike. Measurement of engineering productivity should therefore be evaluated very carefully – even professionals who ordinarily wear their hair short can go on strike if they are insulted by too close measurement of their "labor."

Design for Maximizing Construction Efficiency

The following is a typical problem in construction which may not be taken into account by an inexperienced engineer. The tolerances to which one ordinarily works in masonry and concrete work are much larger than the tolerances required for piping, for example. Loosely, the pipes have to meet "exactly," while it usually does not hurt if masonry is a centimeter or more off. *On a drawing*, however, it is not clear that the measurement for concrete is within a centimeter, while for the pipes it is much more "exact." Now if the two systems depend on each other, it is much more convenient during construction if the connection between them is designed to be adjustable without much investment of work. Such adjustable couplings may have to be designed late, as change orders, when the construction engineer sees they are needed.

A similar problem is that the structural support for a construction can also quite often be used as a structural support for scaffolding, and if proper attention is paid to this in design, much scaffolding cost (and time) can be saved.

By and large engineers are trained to design the finished structure or the finished equipment, rather than to design a construction process. To put it another way, in manufacturing an "industrial engineer" who designs a manufacturing process is a different specialization than a design engineer, but specialization in construction is usually only by experience. This means that optimizing the construction process tends to be neglected in the design of construction projects.

Where similar work is done on a manufacturing basis, as for instance in shipyards which have produced several very large oil tankers, the ship design and the manufacturing process design can be integrated so as to produce greater construction efficiency. If experienced construction engineers were not so valuable in construction itself, it would be wise to add them to the design engineering force.

Note that the argument quoted above (Miller, 1978) argues that this is an advantage of having the detailed engineering done by the building contractor. One of the competitors for the engineering contract for Statfjord, Bechtel, uses its "construction orientation" as a principal selling point. Whether this is organizationally rational or not, on net balance, the fact that the argument is made by distinguished and experienced people indicates that the design orientation of engineers often presents a problem. It has been argued that much of the reduction in costs between the various Condeep platforms built by Aker (*before* Statfjord A that is) was due to relatively minor redesign for improved construction efficiency of platforms that were basically similar.

The Costs of Engineers Changing Their Minds

The complaints about working under "change orders" are constant among the Norwegian building contractors. The normal percentage of added work between letting the contract and contract completion in the North Sea has ranged around 15 to 20 percent, which is very much larger than is usual in shipbuilding or building construction. The general problem this creates for project management is that a sixth to a fifth of what one has to plan for is not known in advance. This entails various sorts of difficulties.

The first difficulty is that the costs of work done under a change order are generally considerably higher than costs of work done under the original plan. Since the contractor's added costs are calculated more or less exactly, it should be possible to accumulate data on this cost difference, on a per ton of equipment or per dollar of increased output basis. This seems not to have been done. And of course a change order not only involves work by the contractor, but also extra administrative work by the engineering consultant and the owner. We can lay down a general rule that if costs are not calculated, they are almost always underestimated when the decision is made. When costs are calculated only *post hoc*, as they typically are for work done under change orders, nobody really needs information on whether the change was rational to make a decision. The decision has already been taken, for better or for worse, and it is water over the dam.

Only for formulating rules of thumb (e.g. a rough estimate of the internal rate of return for a change order might be required to be twice as large as the rate of return used for added features in the original design period, as a rule of thumb for deciding whether the change was justified, on the supposition that changes usually cost twice as much as they appear to) does one need hard information on how much changes cost. Let us, however, note some features of working under change orders that are relevant to costs.

A first difficulty is that changes are done under pressure of the schedule, because the completion of other work depends on the work involved in the change. In general this results in lower quality of decisions. For example, in general a separable part of a project which involved 15 to 20 percent of the costs would have a separate rate of return calculated, and there would be some considerable attention devoted to whether it was worth the while. This economic evaluation is foreshortened because of the pressure of time in change orders. Very often the work involved in a change order has to go ahead before the order has been formally approved. Practical people know this, so they are very cautious about disapproving changes that have already been built into the platform. But this means that whatever the purpose of the approval process was – whatever the approvers were supposed to see to – has not been incorporated in the decision. So the quality of the decision is generally lower if the decision is taken as a change order.

A second trouble is that there are two rather considerable overhead costs that may not get reflected in the costs charged to the change order. The first is simply the considerable cost of "follow up" of the costs of the change, an administrative overhead. Because it is not included in the contract, any extra work involved has to be separately accounted. But this work involves quite often a half an hour here, a day there, a few hours with a crane, and so on through a lot of details. In the overall cost of an item already included in the contract, a bit of sloppiness in the cost attribution process can be tolerated. But someone has to pay for the added record keeping, and this has to be added record keeping all the way from the foreman in the field to the purchasing office, to the accounting office, to the billing of the construction client.

Besides this follow up, there is also the administrative work by the contractor in getting the decision made, the time of an expensive construction manager announcing firmly over the phone that we have to have a decision on this by tomorrow or the job will be held up. All these administrative costs tend to disappear in general overhead, rather than being attributed to the change order. As a construction client one does notice that the performance of a builder goes down when he does not spend enough on administrative overhead, but part of the reason he needs to spend so much is that it is administratively much more expensive to work under a change order, or in a system that has a lot of change orders.

A very similar problem is involved in the costs of labor flexibility. When, as was pointed out in a quotation by a builder earlier, one has to allocate double the number of workers more as a rule than an exception, that means that one has to maintain an organization ready to double its amount of work in a given specialty on a very few days notice. In Norway, where people are not recruited and laid off as easily as in the United States, this often means maintaining an office in readiness to enter into subcontracts on short notice, maintaining information about who has idle capacity of various kinds, and the like. The general point is that flexibility does not come cheap, and it is possible that flexibility in labor force requirements and "forcing" may be more expensive in Norway, with her superior provisions for stability of employment.

A third and final difficulty is that the change order is very often on the critical path, and has to be completed before other work can go forward. This means that change orders often produce delays. It is likely that the costs of delays are generally underpriced, because the delays tend to be attributed to the building contractor, rather than to the engineering consultant who makes the decision involved in the change order. Thus the incentive system governing the engineers (rewards for showing that they provided the best possible design) does not correctly evaluate the troubles they cause the building contractor. This is a particular case of the violation of the third element of the decoupling principle, that the authority to make changes tends to be located among the engineers, while the responsibility for the outcomes rests with the builder, resulting in inaccurate incentive system. It does not reward the engineer for saving construction time, and punishes the contractor for engineering inefficiencies.

The Engineer and Managerial Information

When two activities are as interdependent as engineering and construction (at least when one is in a hurry), we have argued that they should be under the same authority. But when they are in different organizations, putting the engineers in charge of the construction has serious disadvantages (unless the engineers truly take responsibility for total contract cost and schedule). The difficulty is caused by a violation of the decoupling principle.

The problem is that the owner must assess the performance of both the builder and the engineering consultant, both to decide whether to employ them further and to identify sources of cost overruns and schedule difficulties. If the engineers are put between the owner and the builder in the authority and management system, the communications link between the builder and the owners is biased. Since in this particular situation much of the difficulty is caused in engineering, what the engineers should be telling the owners is that they themselves have done a bad job. Not bloody likely. What the owner is likely to hear is that the building contractor is doing a bad job.

It is significant that when the owners reorganized the Statfjord B project, one of the responsibilities they took back into their own hands was cost and schedule control. And one can find in the comments by contractors that it is important that among the people at the site representing the client, there be not only people from the engineering consultant but also from the oil company. Note that the close interdependence between the "client" and the "builder" is indicated by Storvik's statement about the organization at the site of representative of the client: "For a contract of the order of magnitude of 10 to 20 million dollars, this organization can amount to 15 to 20 people" (Storvik, 1976).

Organizational Options

Each of the organizations in the oil business has a historically developed competence and a built in "orientation," represented in the experience of senior executives, the manpower composition of the staff, the kind of business in which the standing orders and routines were developed, and so on. To take a simple example, O. Usterud of the Aker group says, "Experience has shown that usually, here in Norway, one looks at these types of projects from the point of view of traditional shipbuilding practice, where one is used to being master in one's own house" (Usterud, 1976:1). Because one has to build joint enterprises out of the organizational materials historically available, and those materials have traditions of their own, "ideal descriptions" of what should be done may not apply to the particular case. Instead what I will try to do is to outline alternative ways in which the problems of failure to observe the decoupling principle might be reduced.

One option would be to give the engineering contractor the status of building contractor, rather than consultant to the owner. One trouble with this strategy will tend to disappear in any future activities with Statoil as operator, because the engineering company will not necessarily be American. This means that we can expect a reduction in many difficulties that come from the engineering company having its historical competences in working in the American environment, and its historical orientation toward building with American building contractors and suppliers. The engineering company could then subcontract the actual building work, but they would truly be the client for that work rather than a representative of the client, and they would have responsibility for delivering the whole project on time and within cost. Whether they could add construction management competence to their engineering competences would have to be evaluated.

Another alternative would be to turn over that part of engineering work which is closely interdependent with construction work, namely purchasing of equipment and preparing detailed construction drawings, to the builder. The choice here depends in part on how much one wants to give priority to construction efficiency, as compared with optimum design from an oil-producing point of view.

A third option would be for Statoil to operate in Norway as many oil companies do in the United States, and work on a "direct hire" basis, taking responsibility for the construction process itself. The difficulties of a state organization hiring and laying off people as if it were a mere capitalist enterprise probably militate against this solution.

Perhaps a fourth option would be to reorganize the consulting contract in some way so that the incentives for individual engineers, and for the consulting firm as a whole, would depend very sharply on measures of promptness and completeness in the delivery of engineering information, so that they paid for difficulties they create for the builder. Whether such measures could be designed, whether they would be acceptable to engineering consulting firms, and whether such a capitalist way of organizing things would be culturally acceptable as a way of administering Norwegian state resources, all would have to be evaluated.

Probably, however, such grand designs to solve all the problems with one master stroke are illusions. What probably needs to be done instead is to collect experience on the sorts of difficulties that usually have the worst consequences in practice, to sit down with senior engineers, senior executives from the operator and owners, and senior project managers from the builders' side, and to figure out how to manage such troubles one by one. If our argument is correct, in each case what they should be concentrating on is decoupling activities which cannot be administered under one authority, creating joint authorities (responsible for the information, the management of workers, and the measurement of outputs and costs) for activities that cannot be decoupled, or developing mechanisms of cooperation which subsitute for these ideal solutions.

PART 4: THE APPROVALS SYSTEM

Approvals in Projects with Multiple Organizations

According to E.J. Medley, the General Manager of Mobil Exploration Norway, getting approval of the general design of the Statfjord B platform took a year, and is the primary explanation for the excessive use of engineering time. The apparent cause of this year-long delay (for purposes of comparison, at the end of May 1979 the most-delayed part of construction, that at Fredrikstad Mek. Verksted, is only delayed 5 weeks) is a true disagreement about safety standards (Medley, 1979a).

Roughly speaking Mobil thought that Statfjord A was safe enough, so designed Statfjord B, in the first instance, to the same standards. The Norwegian government decided that Statfjord A was not safe enough, so specified additional requirements for Statfjord B. According to the estimate by Ager-Hanssen, the increased requirements themselves used up about a sixth of the anticipated revenues of the project, about the same amount as the increased costs of materials and labor (Ager-Hanssen, n.d.).

But *coming to an agreement* about safety standards cost a year, and a very substantial number of engineering hours. Thus the cost of the safety provisions is not only the construction costs, but also the costs of a year delay and the engineering and managerial hours required to clear it up.

This case illustrates both the importance of approvals, and why they create difficulties. The reason the approval took so long is that the Department of Oil and Energy was responsible for a different objective, the safety of workers, than Mobil's primary objective, profitable operation. There is true disagreement about the tradeoffs between these objectives also within the Norwegian government – see Ager-Hanssen's statement that "Our North Sea surplus is finite. New regulatory requirements may absorb [a] very large part of that surplus. What will be of utmost importance in the future is that the investments in new safety measures are analyzed from the point of view of their costs and impact on overall safety before they are enacted." (Ager-Hanssen represents Statoil, that is, the part of the Norwegian government primarily responsible for profitability of oil operations.)

That is why three different engineering plans had to be developed before one was approved. But also no one in the Department of Oil and Energy, as the regulatory authority, loses promotions because of the year-long delay, while an executive in Mobil or in the Kværner group who caused a year delay would be urged to look for another position.

The point here is not that the extra safety is not worth the money, even counting in the money involved in the delay and the extra engineering. The point is rather that when different organizations try to secure different objectives with the same platform structure, the problem of working out the tradeoffs between objectives becomes more complicated. And more to the point of our analysis here, the pressure to create a way out of the complication is not proportional to the complication created, so that approving authorities work normal hours, while construction firms work double shifts to make up for it. The core problem is in incentive-consequence correspondence, that the consequences of a delay caused by slow approvals are not "paid for" by the person or organization causing the delay.

But the problem not only occurs at the grand political level of balancing profitability against workers' lives. The difficulty is very well illustrated by the practical administrative problems of sub-contracting. Jamie Bent (Bent, 1979) estimates that subcontract-ing for the construction of a project adds from 10 to 20 percent to the total time required (Fig. 6), and that it adds 25 percent to the space required per worker because the work cannot be as closely coordinated (Fig. 18). The central thing that differentiates admin-istration by subcontracts from administration by direct hiring is that the whole package of subcontracted activities has to be planned ahead by the client, who then has to approve of the package, and of the legal and administrative provisions of the contract, before bids are asked for. The owner or operator must, of course, have made at least rough estimates of how much it would cost, to judge whether or not it would be worth while to ask for bids.

But now the contractor has to estimate the cost to him (and to his competitors) pretty exactly. The contractor is going to end up being committed legally to deliver the specified activities at the specified price on the specified schedule, or pay damages (perhaps specified in the contract itself) for nonperformance. Thus before the bid goes in, it must be approved by authorities with the power to commit the contracting organization.

Now once a subcontractor has agreed to do specific work, for a specified price, he cannot be expected to worry too much about inconveniences he causes other contractors or subcontractors. That is why each of his workers requires more space and more time: coordinating information does not pass easily among sub-contractors, no one has superior authority to adjust each one's work to the others, and their incentives are not to get the overall project done, but to get their own work done.

It is for this reason that it is important to decouple activities which are going to be subcontracted separately (see Tovshus, 1976:12 on the importance of parts-projects being independent from each other). And in part the extra time taken in subcon-tracted projects is due to the fact, argued in detail in Part 3, that a gap or slack in the schedule is important for decoupling activities. So things cannot be run so tightly together when subcontractors are involved.

When all this is said, however, it remains the case that the primary cause of extra delays when there is a lot of subcontracting is that it requires extra approvals on both sides before the subcontract is entered into, and the approvals have to include more of the details of management of construction, than is the case with direct-hire projects.

A bit of consideration will show that the importance of approvals in subcontracting is due to the same basic cause as its importance in deciding tradeoffs in policy objectives. It is due to dividing the responsibility for different *technical* objectives, rather than different policy objectives, between different organizations. The reason one wants to do this is the same, that the electrical subcontractor will be better at reaching the objective of high quality electrical work at low cost, while the platform subcontractor can use his specific equipment and skills to minimize costs and delays in that construction.

The same reasons which make extensive final approvals necessary also make them administratively difficult. The system of incentives, and the corresponding system of responsibilities (a responsibility may be defined as an objective, the measurement of the achievement of which will determine the incentives paid to a worker or manager or to his organization), to which a person is subject is generally within his own organization. Whenever his activity has consequences for another organization, there is a difficulty in the fact that the people who must live with the consequences do not control the rewards and punishments (the promotions, the honor, the pay, the size of the office) of the person on whom they depend.

In much of commercial life this fact is recognized by the system for rewarding sales people. A sales person is exactly someone who must adapt the product of one organization to the use of another organization (or person). If he or she does this successfully, the user pays the producing organization, which uses part of that payment to increase the rewards of the salesman.

For obvious reasons we do not want the Department of Oil and

Energy to sell approvals for workers' safety. It is in fact because we are afraid that economic incentives will override safety considerations that we concentrate regulatory authority in a separate organization, which does not collect profits on the things whose safety it must approve. But in making their safety decisions independent, that is, by making their incentives not depend on the profits, we have also failed to reward them for speedy business dealings, and failed to punish them for the costs of the unnecessary delays they cause.

Even when the organization employing a person whose approval is necessary *does* depend on the outcome to some degree, as in the case of "owner's review," which occupies much of the calendar time early in the project, an outside organization which is inconvenienced by delay cannot easily make use of the authority system of the regulatory agency or even of the owner to get things moving.

The Demand for Documentation

A familiar example of how the cooperation of many organizations results in the multiplication of documents is the international shipping of general piece-goods cargo. In the port of origin, for example, documents have to be generated for the contracts of the freight-forwarder (whose main job is to create other documents), for the insurer, for the provider of transport within the country of origin, for the bank or banks through which payment is arranged, for the shipping company, for the warehousing and longshoring or loading companies (in different countries this may involve different numbers of firms), perhaps for the tax authorities who allow writing off part of the value added taxes, perhaps for export credit authorities if special credits from governmental sources are used, for the client and customs authorities in the receiving country, and then the invoices and checks to pay for all these services. Each shipment, which may average about four tons, thus generates somewhere around a day of clerical labor in the port of origin, just to arrange shipping. If we add the catalogues and technical specifications and bids and orders and all the other documents involved in the commercial export-import business as well, we can see why the labor force of major port cities has such a high white collar component.

It is not clear that the ratio of documents per ton is lower in the offshore construction business, and the documents themselves are more technically complex and demanding so that one cannot have them all filled out by clerks. A clerical worker can certify that four tons of women's slacks have been shipped and insured, but not that four tons of tubes have been welded in the right place, with welds that will not give way under 20 years of North Sea weather.

The general source of the multiplication of documents is that everything has to be referred to many organizations for many purposes, so it must be submitted in many copies, and each of the approvals in its turn creates a new document to be forwarded to the next level. When the process is also technically complex and costly, each document requires more skilled work.

The general problem of incentive-consequence correspondence shows up in the demand for documentation because the work and expense that goes into preparing the document is not paid for by the organization demanding the document. Thus in general one requires more complete information than is ordinarily needed, or even read, by the approving authority. This "free" information is required "in case it might be relevant in some case," rather than because it *is* relevant in *this* case. When much of the form of the interaction is routinized by years of experience and legal arrangements (for example in commercial practice, CIF stands for "cost, insurance, freight," and the terms of the insurance contract are so standard that one need not specify what they are), such routine specification of the information may be easier and cheaper than deciding what is relevant in each particular case. The shipping document may quite often be a printed form with a few spaces for information on the particular case. Such routines are not applicable when it is a contract for building something that has never been built exactly this way before. Thus the offshore industry combines high demand for numbers of documents and numbers of copies with a high level of expense for each document.

An additional cause for documentation delays is that one way to arrange for orderly decision making is to demand that all documents (representing previous decisions) be in order before a given decision – especially the decision to pay – can be taken. For example, consider the following list of documents about a purchase made by a contractor on behalf of the owner, to be submitted to the owner for payment:

Activity	Documentation
Bidders list	Approval
Technical specifications	Approval
Request for bids	Approval
Request for bids, log	For information, every fortnight
Copies of bids	For information (at least 3 suppliers)
Evaluation of bids/choice of suppliers	Approval
Order	Information
Order, log	Information every fortnight
Inspection reports	For approval (Perhaps with participation by owner)
Notice of arrival, inspection	Information
Preventive maintenance at storage	Information
Storage release, transport, receipt	Information
Invoice check and validation	Information
Charge to the owner	Approval

Note that there are six approvals required, only one of which (the charge to the owner) is made by the contractor alone. These approvals are involved merely in establishing that a given piece of equipment, meeting the required standards, and bought under legally acceptable conditions (e.g. that the bidders list had a substantial representation of Norwegian firms), was in fact delivered at a given cost. This set of documents, including the five previous approvals, then have to be approved by the owner (or in the usual case, by the operator as representative of the owners) before the contractor can be paid. The owner or operator does not want to pay unless, for example, the contract satisfies Norwegian regulations about the bidders list, because then it will be liable to the authorities.

But note that the reason all the documentation is required is not that the owner needs the information. Instead its purpose is to maintain the control and incentive system that makes the purchasing system orderly, fair, competitive, legal, and makes it satisfy the relevant technical standards. If one could build up routines on the basis of full confidence and trust, nine-tenths of the above documentation would not be necessary.

Of course, "trust" here is a complex concept. In this case, for example, one would have to "trust" the contractor to maximize access by Norwegian suppliers to the market, and this may well be against its short run interest. That is, "trust" involves believing that the other parties will follow a complex system of objectives and purposes and standards. When the system involves many organizations from several cultures, when it involves also true conflict between the Norwegian public interest and oil company interests and true differences in judgment about the capacities of Norwegian suppliers, and when the tax system allows generous writeoffs of capital costs (writeoffs depend entirely on the content of documents, because no one "trusts" a company to remember the cost of a machine and to write it off properly without documents), in short when the system has multiple reasons why people may be pursuing different objectives, "trust" is not easy to achieve.

When only one organization is involved, the authority system and the incentive system of the organization itself can be used to establish the same system of objectives, purposes, and standards throughout organization. Authority can substitute for documents and approvals. But even there one may, for example, construct a quality control department which is not under the control of the production supervisor, because the objective of quality control often conflicts with the objective of meeting production targets. In this case the internal system of the organization will have quality control "approvals" as if quality control were separate organization.

The Distribution of Waiting Times for Approvals

Cases of serious disagreement in the approvals process, like that over safety standards for Statfjord B, are relatively rare. Most approvals go through routinely. Sometimes, as we have noted, the approval is so routine that the contractor goes ahead to build a change order before it is approved. That does not mean that the approvals are unnecessary – it is often only the knowledge

that something must be approved that makes one obey regulations. It does mean that delays due to approvals that are "matters
of form" serve no purpose *for the case at hand* – they are instead
general prevention of deviance, a deterrence system. Anyone
who has waited several days for a document to be stamped
approved, and then sees a clerk glancing at each document in a
pile for a second or two, then stamping them one after the other,
knows this frustration of being held up for purposes of the
bureaucracy itself, rather than for substantive control.

The extreme of absolutely routine approvals is postmarking
mail that has been stamped. We would not put stamps on the mail
unless our stamps had to be checked but the postmarking is
entirely routine. But the time between finishing a letter and
getting it postmarked is highly variable, depending on how long it
sits on the typist's desk, on the performance of the organizational
mail room, on when and where it is mailed, on the collecting and
postmarking waiting times in the post office. The overall waiting
times between mailing and delivery are even more highly variable, because in order to be delivered a letter has to go through
several sequential steps: postmarking, sorting, transportation,
sorting again, more transportation, sorting at the receiving station, and delivery, for example. Each of these also has a distribution of waiting times with a long tail, that is, with a few letters
being delayed over twice as long as the average delay time. The
mail service is therefore a good place to get analogies for studying
delays in routine approvals.

It takes less than a day for a person to get from Bergen to a
given house in the United States, but it takes an airmail letter an
average of about nine days. This shows that sequences of normal
waiting times in a sequential process can easily multiply the
necessary time for an approval by nine times (even assuming that
the approval process does not take place during July or during
Easter week). And just as an occasional airmail letter takes over a
month, so sometimes the necessary approval work is multiplied by
30 before the approval goes out.

When the series of delay times is in production, rather than in
approvals, and therefore the person waiting is the one who pays,
the purchaser may require that his people be permitted in the

plant to "expedite" the order. One standard contract by an engineering prime contractor reads:

Physical Expediting

When [company name] deems it advisable this order shall be subject to physical expediting by [company name] representatives who shall be granted access to any and all parts of the seller's or sub-suppliers' plant involved in the manufacture or processing of this order.

No authority to change any activities in the supplier's organization is specified. The only thing the expediter can do is to point out that the material is being uselessly delayed. The drawing that lies in the in-basket for three days in an approvals process is in a comparable situation to the material not yet moved to the paint shop in physical expediting, or the letter waiting to be sorted in Copenhagen while the plane takes off for New York.

In some South American countries with oil deposits there is a profession of bureaucratic expediter. This person works out relationships (perhaps involving bribes) to enter government offices and to move papers physically from one bureaucratic station to the next. A normal three-week approval may be cut to a day by judicious expediting. An informal call by an old friend from engineering school, to find out what has happened to the documents about X, is perhaps the Norwegian equivalent.

The general problem here is the incentive system governing the distribution of attention. The reason a person can get from Bergen to a house in the U.S. in a day is that he or she is motivated to see that the right plane is caught, running if necessary and perhaps breaking into queues to make a connection, and if the taxi queue is too long he or she can take the bus downtown to get a taxi there, and so on. A person expedites himself or herself by paying attention. Ordinarily a letter is delayed by waiting for attention to be paid to it, and not by someone pondering for a long time to decide whether to send it by way of New York or Houston. Similarly unless there is good reason to do otherwise, a person in a government office or other approving authority deals with a paper when it comes to the top of the pile.

By the same reasoning, when a matter must be treated in a meeting, the next regularly scheduled meeting will determine the delay time. At that meeting it will probably be treated in almost no real time, with only a brief question "Any problems with X?" But if the next regular meeting is a Monday, and Monday is a holiday, then if there is no incentive for fast decisions the waiting time can be increased by a week.

It generally takes a very small incentive for an individual to pay attention to cases out of order. That is why expediters are effective even without bribes. "It has to be done anyway, so why not now?" But it takes a serious motive to reorganize an office administratively. For example, to cut down the number of exceptionally long (and so exceptionally infuriating) delays, one would need to keep a log of times in and times out, to follow up cases in which there was an exceptionally long delay, and to remedy the procedures (or the people) that lead to long delays. Simply requiring an explanation for all matters delayed over a week would cause a revolution, with mutual recriminations and explosive meetings with trade union representatives, in most offices of regulatory authorities. A superior in a regulatory office will not require such explanations unless the fury of the long delayed client matters more to him or her than the fury of employees.

Communicating Priorities

One of the central difficulties in scheduling approval work for construction is that it is very difficult to get accurate information about priorities. Obviously an approval that lies on the critical path, that is required before the construction can progress, is of much higher priority than something which can be done anytime before completion. The simplest priority system is the queue, first-in-first-out. It also has an obvious fairness, so that even in hospital emergency rooms a less serious patient grumbles when a more serious patient is taken first. If one asks a set of people waiting for approvals to classify their priorities into "Rush" and "Routine," all will end up classified as "Rush," just as all patients will classify their emergencies as urgent. The post office lets us pay for special delivery or express mail, and so cuts down the motivation for calling everything "Rush."

7 - Organization theory.

The simplest innovation in most regulatory offices would be to create an internal priority system, "Rush" and "Routine," and to classify approvals into the two categories on arrival in the office. Various rules of thumb could be used (e.g. all matters currently under construction might be in Rush, all others in Routine). Then a simple requirement that each person in the series of bureaucratic stations should date his treatment of the matter, and explain any delay of more than one working day, would probably create a motivational system of sufficient power for the purpose. People do not delay on purpose, but because they are not motivated to pay attention.

In order to allow a client – who finally has the best information about the true priorities – to influence the priority system, it would be necessary to create a cost to the client for higher priority, similar to the charge for express mail. Corruption in poorer countries or in American city political machines partly serves this purpose, since it creates a minor charge for "expediting." It is not my place to suggest a more corrupt Norwegian public administration, but ingenuity should be applied to invent a reputable functional equivalent of corruption, a system for the client of regulatory agencies to pay for priority treatment.

When an approvals process is sufficiently important *to the approving organization*, the usual solution is to set up a special fast approvals service for a particular project. For example, there is often a "project manager" with associated staff in the operator's organization, in Statoil, and in the engineering organization (besides the one in the construction contractors' organization). Much of the function of these project organizations is efficient management of approvals. A project manager in the operator's organization can use his authority to make sure the engineering and budget committees both produce their decisions in their meetings this week, instead of engineering this week, budget next week. That is, by reorganizing approvals sequences, one can avoid the long delays due to inattentive sequencing, with delays between each station.

There are several ministries and quasi-governmental organizations (e.g. Det norske Veritas) which have to approve various matters connected to oil projects. When the government must act fast, as in the Bravo blowout, it creates a special "project" authority with delegates (and delegated authority) from the various concerned departments. So the state also uses the "project manager with staff services from other departments" organization when it, too, is in a hurry. When the Norwegian state pays almost all the costs of delays, it may use its own experience in Bravo, or the example of Mobil and Phillips, to concentrate authority from various approving departments under one head, for expeditious treatment of matters on the main time line in oil construction projects.

Information Demanded for Approvals

A sample "Factory inspection report" for placing firms on a bidders list had 71 places where entries could be made, including a number of places that were for lists (for example, a list of cranes, a list of cutting and edging tools, a list of projects previously completed). Much of the information is about technical limits on projects that could be handled (maximum sizes and weights that can be received by road, by rail, and by sea, maximum lift of overhead stationary cranes, ect.). Other questions cover information affecting productivity (labor force, subcontractors available, drafting capacity for detailed drawings).

This information will be used to draw up the list of firms that may be asked to bid on specific projects, and it is fairly likely that only a half dozen of the facts will be relevant in differentiating into eligible or ineligible for any particular contract. Thus even when the approver pays the wages of an information collector for the information (the form is to be filled out on a plant visit by representative of a prime contractor) it is normally rational to collect about 10 times as much information as one needs for a particular decision, "just in case."

When the proportion of the facts collected in a document which are read before taking the decision or making the approval falls below about 10 percent, it usually indicates that the people who drafted the document requesting the information do not have a clear idea of what they are doing (and that they do not pay for the time used to fill out the forms). A short study of the reading habits (or of the requests for searches of the information on a computer file) in the approving organization could indicate that the information was being requested without regard to the burden it creates for the respondent.

Conversely, of course, an issue that has to be decided without the relevant information indicates an inadequacy in the forms on which information is provided.

For deciding whether to collect a given piece of information, computing a fictional charge is useful. Merely multiplying a minute per item on the form by an average executive's per minute cost, multiplied by the number of firms which have to provide that information, can give an idea of the true cost of information. If the regulating organization would not think it worthwhile to pay that much if it had to collect the information itself, it should probably omit the item from the forms. There is no indication that such a calculation is routinely made for the forms of regulatory authorities, and probably for this reason the percentage of documentation that is read by the approving authority falls well below the norm of 10 percent.

Notice of Impending Approval Problems

Part of the difficulty of scheduling approvals in a regulatory agency is that work loads have to be distributed in the face of low information. The queues vary in length for the reasons normally studied in queueing theory, but also because the jobs that come in for approval are of very different sizes and degrees of complexity. Consequently, a normal queue norm, first-in-first-out, creates a distribution of waiting times with a larger variance than would be computed in queueing mathematics. Part of this is inevitable, and can only be solved by the device of priorities, of breaking into the queue. But some administrative measures depend on having previous information about large, or high priority, decision processes that are coming up.

Of course, having an additional bureaucratic station which receives information about approvals coming up may create simply another cause for delay, for one has to announce that one wants an approval before anything else can be done, and the person to whom one announces it is busy. And there is an additional cost of processing another set of information about approvals coming up. The estimates of the size of the approval work to be done on a case by the clients of the regulatory agency will, in general, be wrong, because they are not in the regulatory business themselves. However, a compromise in which there is someone to call ahead of time *when* there will be an approval to be made which ought to have high priority, because it is on the main time line or critical path of the project as a whole, can provide useful information for dividing up the work load of regulation.

Conclusion

It is hard to know how much of the approvals time that appears in network diagrams of activities is useless bureaucratic waste, due to failure of incentive-consequence correspondence, and how much is simply that it takes a long time to work out reasonable tradeoffs between the objectives that are the responsibilities of different organizations. The difficulty of the process for the North Sea should decrease over time, as the Norwegian government gains experience and as the political process of deciding tradeoffs between, for example, safety and revenues, is worked out at the higher levels. In the long run, as each organization learns to accommodate its behavior to the wishes of the authorities that control approvals, all approvals should become routine. So in the long run all delays occasioned by approvals should be mere bureaucratic impediments to efficient functioning, much as the multiple sorting processes in the mail system constitute an impediment to communication. Then the problem for analysis will be simply an operations research problem, how to arrange sequential systems, and queueing for them, so as to minimize average waiting time and reduce the size of the tails of the few cases that take exceptionally long.

In the meantime one has to start the analysis of the approvals process by sorting out those cases in which there is a serious difference in objectives or difference in judgement between different organizations, and those cases in which approvals merely keep the decision process orderly. These cases have to be analyzed separately, and no organizational tinkering will help in cases of serious disagreement about objectives, purposes, and standards, and the tradeoffs between them.

There are, however, two general strategies that have been suggested above which are very often useful. These strategies correspond to the two different kinds of problems, policy disagreements, and delays because no one is paying attention to a document waiting in the in-basket.

When policy disagreements involve sufficiently important matters, the strategy of the absolutely aloof regulatory authority, the strategy of "you keep trying to redesign the platform until we are satisfied," costs time and administrative confusion. What is required is an acknowledgement that there is a disagreement (and protests of "We too are interested in safety" will not serve the purpose, though they must be made for various other purposes). The problem then is to weigh sacrifices of one good thing (e.g. revenues for the Norwegian government) against another (e.g. the outside chance of serious pollution damage to a valuable fish population).

For this to be done, it is necessary to set up an organization that can take a decision about the tradeoffs and defend it politically. This means that it must have representation from the various interests involved, have access to the government and to people in the *Storting* who can make trouble, and the like. In short, serious disagreements of objectives require politically responsible creation of a decision apparatus which can get at the true issue, and not bureaucratic avoidance and the attitude that "it is not my responsibility that the project is delayed – it is they who have not come up with an acceptable proposal." Creating an integrated approval structure without undermining the special responsibilities of one or another department may, of course, be easier to propose than to do.

Such creation of relevant authorities is, of course, much easier within a corporation devoted to profit, so that reorganizing authority within Mobil or Phillips to create a project manager is not too difficult. The relations between staff specialists and project managers can be sufficiently tense even there, and sometimes a higher authority has to intervene to create a decision-making authority to resolve serious disputes between people representing different responsibilities. But corporations can reorganize their decision-making "constitution" much more easily than governments can.

The second major strategy is to create small substitute incentive systems in regulatory authorities which are sensitive to client inconvenience. Simply measuring and publishing, say average waiting times for an approval to be issued, and the three most delayed cases, at appropriate intervals, can create some correspondence between consequences for the client and incentives whitin the regulatory agency. Similarly, at the individual level a simple device of requiring an explanation whenever a matter is delayed beyond a specified time interval tends to focus the employee's attention on client consequences. The small incentive involved in the special charge for express mail, to get the client to give accurate information about the priority of his document, is a similar case. A good deal of administrative ingenuity has to go into inventing appropriate measures of client inconvenience – measures that are not easily faked by an indifferent bureaucrat. Probably the central "minor incentive" which is available is the attention of superiors, especially negative attention when clients are seriously inconvenienced, but superiors in government agencies often do not have more time to spend on rewarding and punishing subordinates – they have work of their own to do. And then again, subordinates have trade unions in government, too.

PART 5: THE COST AND SCHEDULE CONTROL SYSTEM

Oral and Written Feedback Systems

Generally when practical people use the words "management" or "management systems," they are referring to control and decision-making mechanisms in which much of the communication is written, and when they use words like "supervision" they are referring to visual inspection and conversation by superiors and oral directions or orders to workers. Sociologists have paid more attention to oral systems, because it is in these systems that interpersonal relationships generally grow up and affect the functioning of the organization.

But a brief analysis of which parts of organizations have been growing shows that when the accounting office (a written control system) increases, "supervision" if anything decreases. This is important for sociology because written systems of control are much less hierarchical. They provide summary measures of performance for consideration by a management committee more often than they provide information to a superior about what a given worker ought to do differently. But the growth of written control systems is important for project administration because the relationship between the two systems is especially difficult when there is no routine repetitive production to measure.

The general reason that oral feedback is so important in project administration, and why clear personal authority by project managers and field supervisors is so important, is that activities have to be adjusted from day to day. A written control system never "sees" what has to be done next. Instead a written control system measures certain crucial aspects of overall performance, and abstracts from the fast oral feedback system required for control of the detailed activities of workers. For instance, in a typical industrial production process the measures of overall performance that enter the written control systems may be: (1) percentage of "down time" when the line is not running, (2) percentage of scrap, (3) working hours charged to each separate lot that goes through the line, (4) list of orders which are behind schedule for delivery. Because the process is repetitive, the meaning of these indices of difficulty and cost remains stable, and they provide an accurate abstraction for the purposes of overall cost and schedule control.

Project administration of unique projects has the distinctive characteristic that peoples' activities have to be changed frequently, so that they need orders rather than standing orders. This increases the need for supervision. And the activities always changing means that physical measures like down time, percentage of scrap, or working hours per ton produced, all change meaning from day to day. In a tube mill, working hours per ton of tubes produced may be a reasonably accurate measure of productivity – working hours per ton of concrete poured are very different in meaning than working hours per ton of equipment connected by welding, and this is much different than working hours per ton of scientific and control measuring instruments installed.

Even in highly repetitive systems, the written system is very stiff and inflexible when it is first installed. When one tries to convince the electricity company's computer that there is a mistake in the bill, convincing a half dozen people in the organization is usually not enough, until the computer system has been revised so that exceptions and corrections are easily managed. Some computer programmers never learn to write in provisions for flexibility and exceptions.

In industrial administration there are a lot more exceptions which an experienced industrial shop supervisor handles immediately orally than is usually realized when the written control system is introduced. There is therefore usually a good deal of slippage and inaccuracy for example, in the cost accounting system, even when it is highly developed and in a favorable environment of repetitive processes. Coffee breaks, for example, are never properly charged.

This stiffness and inflexibility of written control systems means that people in highly variable and uncertain technical environments, like the North Sea constructions, never quite trust the written system. Even people in charge of the written systems, if they are much good, go out in the field to see what is really going on, to talk to the construction manager, to find the documents that have not been forwarded to the cost control office as they should have been. It is not quite true to say that those in charge of the written control system, the cost and schedule engineers, do not really believe in the system as much as they believe in the construction manager. But if even they are doubtful, it is not surprising that the people experienced in oral supervision often think of the new fangled "systems" as a lot of foolish American bureaucracy.

In almost all such combined oral and written control systems, the operative part which completes the feedback loop by changing the behavior of workers in the field is an oral part. When the percentage of scrap goes up in a tube mill, one sends the manager of the mill out to talk to the line supervisors to locate the difficulty, and the line supervisors talk to the workers. Even less in a construction project would one point out that the project was behind by writing a letter to the foremen.

The general problem of the written control system is to get the information that is seen and experienced physically at the field level of the organization translated into abstractions in the written system that accurately measure what is going on, and then to translate the "system's" analysis of where there might be difficulties back into activity in the oral supervisory system. The original supervisor's and field clerk's encoding of physical reality is a good part of this, but then afterward the encoding by cost engineers into measures of performance is a difficult process.

The problem is to choose the right level of abstraction for the encoding, so that the details of what has to be done next disappear, and the general problem that the project is delayed in, for example, equipment installation appears. The line supervisor is looking for a foothold in order to take the next step up the mountain, while the cost control engineer has to be able to translate the report about which step is now being taken into a location on the map.

Three Basic Maps of Project Progress

The highest level of abstraction of a map or chart of project progress is the investment plan, or authorized budget; next in level of abstraction is the S-curve of hours of work expenditures, sometimes divided up into different kinds of work (e.g. engineering versus construction work): the lowest level of abstraction is the network diagram of specific named activities arranged in sequence. Below this there are indeed written aids to the oral management system, such as the monthly report to the owner or the agenda for the biweekly engineering meeting or the weekly construction meeting (for typical contents of such meetings, see Usterud, 1976:Vedlegg 2). But these three levels of abstraction represent the "higher management" written control system.

It is easiest to see the relationship between the three maps if we start at the bottom with the relation between the physical activities and the activities network, and work up to the investment authorization, noting which things are left out of the abstraction at each stage.

In order to construct the activities network map of the project as a whole, one has to take the engineering plans and identify important subsidiary objectives, which can be the milestones in the network diagram (or the nodes, as they are sometimes called). These must satisfy the criteria that they are clearly observable so they can serve as milestones (for example if about a third of the street intersections in a city have no street signs, as in Bergen, a map with street names is very little use), that the activities needed to complete them are clearly identifiable, and that they identify the steps that need to be executed before going on to the next stage.

The reason we must be able to identify the activities that are needed to reach the objective is that we must estimate calendar times (and also usually hours of work needed), so that the milestones not only name events but can be compared to a reasonable plan. So the lowest level of abstraction of the written control system is to abstract from the multitude of actual actions carried out by this and that welder or cement mason or carpenter in the field, and to keep only information about which milestones the activity is devoted to, which milestones have been passed, and estimates of how long it will take to reach the milestone we are currently working on.

The coarseness of the activities network (i.e. the amount of abstraction involved) may range from very fine (with thousands of activities) to very coarse (with big blocks of important activities). The finer the network, the more we depend on computer processing to abstract for us and to locate the difficulties, for the purpose of control. Usually the network is arranged hierarchically, so that there may be a master network diagram with, say, 80 to 100 major activities, and then a breakdown of each of these major activities into detailed scheduled objectives.

The activities in the network diagram still, so to speak, have proper names. A construction worker might well be able to look at the diagram and figure out where on the diagram the work he is doing right now fits in, because the abstraction is still very commonsense, very much tied to concrete practical engineering objectives. In the next data reduction stage, the next level of abstraction, this commonsensical description of activities by their substance and their concrete objectives disappears, and only quantitative aspects are preserved.

The S-curve map of project progress depends on translating the activities diagram into hours of work. For each week or month or other calendar time period, one can translate the activities planned into hours of work required (sometimes described further by specialty or discipline, and sometimes – especially in the case of higher management – described with proper names, to make sure the right person will be available when his or her special talents are needed). Very often such a planned expenditure of working hours is required of the contractor with his bid, so that the owner can be assured that the contractor can supply the required labor at the required times, that the contractor "knows what he is getting into."

If we graph the quantity to be expended *each* month, according to the plan for project progress, we usually find that there is a period of relatively small expenditure of hours of work at first, as preparatory activities and startup activities are being done. This gradually increases to an upper limit, set in practice either by the labor force available or by the point at which workers start falling all over one another, and perhaps stays there for some period of time. Then the working hours planned for each week or month start to decline, as major parts of the project are completed and there remain only details, final checks, repairs of mistakes, final finishing, and the like. The uniqueness of each construction project is reflected most strongly in the first and last stages – it is the first connection and the last connection that take longest, the first and last weld that create most difficulty.

The graph of planned expenditure of labor time each month then typically takes on a bell shape, such as that sketched below.

Figure 1.1: *Hours Planned to be Expended Each Month During a Project.*

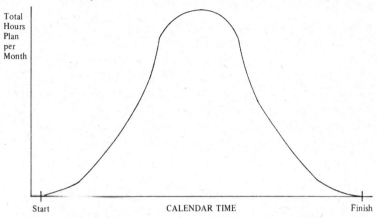

If this graph of expenditure of hours each month is cumulated, we get a graph of total hours of labor time planned to be expended up to a given data on the calendar. Since the expenditure is slow at first, rapid in the middle, and slow at the end, the cumulative curve takes on an S-shape, such as in the following sketch.

Figure 1.2: *Cumulative Hours Planned to be Expended by a Given Month During a Project.*

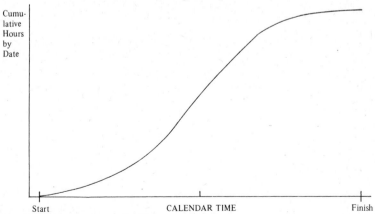

If we now compare the total hours of work actually expended with the hours of work planned to be expended, we have abstracted from all the details of which activities have to be carried out, and pay attention only to the quantities of activities, as measured in hours of work.

Each of these activities costs money. In construction projects of this kind, roughly 85 percent of the cost is labor cost, if engineering is included as labor. In order to have that money available, and the money for materials and equipment, there has to be an investment plan. Since usually money is allocated each year, time here is more abstract – we no longer care which month things are done in, but which year they are paid for in. And the human practical quality of the working hour disappears, and a construction worker cannot identify which crown in the budget is the one that pays him. Activities are described only by the costs attached to them.

It is important to note that all these abstractions involved in the plans, whatever their degree of detail, are based on two fundamental sources of information: physical engineering plans and the constants for translation of physical plans into hours of work (or in the case of materials and equipment that is purchased, into dollars or crowns). When the engineering plan is just a sketch, the investment plan is just an abstraction of a sketch. When the constant that translates a physical quantity of welding into welder hours required (i.e. the constant that measures welder productivity) is a guess about what a welder can produce under crowded conditions on the platform at sea, the S-curve and the investment plan are guesses.

To understand what a given estimate means (for instance, an estimate of "cost to complete"), one has to know what its basis is in physical engineering plans, and what its basis is in the productivity figures used to translate physical quantities into costs.

This is so important that it bears some repetition and elaboration. When one learns arithmetic in school, all the numbers one works with are really solid. When A foolishly rows upstream while B coasts downstream, the stream goes at exactly 3 kilometers an hour, unlike real streams that go faster in spring and stop, frozen, in winter. Even engineering school does not really teach people how uncertain a number used often is in practice. We can always depend on the arithmetic textbook to have abstracted correctly, and when we calculate with the numbers it gives us we get the right answer. We know it is the right answer because we look in the back of the book (unlike poor A, who gets tired before the problem is over). But when the engineering plan is a sketch, and the productivity figures are a rough guess that this thing will be about 12 times as much trouble as a platform in the Gulf of Mexico, the number is not nearly as real as it was in the textbook.

It is typical practice for example in using an S-curve for control in projects of this kind to allow for about a 20 percent overrun – engineering changes and troubles generally will cause the contract to take about 20 percent more hours of work than originally estimated. So one very carefully draws a map (an S-curve) of planned project progress and then estimates that this map is about 20 percent off. A mountain climber whose map is 20 percent off may fall off a cliff.

The main difficulty is that practical people do not like to admit they do not know quite what they are doing. If they did know, of course, the plans would not be 20 percent off the final structure. But in practice, we find each engineer, each manager, being perfectly sure about what *he* or *she* is doing – it is all those others who create the uncertainty. Partly this is an illusion which is created by the exactness of the physical quantities. These are not nearly as exact as they look, as we pointed out for instance when we talked about the problem of concrete work being done to different tolerances than piping. And even the physical translation of design parameters (e.g. earth to be moved) involved a great deal of uncertainty, usually resolved not by engineering but by experienced construction managers.

But even if we were to assume that physical quantities were exact, it is humans who have to carry out activities, humans managed by the human management systems that we in fact have in place. If it is hard to predict how much earth will actually have to be moved, predicting which days the machine operator who moves it will have been up fighting with his wife all night is even more difficult. The number in the estimator's manual about hours of work per cubic meter of earth moved is a sociological and psychological number, a number about average human behavior of bulldozer operators, and about their foremen and managers. In the arithmetic textbook, A is never rowing while muttering to himself about his wife, but in the estimator's manual the number takes account of the average number of minutes muttering. Being a sociological number, it has the degree to accuracy, the tolerance limits, that we expect of sociology rather than of physical science.

It might be a reasonable innovation to publish the numbers in estimator's manuals, for translating physical quantities into hours of work, with standard deviations. Part of the reason people imagine numbers are more exact than they are, is simply that they can calculate with them and get the right answer. Since most engineers would not know how to calculate with the standard deviation, to get the standard deviation of the total cost, it would at least induce modesty in their sense of the exactness of their final figures.

The Resolution of an Abstraction System

If we compare the picture printed in the newspaper or sent over television with an original glossy print, we may recognize the prime minister in both. If we magnify the center of the picture several times, the glossy print still clearly shows that it is a nose. Further magnification of the print may show a blotch for what is a well-defined freckle on the prime minister, while the newspaper photograph shows only a dark dot. The maximum degree of detail that be recovered from an image is called the *resolution* of the image.

Similarly the cost overrun on Statfjord B is clearly recognizable from a distance, and *perhaps* can be resolved into increased costs of reengineering for safety approval, increased costs of building a safer platform, increased costs due to more difficult seabed conditions, general inflation, lowered productivity of inexperienced engineering organizations, increased percentage of work done under change orders rather than in the original drawings, and so on. A further level of magnification might then give us details of lowered engineering performance, such as more hours per drawing, more drawings redone, more waiting for the major design parameters before the detailed work can be done, and the like. Or a detailed analysis of change orders might show the percentage due to inaccurate drawings from equipment makers, percentage due to new safety demands, percentage due to the fact that an alternative design is easier to construct, etc.

Someplace in the total administrative system the pieces of information required for resolution of the details must exist. For many purposes we want those details ignored. Occasionally we might even want them concealed – the lack of availability of accounting details to journalists and critical engineers in the Statfjord projects clearly must be a conscious decision by Statoil, which by agreement has a monopoly of issuing information. While there may be many reasons for this from a business point of view (the figures are about the performance of private companies, and may be considered business secrets, for example), the fact remains that the abstraction system accessible to outsiders in the Statfjord projects has very low resolution.

It seems that the written control systems in administration of unique large projects generally have lower resolution than the written system in factories. For example, a typical recording system for "down time" in a tube rolling mill will record down time for each line separately, and will record which motive system was affected (hydraulic, electrical, mechanical, and other). While by the time it gets to the cost-accountant's office we may only know that costs are high on a particular line, in the maintenance office of the mill one may be able to find out enough from the papers at hand to set up a policy of more frequent overhaul of the hydraulic system, and prove that what one loses in down time for overhaul will be made up in less down time by hydraulic failure. That is, one can descend the hierarchy of abstraction to locate specific problems which give rise to bad performance that shows up in the more abstract indices.

In project administration one very quickly must leave the written system and start consulting managers, supervisors, and workers. The written control system has low resolution. The general reason is that the abstraction system, to a considerable degree, has to be set up anew for each project. Teaching all the supervisors and clerks a whole new system for charging working hours for each project is unduly tedious, especially when the clerks and supervisors are in a bunch of different organizations.

Presumably, what is needed is a flexible system for connecting work activities to a system for encoding the information which does not depend so much on teaching a full new control system to all the supervisors. To produce a two volume manual of administrative procedure for each project, to be mastered by each foreman, will just produce evasion and lowered morale at the working level.

I suspect that the key to this is to map both the activities at the working level, and the system of codes, to the detailed engineering drawing. It is the engineering drawing which carries the information that is new to each project. In the cost and schedule control office each drawing can be given a detailed code, specifying the activity in the activities network to which it is relevant, identifying major subsystems related to that activity, specifying when the activity was planned to be done, and so forth. Then this set of codes locating the drawing in the activities system can be set up in a dictionary in a computer file, which says for each drawing where it will fit in the activities system and any other distinctive features that may be relevant to the overall control process (e.g. whether the drawing pertains to a change order or was in the original).

Then if the foreman can identify the drawing for which given working hours were to be charged, he need not remember what the code is for "plumbing subsystem, utilities, residential section (sprinklers)." The coding of the day's or week's work, then, is done at the working level by identifying the drawing which governs it. The other data normally given by the foreman (e.g. the specialty or discipline of the workers, subcontractor code name, etc.) can then be matched with the activities analysis through the engineering drawing number, and this can then be translated into the code system used in the written control system.

The purpose of this scheme is not to propose any innovations in practical administration (the system above may be in use), for these would have to be evaluated by discussion with practical people. Rather the point is to outline the administrative problem, that the usual way one constructs a cost control system with detailed resolution, with the capacity to analyze problems at progressively descending levels of abstraction, depends on teaching each supervisor or field clerk an encoding system which is fitted to the repetitive processes being analyzed. Such a solution is not really possible in project administration, and one has to locate the encoding system in the analysis subsection itself – probably in a computer dictionary, developed specifically for each project, which identifies activities done by particular workers in commonsense terms that are obvious to the workers and foremen (such as what drawing they were working on), but which translates this into codes that can be used in the analysis system at any desired level of detail.

The codes themselves need to be arranged hierarchically, so that when one is producing, for example, a summary of progress by the electrical subcontractor one does not have to tolerate a lot of irrelevant detail about which wires pertain to the kitchen, which to the compressor control system. One should be able to produce summaries comparing plans to actual performance at any degree of detail, by using the code attached to the detailed activities which has the appropriate level of abstraction in it. This will have to be developed for each specific project, but the general analysis schemes should be common across projects.

It is important to remember, however, that at the present time the method of going to ask the construction manager why the piping is behind is a way of getting higher resolution in the abstraction system, and that this method is working. Often the kind of people who like to monkey with computer systems to make the written system work do not like to go out and ask what the problems are in the field. If the time spent in a hard hat gets too low in the cost control offices, the chief cost control engineer should start to worry.

Comparing the Plan to Reality

As the project progresses, planned activities are turned into actual activities. There are four main sources of deviations between the plans and reality about which something may have to be done, four main occasions on which administrative attention has to be redirected to get the project back on schedule.

(1) The plan itself may have changed, so that additions (or occasionally subtractions) have to be made to the total work to be done, or the sequence of activities becomes tighter (or occasionally looser because a new plan results in decoupling two activities).

(2) Productivity may have declined, occasionally because the workers do not work as hard as planned, but more often because of management failure, more difficult conditions of work than anticipated (e.g. at sea rather than on land, forcing the project with extra labor, overcrowding of the work site, etc.), or difficulties with coordination (e.g. late deliveries of equipment).

(3) Total input of labor may be below that planned, so that overall not enough work is getting done.

(4) Critical activities required for other activities to proceed may not be getting done on time (e.g. drawing may be delayed so that construction cannot go forward).

At any level of resolution, at any degree of detail relevant to a particular analysis, one wants information about these four sources of deviation. Conversely, of course, a low level of change orders, high productivity, labor input when planned, and orderly passing of milestones so later activities do not have to make up for delays on earlier ones, indicate effective project management. Information on all of these deviations is also required for estimating (at the appropriate level of resolution) the cost to complete, and the anticipated schedule, with the consequent inputs into the economic decision making apparatus and the project management system.

This requires rapid and accurate input from the working level to the cost and schedule control system. There are several reasons why this information is often delayed, but most of them seem to have to do with the approvals system. For example, while the contractor goes ahead to build a change order on the say so of the client's engineers for the project, the change does not reach the planning and cost control engineering office until some time later when it has been approved. Similarly a report of the hours input into the change order is only available after all the follow-up work in the contractor's organization has been done, the charge has been reviewed by the contractor for completeness, and the invoice has been sent to the owner. So both the incorporation of the change order into the plan, and the incorporation of the hours of work into the performance figures, tend to be late. Usually the implications of the change for the rescheduling of critical activities can only be found out by talking to the construction manager, and the network diagram remains outdated until the end of the project.

But even if the map were perfectly accurate, one must compare reality to the map to find out where one is. Control requires coding the activities actually done, by the same system as the coding involved in the activities network planning diagram. This is why the question of whether the foremen understand the cost control coding system or not was so important in the previous section. It is one thing to code a set of engineering drawings into convenient set of activities for a plan, and quite another to get information from tough construction foremen who learned to weld rather than to keep a cost accounting system running. From the point of view of the foreman, of course, anything that he can code, he already knows, so the whole cost control system does not help him. To him, it is burden on the construction process to help higher management. Sometimes that burden gets heavy enough, when combined with plenty of construction troubles as well, so that the charge records get coded rather carelessly.

The basic measure of productivity depends on an estimate of "hours earned". Suppose for example we have estimated that it will take 12 hours of work per cubic meter to pour concrete. Then if 5,000 cubic meters have been poured in a given period, the "planned hours" that should have been spent are 60,000 hours. These may be regarded as "hours earned, if the productivity is what we originally estimated – i.e. if productivity equals the number in the estimator's manual, with the adjustments we made in it for Norwegian conditions."

First, it is the earned hours, the hours that depend on physical measurements of accomplishments, which should be compared with the expected accomplishments by a given date to get an estimate of the overall delay. If we planned to have earned 65,000 hours by this date, we are 5,000 hours delayed. Second, if we have spent in fact 65,000 hours in pouring 5,000 cubic meters of concrete, rather than the 60,000 planned, our productivity is about 8 percent lower than estimated. So the earned hours, when compared with the plan, estimates both productivity deviations and also anticipated delays.

The actual labor input can be compared not only with the earned hours, but also with the anticipated or planned labor input by a given date. This may give some idea of the cause of the delay.

The information above is usually useful for estimating the expected date of completion of some particular milestone which involves pouring concrete, such as the completion of the concrete base and legs for the platform structure.

The Operational Parts of the Control Feedback System

If a cost control engineer tells a construction manager he is in trouble, he is likely to get the reply, "Tell me something I don't know." Presumably what the construction manager does not know is what to do about it (or else he would have done it). What is needed in a particular case is an analysis of the cause of the deviation, and one or more proposed remedies. What the cost engineer generally has is a measure, in more or less detail, of the result. This may give a clue to the cause (the greater the resolution of the abstraction system, the more likely the cost engineer is to be able to give useful information about where the cause lies), but generally cost accounting systems are not designed well for causal analysis. Supervisory systems are better at finding causes and devising remedies.

What then is the function of the cost engineering and schedule control system? It has three main functions, having to do with usefulness for decisions at a higher level. We can call them the early warning function, the charge documentation function, and the redirecting of administrative attention function.

The early warning function is the easiest to understand. If the platform structure is five weeks delayed, there is not much sense having electricians show up at the time previously planned to install wiring on it. A notice to the manager (or subcontractor) in charge of electricians, that he ought to set his schedule back (or figure out how to prefabricate parts of the installation), will be of much use. Similarly an early notice to the section which has to defend the budget to the Storting that next year it is likely to be 50 percent over the earlier estimate may help alleviate their panic.

The charge documentation function is built into the system as a whole, and the same documents that end up on the S-curve as hours earned also show up as charges to the accounting office. Particularly when much of the contracting is cost-plus (as, for example, change orders very often are), the contractor's part of the cost control system is essential to justify the charges to the owner.

From the point of view of efficiency, however, the most important function is the direction of administrative energy and attention to problem areas. The greater the resolution of the system of abstraction, the more exactly the system can say where causal analysis has to be carried out, how much an investment to cut down a delay in a given activity will pay (in project time saved or in costs saved), and the like.

But in order to redirect administrative energies, there have to be fluid resources of administrative energy in the project. There is a certain sense in which the project manager is supposed to have infinitely fluid attention to pay to whatever is causing problems. And there is some real function in just increasing the pressure on the men in charge of a project to achieve a given purpose, to direct their attention to the lagging output indices – whatever they are. But there are already a lot of pressures on the project manager or the construction supervisors, and a cost engineer with a gap between the S-curves and a projection of 5 weeks delay may have low priority, especially if he is young and does not get out of the office much. There is an upper limit to what a project manager can pay attention to.

In industrial management the fluid resources are often in an operations research or industrial engineering group, a set of engineers or other specialists primarily concerned with managerial problems, but not in line supervisory positions. They then form a fluid resource which can be devoted to finding causes and remedies of special problems located by the more general feedback and control system. That is, one operative part of the feedback system is a special reservoir of administrative attention, which is more fluid than most such attention because it is divorced from line responsibilities.

A comparable resource on a smaller scale, but often with more weight behind it, is the "trouble shooter" who is often attached to very high executives in an organization. A trouble shooter takes on special projects requiring high level administrative attention, involving investigation of problems farther down the line but out of the line of command. These special structures in industrial management would not be appropriate without modification in project management, but they make the general point. In order to complete the feedback loop, deviations in the output indices, however fine the resolution, have to be translated into proposed lines of action to remedy the difficulty. What is needed to find causes of the trouble and develop remedies is administrative attention, and in general administrative attention is scarce, and already committed to other tasks. Consequently the institution of "staff managerial specialists with fluid responsibilities" provides a chance to translate output index deviations into plans for remedial action.

The reason for emphasizing this translation operation, and the fluid administrative resources needed to make it work, is that ultimately activities have to be changed. And this generally speaking means entering the oral, hierarchical control system, the system of field supervision and labor relations and human actions of skilled workers. To enter that oral control system, one needs to have translated a diagnosis into a treatment plan, a plan of remedial actions for specific people to take. Otherwise the written feedback and control system tends to dangle in the air, gulping in great quantities of paper and turning out graphs to be filed in the offices of higher management. A functional equivalent of operations research or industrial engineering, as staff functions, responding to problems located by a written cost and schedule control system, combined with a system of abstraction with high resolution, is what is needed.

CHAPTER 2

CONTRACTS AS HIERARCHICAL DOCUMENTS

Arthur L. Stinchcombe

PART 1: INTRODUCTION

Coase, Dahl and Lindblom, Williamson, Teece, and Lindblom have all built and used a contrast between market transactions among firms and hierarchical administration within firms (Coase, 1937; Dahl and Lindblom, 1976; Williamson, 1975; Teece, 1976; Lindblom, 1977:27-29, 237-309). The basic notion is that when many adjustments will have to be made during the course of contract performance, the transaction costs of negotiating and enforcing a contract rise, and the great flexibility of a labor contract used to create a hierarchy saves transaction costs (see Williamson, 1975:64-72). Thus whenever it is difficult to specify the required performance in advance (Marschak, Blennan, Jr., and Summers, 1967:190-321), when the costs, prices, or quantities to reign at the time of the performances are uncertain (Macaulay, 1963), when team interdependences do not allow separate measurement of performances (Alchian and Demsetz, 1972), hierarchy is preferable to market coordination through contracts.

The argument of this essay is that contracts are often signed between a corporate client and a corporate contractor when this theoretical tradition predicts hierarchical integration. Although research and development in commercial life is ordinarily carried out by a subordinate R&D staff as Mansfield predicts,[1] the government buys weapons R&D by contracts under the same conditions of uncertainty of performances.[2] Uncertainty about costs, prices, and quantities frequently leads to vertical integration as Thompson predicts (Thompson, 1967), but automobile franchises and weapons procurement often involve contracts for shifting quantities, uncertain costs, and prices to be determined (see Macaulay, 1966; and Scherer, 1964). Team performance of technically interdependent production often leads to hierarchical controls, as predicted by Alchian and Demsetz, but airlines penetrate deeply into the technical work of airplane manufacturers.[3] And in rushed megaprojects in energy production the intimate technical dependence of engineering and construction does not prevent their being split between contractors (Stinchcombe, 1979:67-86). Performances can be adjusted to changing situations by contractual means; administrations of performances can be set up by other kinds of contracts than labor contracts.

If the easy way to get flexible continuous performance over time is a hierarchy isolated from direct market processes, we need to ask how people manage who are forced by their situation to do it the hard way. The literature that predicts why, for example, weapons development or building construction will be vertically integrated should predict what kinds of difficulties weapons and construction contracts will run into. Then we can look for attempts to solve such problems by writing administrative provisions into the contract. What we will be looking for is ways to construct social structures that work like hierarchies out of contracts between legally equal corporate bargaining agents in a market.

In Part 2 below, we will analyze very briefly what kinds of social relations hierarchies consist of, and what functions they perform. This then provides an outline of what are the functions whose occurrence in contractual situations will lead to hierarchical elements in contracts. It may also suggest the nature of the structures that may intrude into the ideal type market transaction, producing a variant of the ideal type contract. The ideal type contract is defined here to include all market transactions in which one firm or person makes an offer and another accepts. An offer and acceptance create legal obligations, whether or not a written contract is signed. In the ideal type contract the performances the offering party offers to perform are clearly specified, and the performances it will require in return are clearly described, though they may be implicit. Thus a store's display of papayas with a sign, "Papayas, $2.39 each," is an offer, and carrying them to the cash register and paying the money is an acceptance, creating a contract. This contract is hardly ever written, except as a cash register receipt. The papayas are specified by being on display; the performance of the buyer has a meaning defined by laws of legal tender and sales tax laws, and by the sign. Legal obligations created include the store's obligations to let the customer have the papaya, and the customer's obligation to take it away, to suffer the consequences if it is dropped on the way home, and the like. A contract with hierarchical elements departs in many ways from such an ideal type, and those bring it closer to the description of a hierarchy we offer in the first section below.

Some conditions make it difficult, uneconomical, or impossible to specify the performances to be required at the time a contract is signed. Our argument in Part 3 is that difficulties in arranging market transactions in the way specified in the ideal type papaya buying contract tend to cause the addition of hierarchical elements to the contract. These may be divided broadly into (a) difficulties of prediction of specifications the client will want to make of a contractor's performances (e.g. one cannot describe what weapon one wants manufactured until one has done the development work, yet one wants to start tooling up for manufacturing early so as to reduce the time between development and operational availability: Marschak, 1967:49-139; see also Stockfisch, 1973), (b) client or contractor uncertainty about the costs of carrying out the performances, resulting in a wish to make strategic readjustments either in the performances or in the compensation during contract performance, and (c) inability to measure clearly the performances to be demanded or the conditions determining compensation (e.g. the inseparability of engineering mistakes and construction inefficiency in cost overruns in major construction projects means that engineering and construction performances cannot be measured separately, even though they are often in separate contracts: Stinchcombe, 1979).

The "markets and hierarchies" literature assumes that the usual optimal way to arrange work is through a market. Hence what has to be explained is "market failure." Since most work by individuals is not arranged directly through a market, there is a good deal to be explained. The explanations of market failure most often have to do with failures of information (or "uncertainty"), monopolistic advantages of either the buyer or seller (small numbers in a given market), or difficulty in measuring outputs or commodities ("teamwork," etc.). Hence they predict that uncertainty, small numbers bargaining, and teamwork should produce nonmarket arrangements such as vertical integration or hierarchy. Our general argument takes the form of finding situations in which work is arranged through contracts (and hence through markets) which are characterized by uncertainty, small numbers bargaining, and teamwork. Hence the received theory predicts hierarchy, but we observe contracts. We will show that hierarchy can be arranged through contracts, hence "through the market."

Part 3 below then sets a series of functional requirements that various contract devices will be called on to solve. The general argument of the literature is that hierarchy is a general purpose structure for fulfilling these functions, for adjusting performances to an uncertain future flow of events. But since we will observe these functions being required in parts of the economy that are in fact arranged through contracts, there must be contractual functional substitutes for hierarchy, perhaps ordinarily of lower efficiency but called forth by the special circumstances of particular industries.

If hierarchies ordinarily do some things better than contracts, we can look for those contractual devices that simulate the operation of hierarchies to do those things. Part 4 below decomposes the functions served by hierarchies in adjusting to a changing world, in order to specify what contracts have to do to simulate them. We will argue first that contracts often specify authority systems, in the sense of specifying how one will recognize a communication requiring a change of performance as binding. In particular if a client specifies a change in contractual conditions in midstream, it will ordinarily have also either to assume the risks this exposes the contractor to or to compensate the contractor for assuming the risk. In short, to specify the right to change the contract, one must ordinarily specify many aspects of the consequences of issuing an authoritative communication.

In order to back up this authority, contracts often specify an incentive system, in the sense this has within the firms: a method of tying rewards to performances which does not give all the revenue due to better performance to the employee. In order to achieve the maximum flexibility, the client should reserve the right to change the incentive system as conditions change. Within a firm, for example, one may get a lower commission for selling popular goods, bonuses for moving things that turn out to be turkeys. Similarly a contract may specify how the compensation scheme may be changed.

In order to control uncertainties in costs and prices, contracts often provide an administered pricing system. This may in some cases mean an authoritative way to determine the market price – the "administered" aspect in such a case is then only that the parties to the contract are required in the future to accept the market price so determined, whether they want to or not at that time. But the devices may be much more complex than this, as for example in the English system of bidding on bills of quantities in construction projects. The quantity surveyor describes the project as a list of quantities of various kinds of work (such as cubic feet of concrete foundations poured). The contractor bids a price for each quantity in the list, which then specifies a unique pricing system for change orders for that particular contract: they are described in the same way by the quantity surveyor, as a list of quantities, and priced according to the prices originally bid by the contractor.

A hierarchy provides for resolution of conflicts within the firm, without routine appeals to a court. Similarly contracts often provide a system for resolving disputes, sometimes with several layers. English construction contracts for example often provide that a named engineer (presumed to have non-partisan professional standards) will resolve all disputes between the client and contractor for the interim so work can proceed, but that the engineer's decision can be appealed to a named structure of binding arbitration. These structures internal to the contract are subject to the usual appeals to the courts (as are decisions in hierarchies in firms), but they are intended to serve the functions of keeping disputes from hardening into expensive and disruptive legal battles.

Finally hierarchies establish standard operating procedures for organizations, to secure efficiency and dispatch in processing organizational matters, to secure that unobservable qualities in the output will be regularly achieved by quality control, to prepare for unusual dangerous events such as fires, and for other purposes for which established routines are useful. Similarly contracts for large projects often include a schedule (whose legal status is in general precarious), orders for components of nuclear plants often specify a series of quality control documents and X-ray films to be supplied for each weld, and marine insurance contracts implicitly specify standards of readiness for emergencies ("seaworthiness": see Heimer, 1981).

A structure with legitimate authority, with a manipulable incentive system, with a method for adjusting costs, quantities, and prices, with a structure for dispute resolution, and with a set of standard operating procedures, looks very much like a hierarchy, very little like a competitive market. Yet all these features of hierarchy are routinely obtained by contracts between firms in some sector of the economy.

Part 5 below asks what it means for the theory of the market that one common use of the market is to set up joint administrative structures between a client and a contractor, rather than to trade specified performances for specified compensation. That is, the model of the market in Coase, Williamson, Teece, and others is not a description of the construction contracting market, the market for weapons R&D, the market for the services of franchised automobile dealers (see Coase, 1973; Dahl and Lindblom 1976; Williamson, 1975; Teece, 1976; and Lindblom, 1977). Instead it is an abstraction from the economics textbook, in which the administrative ingenuity embedded in the contents of contracts has disappeared. But when hierarchy is defined by contrast to this idealized version of the market, its features are indefinite. A common danger of the ideal type method used in this literature is that one of the types, usually the most interesting one, is defined residually, by contrast with an empty ideal type into which few empirical observations fall. This means not only that intermediate cases are misanalyzed, but that even the poles of contract and hierarchy are poorly defined.

PART 2: AN EXTENDED DEFINITION OF HIERARCHY

We will describe below how a series of functions that are not included in the simplified ideal type of a market contract can be achieved through modified contracts. We need to show that they are in fact routinely achieved by those structures we usually call hierarchies. It will therefore be useful to show how hierarchies themselves, created in the usual way by chartering corporations and by decisions of boards of directors, carry out the functions which can be done by contracts. We will try to show how corporations create a structure with a working authority system, and effective incentive system with observations of individuals' performances and rewards for differential performance, accepted operating procedures, legitimate dispute resolution structures, and internal pricing systems that contribute to organizational rationality.

First we will try to specify the elements out of which these functions are constructed within firms, the formal elements of hierarchies. Then we will try to describe briefly how the structure so constructed deals with uncertainties of specifications, uncertainties of costs, and unobservability of performances. Our main purpose here is to cast our traditional knowledge of organizations into a form that describes its relation to the contractual materials we will go through.

*(a)Formal Elements of Hierarchies:*We will argue that most of the hierarchical intra-firm structure we need to analyze is made up of five elements: (1) labor contracts yielding subjection to authority systems by employees, (2) fiduciary relations, especially involving boards of directors, entrusting them with wide discretion as representatives or trustees of the stockholders and others, (3) the legal personality aspect of organizations which defines them as origins of decisions, allowing them to set up performance measurements and wage, salary, pension, career development, or other incentive systems, to enter into contracts to motivate other

firms by appropriate incentive systems, and to change these by organizational decisions, (4) the governance of the activities set up under these structures by production programs or standard operating procedures, and (5) meetings (with agendas controlled by the hierarchy or by standard operating procedures) for internal dispute resolution. A normal hierarchy, then, consists of labor contracts, fiduciary relations, the exercised right to measure and reward performances, standard operating procedures, and decision-making and dispute resolving meetings.

(1) Labor Contracts: Simon, in a fundamental paper on the theory of the employment relation, showed how the central phenomena of authority can be generated in exchange relations.[4] Briefly the argument is this. The central phenomena of authority are related to a "zone of indifference" of the subordinate (the term was invented by Chester I. Barnard). By a "zone of indifference" we mean a set of activities, all of which it would be rational for the worker to exchange at his or her wage rate. The higher the wage rate as compared to alternatives available to the worker, the more costs in terms of unpleasant or dangerous jobs the worker would be willing to do to retain the advantage of the wages. The higher the wage rate in a given job as compared to the competitive wage rate, the larger in general will be the zone of indifference of the worker. Conversely, as the competitive wage rate goes down, e.g. by unemployment during a recession, the size of the zone of indifference at a given wage rate goes up. Authority is strengthened by paying high wages, and by bad times outside the firm. The zone of indifference is also increased if the tastes of the workers do not make a less desirable activity much more costly to him or her than another activity. The more equal different activities are in the minds of the workers, the more flexibility authorities have. One hires as traveling salespeople those who do not mind traveling, and one tries to so arrange work activities so that one particular choice of activities does not result in the employment of the worker's lover at high wages.

Under what conditions will an employer prefer to buy a zone of indifference rather than particular activities (e.g. by subcontracting)? If the employer knew it wanted particular activities in advance, it could buy them on the labor market at the competitive wage rate, or set up an incentive system in which one could mobilize the powerful motives of, for example, employing one's sons and lovers at high wage rates. And clearly this is often done. Rather than run automobile sales bureaucratically, car manufacturers allow families or small corporations to own the job of selling cars through the franchise system. This allows car dealers to use their business power to reward their children and relatives, and produces a small aristocracy with inheritable status in the core of the most modern bureaucracy. Presumably car manufacturers do this for rational reasons, since they know perfectly well how to run bureaucracies of employed people, with nepotism rules, orderly careers, and all the rest.

Clearly the central question of rationality from the point of view of an employer is the distribution of uncertainty. An exchange partner is likely to want authority when it does not know which particular activity it is likely to want, but is reasonably sure it will want some activity. Under these conditions it is rational to become an employer, to buy a zone of indifference rather than a set of particular activities.

Provided one is continuously in a given line of work, if one is faced with uncertainties of specifications, uncertainties of cost, or inability to divide up the work so that it forms decoupled packages, one will prefer to buy a zone of indifference rather than specific performances. But the situation in which we will find the uncertainties and the coupled activities above, and yet find contracting, are situations in which either one is not continuously in a given line of work (as, e.g., when one is a client for a building of an oil refinery, one is not continuously in the construction business), or when one is not competent to run such a business (as in weapons development or buying a software system). Under those conditions one wants a zone of indifference but also wants to contract for the work.

For our purposes, however, it is enough that authority systems can be constructed if one can buy zones of indifference, and the labor contract combined with careful differentiation of family from work will usually do the job. Organizations which have tasks requiring hierarchy will tend to have employees.

(2) Fiduciary Relations: Historically the law of corporations

developed out of the law of trusts and the law of agency, rather than out of the law of master-servant relations. That is, from a legal point of view the central element of a corporation is not that it employs people, but that others entrust it with their money. Boards of Directors are also employees of the corporation, but they are mainly legally trustees. And operating executives of a corporation are also employees of the corporation, but mainly legally agents of the Board. Stockholders, like the minor children for whom a trust is created, cannot legally exercise their ownership of firm's goods by disposing of them or using them. Only the Board, like the trustee, has operating legal control (e.g. "possession") over the resources of the firm. Likewise an officer of the corporation is bound legally to exercise his or her agency in good faith, not to exceed the authority granted, but his or her acts (if legal within the law of agency) commit the corporation and its resources.

What the stockholders buy in hiring a Board, and what the Board buys in hiring officers, is not so much a zone of indifference, as a promise of responsibility, a promise to carry out a fiduciary role as a trustee or as an agent. The capital market is shot through with these fiduciary exchanges, and the ponderous conservatism of bankers and stockbrokers and corporation lawyers is more an ethical imperative of fiduciary exchanges than a character type of the very rich.

Inheritance law provided for trusts because the heir was often not trusted (either by the court or by the person who died) to administer the estate rationally. Children were always presumed incompetent. So the basic purpose of the trust was to provide wisdom in the management of an estate when wisdom was presumed lacking. The choice of a trustee generally required not only wisdom, but also either disinterestedness or identification with the interests of the heir.

The first of these, wisdom, is reflected in the legal provision for trustees (and often agents) that they must act as "a reasonable man" would act in the circumstances. The norms do not specify what specific actions the trustee or agent should carry out. Nor is it any excuse in the law that the action taken is not forbidden in the document creating the trust or the agency; if that action was not one that a reasonable man would have taken under the circumstances, the trustee or agent can be held liable. It is a defense for the agent, but not for the trustee, that he or she was specifically instructed to carry out the unreasonable actions.

The second of these, disinterestedness, is reflected in "conflict of interest" norms, which try to ensure that the trust or agency is used in the interest of the beneficiary or principal rather than in the interest of the trustee or agent. Identification with the interests of the beneficiary or principal is often achieved by norms of election and dismissal, as in the case of Boards of Directors, or precarious or discretionary tenure, as in the case of Cabinet Officers, officers of corporations, or commercial agents.

The problem with both of these normative provisions is that they are easily corruptible, and that the law is a very inefficient way to prevent corruption. Hence the norms of wise and disinterested service are often supported by structural devices providing for continual review of performance of these central normative provisions. The most common of these are collegiality (a committee as trustee, as e.g. a Board of Directors), publicity (e.g. annual reports with specified contents), and auditing. In their full development, then, the norms of trust or agency provide for six features (aside from the obvious one that the trustee should be well paid for the service): (1) reasonableness or wisdom as the performance standard, (2) disinterestedness, (3) election or precarious tenure, (4) collegiality or committee decision making, (5) publicity, and (6) audit. In general large transfers of capital to new enterprises take place in the context of exchange relations with all these features. These formal provisions are ordinarily supported by extensive norms of gentlemanly business behaviour, and mutual relations among the people involved as trustees and central agents of the corporation that are well described by the Spanish phrase for the group, "*hombres de confianza*," men of (i.e. in whom we have) confidence.

(3) Status Systems and Performance Incentives: If a central distinction between the times when a client uses contracts and when it builds a department to do the work is the continuousness with which it is in that line of work, we should expect that a chief feature of the hierarchical incentive system would be the con-

tinuity of the exchanges between employee and employer. When an exchange relationship is continuous, such as bureaucratic employment, marriage, or the exchanges among subsidiaries of the same corporation, current exchange is modified by the expectation of future exchange. That is, in the future there will be a flow of valuable goods if the exchange relationship is not destroyed by the current exchange.

The rule of *caveat emptor* is not appropriate to the current exchange because the person who commits fraud or renders a poor performance gains only a small amount in the current exchange, but sacrifices the whole (discounted) value of the flow of future exchanges (Becker and Stigler, 1974; see also further work in the same tradition). Norms about "fair" exchanges thus serve the interests of both parties, in that whatever disadvantage they may sustain from unfair norms of fairness, those norms protect them from the destruction of the relationship, and hence protect the capitalized value of future exchanges. Further, a reputation for fairness may advantage one or more of the parties, so that, for example, an employer may keep on high seniority workers who no longer pull their load because firing them would undermine profitable exchanges with younger workers who hope someday to have seniority themselves (Becker and Stigler, 1974).

The first requirement of such a system is that the future exchanges should in fact be secure, so that the future advantages for which one sacrifices his or her current interest will in fact be there. The basic phenomenon in an effective commitment is that each party be satisfied that at all relevant points in the future, the value sacrificed by the partner by stopping the exchange will be greater than the advantage that the partner can get by stopping unexpectedly. For example, giving hostages does this by the hostage being more valuable to the person giving the hostage than to the person receiving the hostage, so that the latter can sacrifice the hostage if the relationship is broken. Evidence of giving the partner a monopoly position by leaving the market (e.g. by stopping flirting upon marriage) shows that one intends to sacrifice the whole value of the relationship in case of rupture, rather than only sacrificing the difference between the value of this stable exchange and the value of well explored alternatives.

Passing control to the partner, for example by a supplier selling out and becoming a subsidiary to its customer (see the analysis of Fisher Body and General Motors in Klein, et al., 1978:308-310), guarantees the relationship by transferring control over the fulfillment of the selling partner's obligations to the parent.

An important concrete manifestation of commitment norms are norms of seniority. If the contract of commitment were established in a timeless instant, on model of a marriage that starts at the wedding and lasts "until death do us part," this creates the risk that only one of the parties will turn out to be truly committed. A one-sided holding of hostages, a one-sided monopoly, a one-sided transfer of control over one's resources, all lead to slavery. One general solution to this is to move the commitment by small stages, so that at each point (if all goes well) the partners will lose more by bugging out than is being risked by increased commitment. And in the employment relation and its analogues, the growth of seniority rules, or of security of tenure in an agricultural tenancy, or of tenure in a university, is sufficiently vital to the nature of the relationship that its absence is a sign of ruthless exploitation.

If a commitment is effective, it establishes an area of bilateral monopoly for the two parties. The skilled autoworker has seniority only in Packard Motors, and the workers who know Packard's production process are the workers with seniority. Within the range between the price of labor at which Packard is willing to go out of business, and that at which the workers will quit in spite of their seniority rights, any price is possible. A bilateral monopoly does not have a unique equilibrium rate of exchange, and the range of possible rates is set by the degree of commitment.

The reason all of this is important to the incentive system of continuous hierarchies is that many of the incentives used, especially at the lower managerial levels, are status system rewards. The value of a promotion is not mainly this month's increased paycheck, but the expectation that the rate of exchange in this particular exchange has permanently altered for the better. Thus the reward for a worker improving his or her human capital is a commitment at a new rate of exchange. Unless the whole system is organized as a permanent status system, the investment (and the continuous disciplined pursuit of objectives specified by the superior) does not seem so worthwhile.

Status systems with promotions as incentives are also more appropriate for executive and managerial jobs, in which one wants to reward discretion whose results are only observable over a quite a long period (Jaques, 1956:22-42). It would be quite hard to devise a piece-rate system for jobs whose span of discretion was a month or six months.

Thus continuous exchange between the firm and its employees makes it possible to construct a more effective, career, incentive system. Max Weber's specification of career incentives as a central defining feature of bureaucracy was shaped by his realization that such an incentive system produces the highest level of discipline for complex interdependent tasks. Thus we will expect hierarchies to have a permanently organized status system in which rights are attached to positions rather than to performances, and an indirect attachment of rewards to performances by attaching promotions to judgements of competence (but see Cole, 1979).

(4) Standard Operating Procedures: Continuity of work in the same line makes standard operating procedures productive. Much of the transaction cost of contracting for specified work is actually the inefficiency of prototype production. If experienced airplane manufacturers can produce the second airplane of a given model for about 73 percent of the cost of the first, the fourth for about 53 percent, and so on, then contracting one at a time with unique specifications rather than buying off the shelf can be extremely expensive. The virtue of standard operating procedures and of production programs is not that they are standard, but that they embody organizational learning (Newhouse, 1982b:66; also Scherer, 1964:120-121).

One of the main things a hierarchy uses its control over a zone of indifference for is to improve between the prototype and the second, between the second and the fourth, between the fourth and the eighth. At the beginning of a production run there is not much one can do that is as inefficient as buying the same activities today that one bought yesterday. Even after the production process is running smoothly, we can project from experience producing software that about another 40 percent as much again as the investment to that point will be spent on improvements of the sort that programmers call "maintenance."

In production processes these improvements range from simple jigs or patterns to the trained efficiency of an experienced machinist's movements (Burawoy, 1979:46-73). In cost accounting the categories of the system evolve so that they can be efficiently aggregated for all relevant cost analyses for deciding about products, or about executives, or about investments to improve a given process. Production line maintenance programs are improved by better estimates of when parts should be preventively replaced, by development of better diagnostic tests of what ails a machine, and by replacing hard to repair motive systems with easy ones. In many ways the central thing one sets up firms to do is to develop standard operating procedures, and then to improve them incrementally.

(5) Meetings: Perhaps the central illusion of the novice organizational analyst is that the organization chart is a picture of the authority system. In the upper part of the corporate hierarchy the relations between ranks are more like that between courts of original jurisdiction and the appeals courts over them, than like that between privates and sergeants. The higher ranks organize meetings in which problems and disputes of the lower ranks are ironed out. The organization chart serves as a constitution that specifies who will organize committee meetings, not who will make decisions.

Further for most important decisions there will be a sequence of meetings, or at least a sequence of reviews and initials culminating in a meeting. Standard operating procedures usually specify the route of the paper on which the decision contents are recorded, and this specifies the sequence of meetings or reviews that make decisions; in practice all important decisions appear as authoritative after a meeting on them. Tyranny in such organizations is most often organized as it was in 18th century France, where the King expressed dissatisfaction with a series of outcomes by inventing a new court, more under his thumb, to treat matters of interest to the King (mainly taxation matters; Stinchcombe, 1982:90-92). Executives institute tyrannies by controlling meetings.

Using the hierarchy as a constituting mechanism for meetings creates an agile system for resolving disputes – though perhaps not one we would be happy to entrust the administration of justice to. The agility is particularly important in securing decision on things that have to be decided in a hurry. If disputes are appealed up the hierarchy, of course, the meeting of the Board of Directors has the final say. Hierarchies are seldom paralyzed by internal disputes, though the late 18th century French royal administration shows it can happen.

(b) Hierarchy and Uncertainty: The combination of labor market contracts involving a zone of indifference with career incentives in a more or less stable status system makes it possible to embark on a line of activity without knowing precisely what one is about. Within a wide range the employees will obey, and a career executive who has done his best on a cancelled model is happy to be promoted to assistant production manager for the successful model, though perhaps a bit piqued that it is not production manager of his own model. Thus the progressive concretization of specifications, that we will find below created by contractual contortions, is a normal hierarchical course of events. Dispute resolution machinery produces the legitimation of the decision on the model, and the disappointed executive was probably cowed in a meeting he attended.

Similarly the cost uncertainties do not require the payment of a risk premium to the department that may overrun its budget. The corporate funds that bear the cost uncertainties are the same ones that obtain the returns. The incentives to manage costs for the firm are as good as can be arranged, for the firm collects all the benefit of all the cost savings.

Finally, the capacity to reorganize information flows, authority, and measurement of outcomes so as to administer interdependent activities together reduces the problems of unobservable performances. The career incentive system can rely on the overall judgment of the superior on the quality of work, rather than observing separate performances.

In spite of the tendency of superiors to give all their subordinates equal ratings, and in spite of mutual recriminations between interdependent people about who caused the difficulties, one can keep an incentive system going and more or less correct its faults. One might still have to agree with Ecclesiastes, "under the sun, that the race is not to the swift, nor the battle to the strong, nor yet bread to the wise, but time and chance happeneth to them all." But time and chance can be adapted to in organizational performance measurement better than they can in the rigidities of normal contracts.

PART 3: PREDICTION OF PERFORMANCE REQUIREMENTS AND PERFORMANCE MEASUREMENT

The central reason for writing administrative provisions into contracts, provisions that contractual stipulations may be changed by specified methods, is that the future is uncertain. When that uncertainty involves so many contingencies that it is too expensive to give alterations of contract performances for all of them in advance, some mechanism for change or adaptation needs to be built into the contract. For convenience we can treat these uncertainties under three broad categories: (a) uncertainties of the client about what it will want, or uncertainties of specifications, (b) cost uncertainties, due to contractor technical or cost uncertainties, to client ignorance, or to commercial or legal uncertainties in the client-contractor relationship, and (c) problems of observability of contractor defaults, so that without continuous intervention the client does not know whether the contract performances have been delivered.

If the client changes its purposes, and can anticipate that it might, it will want to provide for changing the performances. If the costs of performances change from the estimates at the time of signing the contract, the rationality for the client of completing the contract may change if the client has to pay those costs; the contractor might not be willing to sign the contract without a prohibitive risk premium if all cost risks are to be assumed by it. If the client anticipates being uncertain whether the contract has been fulfilled, it will want to be able to institute detective work or record keeping to reassure itself.

(a) Uncertainties of Specifications: Clients may anticipate that

they will want to change their specifications of performances over the course of the contract for three main broad classes of reasons. First, the contract itself may involve exploration of the possibilities in the world – for example in an R&D contract: one wants to buy research and development work on a particular airplane engine concept only if such an engine could be built, as judged after some preliminary workup is done (Marschak, 1967:63-90). Second, the client may anticipate changes in the state of the world to which it wants contractor performances to adapt; for example, a car manufacturer will want the car dealers to adapt to which models are selling slowly by pushing them so one will not lose money on the tooling of the production line for that model (Macaulay, 1966:12,15,18,33,46,89,167-8,171). Finally, client preferences may change because of a change in the regime of the client organization or because of experience with the performances or products of the contractor during the contract. Sometimes such changes in preference can be anticipated; for example, the Department of Defense knows that operational experience will suggest modifications of the engineering specifications for weapons, but the exact modifications cannot be predicted (Stockfisch, 1973).

The anticipation that one will know more about the possibilities as the contract runs its course is at the core of "contracts for professional services." When people contract for a physician's advice, they find out what medical services they want. The special institutional protections of professional-client relations are designed in part to protect buyers who cannot know what they want until they find out what the world is like, what disease they have (Parsons, 1964:34-49).

When professional contracts are signed for large scale projects, as when an oil company contracts for an engineering consultant firm to develop the specifications for an oil platform, the exploration of what is possible is part of the contract (Stinchcombe, 1979:24-53 and 1984). Such contracts are very generally negotiated on some sort of cost-plus basis, almost a sure sign of "hierarchy" penetrating market relationships.

In weapons development the R&D part of the contract is very often written on a cost-plus basis, while production contracts after a weapon has been shown to be a real possibility are much more likely to be fixed price incentive fee or fixed price contracts.[5] This shows that what performances the government will require in an R&D contract depends on what engineering possibilities turn out to be viable. Engineering theory is quite uncertain in predicting the performance characteristics of a high technology system from an early paper plan. It is also very uncertain as a basis for predicting the costs of reaching a given technical possibility until that possibility has been specified in detail (Marschak, 1967).

Even after a possibility has been developed and manifested in prototype production, the client cannot always explore its costs in the market without additional expense. A drawing that lacks many details of exactly how to produce it can be clarified (within the same firm that did the development) by conversations between the engineers and a crew of skilled workers. To translate this into detailed shop drawings for the production process for a complex weapons system or a computer, so these can be produced elsewhere, can cost millions of dollars.[6] That is, to draw up the clients specifications in specific enough form so that the client can buy from several suppliers rather than only the developer costs a lot of professional work, because the R&D contractor rather than the client knows what the client wants.

Sometimes the uncertainty about the possibilities involves determining natural facts rather than exploring technical possibilities. In the development of the large Ekofisk field in the southern part of the Norwegian North Sea, the first technical judgment was that the field probably was "not commercial" because the rock type was not permeable enough, so each well would only drain a small area and would not pay for itself. In the "contract" between the Norwegian state and the oil companies exploring the field there was a limitation on exploiting the field too fast, e.g., not wasting the gas by burning it off but waiting until the gas pipelines were built. But the only way to get information about the permeability in a reasonable amount of time was to exploit a few wells "too fast," to estimate when the production started to fall off. Uncertainty about the state of the world a couple of miles down then required that the application of the exploitation rate conditions of the contract be suspended for a time, until the production features of the rock were determined – then to reinstate them. This is a shift in specifications over time due to exploration of production possibilities (Moe, et al., 1980. Part II:7,11). Hidden features of the world may be revealed by contractual activity, and may require changing specifications as the hidden becomes manifest.

One very common form of client change in specifications in construction is due to failure of the imagination. The classic example is the light switch behind the door as drawn – when the craftsman sees it he can tell it would be better on the other side of the door. A typical more subtle example occurred in the building of early concrete drilling platforms in Norway. In the tall concrete shafts of these rigs a lot of plumbing and electrical work has to take place after the shaft is poured. If the shaft has supports for scaffolding poured into the inside wall, one can install and repair equipment by scaffolding supported by the walls, rather than building scaffolding from the bottom. But scaffolding does not appear on design drawings, so no one saw this possibility until a prototype existed. Contracts for the other rigs under construction were changed to specify such supports (Stinchcombe, 1979:77-79).

The general point is that in some kinds of contracts it is contractual activity which finds out the production possibilities. As those possibilities are progressively revealed, one wants to change the specification of performances in the contract. To specify all possible states of the world would be expensive and otiose, since mechanisms to adapt performances as possibilities are revealed can be built into the contract.

The purposes of the client may change not only because it finds out about the world, but also because the world changes. In many contractual situations the client can anticipate that some general kind of change in the world may change client purposes, without wanting or being able to specify all possibilities in advance.

Perhaps the simplest of these is a change in the overall volume of the market for the line of goods a client produces. In contracts with franchise car dealers, for example, it may be reasonable to specify a market share for a dealer, but not an absolute number of cars to be sold. In a recession there is no reason to expect the proportion of Ford Motor Company cars among all those sold to decrease, but every reason to expect the absolute number to decrease. In developing informal standards of reasonableness to define the operational meaning of franchise contracts that allowed the manufacturer to require "satisfactory" sales, market share calculations of dealer performance requirements became standard. This replaced practices toward the beginning of the Great Depression in which Ford continued to force a constant stream of unsellable cars on the dealers (Macaulay, 1966:13).

In high technology industries, technical developments outside the client-contractor relationship often make specifications of performances archaic. This is most obvious in military technology when technical development is carried out by the potential enemy. Military supply contracts change as the USSR develops defenses or offensive weapons. But in addition, for example, IBM has in the past followed the strategy of keeping its technical specifications secret for as long as possible so as to preserve its monopoly over sale of peripherals for longer, while Apple has followed the strategy of encouraging others to develop and sell add-ons and software. Both clearly expected technical developments elsewhere to change their relations with their clients. IBM thought that others would undermine contracts for peripherals. Apple thought that others could increase the value to the client of their computer, and so increase future sales (Toong and Gupta, 1982). In both cases the companies could be expected to modify their contracts with suppliers so that the monopoly or developments would be encouraged, and would respond differently to technical developments among those suppliers.

When an accident happens to a given sort of ship, the classification societies which certify the ships for insurance companies often require changes in the ships before they will recertify them. Such societies routinely investigate accidents with a view to requiring preventive measures on other ships. Thus the provision in marine insurance contracts that ships must be classed by a named classification society is an indirect requirement that the policy holder respond to changes in knowledge of the world, in particular knowledge of causes of accidents as represented in classification standards (Heimer, 1980:63-67). Changes in the standards of regulatory authorities, such as the CAB requirement for new inspections and new maintenance procedures for the engine supports of the DC-10 after the Chicago disaster (Newhouse, 1982c:82), are also embedded in insurance contracts by provisions that the policy is not valid unless the planes satisfy government regulations.

Accidents that often happen during the course of construction, such as cave-ins, collapse of heavy structures before completion, weather or fire damage to partly completed structures, will cause clients to want to change the activities required of contractors in order to achieve the performances specified in the contract. The reason construction has a much higher accident rate than the operations phase of the same buildings is that the construction process is not carefully designed for safety, and there are stages when the incomplete structure is weaker, more exposed, more unstable, than the complete structure will be.

Theoretically this is the contractor's risk or the risk of the contractor's bonding company, unless otherwise specifically provided in the contract. However the schedule, the degree of financial stability of the contractor and hence its financial capacity to carry out the performances, and sometimes even the technical possibility of construction plans, are generally affected by severe accidents. Various standard contractual clauses are traditionally generously interpreted by the courts in such a situation, creating a requirement of both parties to adapt to the situation. The requirement for such adaptations are therefore generally implied in the contracts by the traditional legal interpretations.

Uncertainty of the law itself, especially uncertainty of substantive regulations such as environmental standards, create changes in client purposes. For example, nearly a year of work by an engineering crew was required to modify the design of the Statfjord B platform in the Norwegian North Sea to conform to new stricter safety standards (Stinchcombe, 1979:87 and 1980). The extra engineering work this entailed involved a change in the contract between the oil companies which held the concession in the field and the engineering contractor. Environmental and safety regulations virtually always change during the construction of a nuclear power plant in the United States, requiring changes in the performances demanded of both the engineering contractor and the fabrication and construction contractors (Cohen, 1979:76-77, 90-95).

Where it is very difficult to specify in advance what the client wants, as in the case of software development, adaptation of the software to client needs depends on establishing the user-oriented members of the programming staff (the "architects") in authority on the project team, so they guide the implementation programmers. When this authority structure in the contractor (the "system producer") fails, then it takes more time to repair the software system to satisfy users than it would have to design it correctly in the first place (Brooks, 1975:47-50). In this case, the client's preference is not really changing, but instead the departure of what the client really wants from what the contractor is interpreting as its specifications increases over time unless architects have authority.

Finally we can recur to the contract for professional services, in which client specifications, for weapons for example, are developed by professionals. Professional "malpractice" or incompetence then produces specifications which do not in fact reflect client preferences. The avionics for the F111 fighter airplane (the F111 was also known as the TFX; avionics are the plane's navigational and aiming electronic systems) ended up being much more expensive and much less reliable than previous systems, though they did do more whenever they worked. The Department of Defense revised specifications in mid-production to get a cheaper and more reliable system. The bad performance was due to a mistaken set of engineering predictions about what was possible in the given "state of the art." Contractual activity can change specifications of performances by showing that some performance is not among the production possibilities as well by finding some that are (Coulam, 1977:127-132).

The specifications changes we have discussed so far basically reflect changes in knowledge of the world or changes in the world. But client preferences can change in a more direct way.

A simple example is a change in regime in the client organization. When Kennedy was elected and MacNamara became Secretary of Defense, the military philosophy of the government changed. In particular, for example, the role of aircraft in support of ground troops increased in importance compared to the nuclear bombing mission, and the objective of common weapons for several services was introduced. An attempt was therefore made to modify the TFX airplane, whose range and speed (and therefore weight) were adapted to strategic retaliation, for carrier operations and support of ground troops. The management of the actual design was delegated to the Air Force. The fact that the modification was a failure enables us to observe the conflicts in objectives between the new top regime and the Air Force, for the Air Force preference for fast, long range planes warred with the new preferences of the President and the Secretary. In the long run the Air Force won over McNamara and the plane was not useful for the missions of the other services (Coulam, 1977:237-336).

A second source of direct preference change is client experience with the product. Operational testing of weapons almost invariably shows that the military did not want what they specified in the engineering specifications, but instead wanted a modification of it (Stockfisch, 1973). And in order to sell a satisfactory software system, one needs to adapt it in the design stage so that clients can modify it easily when they learn from experience what they really want to use it for (Brooks, 1975:117-118). Even those modifications of software that are called "maintenance" which are done by the supplier and are included in the contract of sale are really changes in client specifications due to client experience. They come about because the test problems that software designers use to debug software do not adequately represent the problems the clients will use the system for. So client experience finds the new "bugs," i.e., functions for the programs which the original program design does not allow for, but which can reasonably be construed as a legitimate expectations for system performance by the client. For a heavily used software system such post-sale redesign or "maintenance" may easily amount to 40 per cent of the total development cost (Brooks, 1975:121).

A third direct source of changes in client preferences derives from the fact that most clients are organizations. When a central authority in an organization delegates decision-making power (or revokes a previous delegations), it often changes the operating organizational preference function. The Air Force predilection for heavy, long range, fast airplanes, poorly adapted for ground support or carrier operation, meant that the delegation to the Air Force in the TFX-F111 development resulted in a fighter only adopted by the Air Force (Coulam, 1977:237-336).

A common shift in preferences by delegation is due to professional perfectionism. Many professionals have a strong preference for technically elegant solutions, which often overrides cost-benefit considerations that are more important in the centers of ultimate power in the client organization. Organizations often go to great lengths to put "more reasonable" professionals in charge of design units (Kidder, 1981:119,142), which shows they fear that internal delegation may change organizational preferences. For this reason contracts normally administered by a professional department may provide for periodic review (with possible reorientation away from technical perfectionism) by higher authorities or operational arms of the client organization. R&D contracts and engineering contracts are especially likely to provide such review points.

Many client organizations determine their concrete preferences by a general preference for profits. Shifting profitabilities therefore change their preferences among concrete alternatives. For example, car manufacturers tool up each year for a large number of model changes. Some of those models sell well, but some move slowly. Since tooling for slow moving models is a sunk cost, and not useful for other purposes, the addition to profits made by selling a less popular model car is greater than that made by selling a hot model car. But if franchise dealers control investments of selling efforts, car manufacturers would like to change performances demanded of franchise dealers to get them to move the slow models.

The purpose of this extended list of examples is to show that there are large parts of the economy in which the basic assumption of the labor contract, that the employer may change its mind about what it wants the worker to do (Simon, 1957), holds between organizations.[7] Corporate and governmental clients change their minds about what they want from corporate suppliers and contractors. They know ahead of time that they may want to change their minds without destroying the contractual relationship, just as employers do not want to to hire new workers on the open labor market for each change of task. Of course the court will demand that the contract be written in such a way that the performances required at any particular time (or the options, such as contract cancellation, which can be used to reward or punish conformity with changed requirements) be definite.

Both the normal economic models of a market transaction and the legal model of a contract tend to obscure the degree to which large numbers of contracts are (realistically though not legally) agreements to deliver an indefinite good or service for an indefinite price. A system for adapting to clients' shifting purposes as they discover production possibilities, determine how the world has changed, or change their preferences, can render the performances required by the contract "piecewise definite," yielding an unfolding definiteness to be enforced by the court. And as clients will have been making those piecewise respecifications in the light of costs or of forgone alternatives as specified in part by pricing mechanisms built into the contracts, the contractors' compensation will likewise have been rendered piecewise definite.

The assumptions of our simplest models of market transactions, that clients know what they want and will continue to want the same thing throughout the transaction, do not therefore fit a large number of actual market transactions. Economists who analyze weapons research and development throw away the Economics 100 assumptions almost without noticing (Marschak, 1967; also Scherer, 1964). Similarly the practical seminars for contracts specialists in the construction industry discuss the techniques for writing the provisions dealing with "change orders" so that work can go forward on the change while compensation for it is in dispute with hardly a glance at the legal theory of definite performances and considerations. Our purpose here has been to focus sustained attention on situations in which rational clients will want to provide contractually for being able to change their minds, without wanting to create a whole hierarchy of which they are the bosses.

(b) Cost Uncertainties: In many of the same industries in which we observe provisions for clients to change their minds, we also

observe contractor incapacity to project costs accurately. Scherer shows that when defense contracts are not renegotiated part way through, the standard deviation of the percentage cost overrun or underrun is about 10 percent. That is, aside from any bias induced in the mean cost estimate by strategic bargaining incentives (which bias in different ways with different types of contracts), sheer variation among contract outcomes causes a particular estimate to be within 10 percent of the mean percentage overrun or underrun for that type of contract only about two-thirds of the time; the other third of the time it is over 10 percent away from the mean (see Scherer, 1964:192, 195-6, and the graphs 196-9). Defense contractors simply do not know how much a weapon will cost. The standard deviation of costs as compared to estimates is large compared to the average percentage profit on the contracts.

Systematic data from other areas is rare, because cost data are not routinely public. A Swedish study of building construction suggested a range from ten percent to 27 percent for working time spent in different projects on coffeebreaks, walking to and from the locker rooms, and other non-work activities (Kreiner, 1969:97). Clearly the contractors could not predict this variation very well, or they would have taken preventive measures. Since labor time is a large share of construction costs, this suggests that cost uncertainty for construction contractors is in the same range as for weapons contractors.

This means that even when the specifications of performances are definite, the appropriate compensation is very generally misestimated. Since often a single project is a large share of the total sales of a contractor, such cost uncertainty is a serious risk. This risk may be aggravated by penalties for not meeting a schedule. In one case of constructing missile silos with such penalty clauses, contractors apparently added about 50 percent risk premium to the cost the government had estimated for the work. The government shifted the risk to itself with a cost plus fee contract, and built the silos more cheaply.[8]

Because the client pays for the cost risk, it may be to everyone's benefit to plan to adapt to the risk, to agree to work together to minimize it, rather than merely to shift it between the parties. As background to the devices useful such adaptation (devices short of hierarchy), we can specify some of the causes of cost uncertainties.

The first source of contractor cost uncertainty is uncertain technical information. An R&D contract would have no research element in it if the technical solution were obvious and all that had to be specified were the details, details that could be described (see Marschak, 1967; on civilian R&D projects see Scherer, 1964:178). The part of software development that can be accurately costed, the writing of lines of code, only accounts for about a sixth of the development cost. This is because disaggregating a user functional requirement into an implementation strategy ("system architecture") requires a good deal of expensive time, and then the implementation never works because it has bugs. The inaccuracy of the estimate of debugging time is so great that Brooks says that a software project usually spends half of its debugging time with debugging "90 percent complete" (Brooks, 1975:154-5). Research and development and software development have in common that performance criteria for the product set by the client are not technically routine to achieve. Only routine technology can be accurately costed.

But technical surprises may be met by any large unique project. The soil samples on the basis of which foundations for a building were costed may not have been a good enough sample, and much extra foundation work may have to be done (Kreiner, 1969:95-97). An oil platform base may sink improperly when being settled on the bottom, and have to be discarded (itself not a trivial job)(Moe, et al., 1980, Part II:113-4). A new lighter material for the huge fans that make bypass jet engines practical may break when a chicken corpse is thrown at a prototype fan at a high speed to simulate the engine swallowing a duck in flight; the titanium which replaces it may require new weight adjustments throughout the plane (Newhouse, 1982e:56).

In addition to technical cost uncertainties, estimators' manuals in construction warn the estimator to take account of the state of the skilled labor market in the area.[9] If there are many more jobs than workers, the foreman's authority is undermined; if there are more workers than jobs, both the skill and the discipline of work crews can be increased. But how tight the labor market will be at the time a project is done cannot generally be predicted accurately when the project is estimated.

Tightness within the firm has the opposite effect in the defense industry. If a defense contractor has many employees but few positions on projects because of bad luck at the Pentagon, the projects it does have will have high official overheads inflated by salaries of people working on new bids, and high concealed overheads as projects are loaded up with extra workers. Scherer shows that lean efficient weapons projects are done by contractors with a lot of work, fat inefficient ones by contractors trying to retain valuable personnel for better times (Scherer, 1964:183, 187). Of course this strategy is only possible because many defense contracts are cost plus fee contracts.

The cost of large specialized machines such as airplanes, ships, heavy presses, or drilling rigs, tends to decline rapidly with experience with a particular model. The rule of thumb among airplane manufacturers is that as one doubles the number of machines produced one cuts the cost of each additional one by 27 percent (Newhouse, 1982a:66; Scherer, 1964:120-1). This means that the average cost of production is as unpredictable as the size of the market. The size of the market for capital goods is very unpredictable, highly responsive to the business cycle, and strongly related to the prosperity of particular clients. Contractors cannot predict their costs for large capital machines because they do not know how far down the learning curve they will get. It is in part for this reason that airplane manufacturers will not design and produce airplanes unless they have a large advance order book for them.

Contractors very often depend on subcontractors who are themselves exposed to cost uncertainties. When a large number of large subcontracts are let on a fixed price basis, at least one subcontractor on the project is likely to get the job because it made the biggest estimating mistake. Since such a large subcontract may be a large share of the turnover of the subcontractor, bankruptcy is not out of the question. Rolls Royce went bankrupt (to be saved by nationalization) because of overruns in developing the engines for Lockheed's wide body airliner (Newhouse,

1982e:56-61). If Rolls Royce had not been rescued, Lockheed as well would have gone bankrupt. Similarly the computer development crew featured in *The Soul of a New Machine* was substantially delayed because the chip manufacturer started to go bankrupt (Kidder, 1981:231-2, 268). In this case the contracts for delivery of computers were not yet signed, so the supplier of chips was not really a subcontractor.

Contractors can misestimate their costs also because their historical cost data are bad. For many large contracts, the contractor's estimated cost is synthesized from estimates of what quantities of various elementary actions need to be carried out (e.g., how many yards of excavation), multiplied by a cost per unit derived in part from organizational historical cost data. But if the categories of elementary actions are not fine enough, the finish work may be costed with data including rough work, clearing irregular terrain for a pipeline costed with data on less broken terrain, or the cost of locating survey respondents who are drug addicts costed with data on locating respondents who are physicians, so the cost per unit may be misestimated from the historical data. Further the multiplier may be out of date due to inflation, technical change in the activity, a decline in the quality control standards of a crucial semi-finished goods supplier, or some other cause of inaccuracy. Such sources of inaccuracy plague all cost accounting, but are more serious and harder to detect when production is not continuous. For one thing, since contractors often have to build up and tear down their organizations rapidly, a constant overhead cost such as a competent cost accounting department is often an expensive luxury (Stinchcombe, 1959).

Even when the contractor knows the costs (or "even to the degree it knows them"), the client may be excluded from that knowledge. The cost of bidding on a building construction job runs from three to five percent of the value of the job, even after the specifications are completely drawn up. Contractors therefore are not willing to bid if there are many serious bidders, because that increases their overhead and can make them noncompetitive in the long run. Ordinarily then a client gets a sample of three or so[10] from a roughly normal distribution with a standard deviation of 10 percent (Scherer, 1964:192, 195-6, and the graphs at 196-9).

The client often does not know what accounts for the differences among contractors (Kreiner, 1969:80-81). So the client may not be able to obtain good information from the market about costs even insofar as the contractors know them, and cannot legally penetrate the contractor for direct cost information.

The government sometimes tries to penetrate defense contractor costs. Even when they ask for separate pricing of components of a weapons development contract and devote government engineer and accountant hours to it, they cannot always get cost information to allow them to choose among alternative strategies (Scherer, 1964:204-207).

In addition, in many cases contractors know of technical possibilities which they do not reveal to their clients because they do not effectively have a professional (fiduciary) contract with the clients.[11] I once knew an operations research consultant who had discovered that the main scheduling decision task a skilled executive did could be reproduced by a transformation of variables and a simple linear equation. By concealing that equation he raised the price of his advice on the scheduling problem. A plastering contractor will rarely tell a potential client how much drywall would probably cost. Technical information that would allow clients to cut contractor profits is hard to come by.

The traditional theory in this field says that when clients are confronted with uncertainties that may impinge on delivery dates, on solvency of suppliers, on quality control problems as contractors desperately make up for costing mistakes, they will tend to incorporate the uncertainty within their organization, so they can control it as far as possible and predict when they cannot control (Thompson, 1967:36, 40-42). But we have observed that in much of the economy they build whatever adaptations they do make into contractual relationships. They do this even when it puts contractors in a position of information advantage that may be (and often is) used to the clients' disadvantage, though the theory argues that the chance of exploitation by the contractor is a principal condition favoring vertical integration.[12]

(c) Observability of Performance: When two activities depend on each other (are "closely coupled"), they should be administered together under the same responsibility, and only when

activities are decoupled should they be divided between different firms, or be done by different departments with a firm. The more two activities are interdependent, the more information has to flow between them, the more combined authority is necessary for making adjustments in both, and the more difficult it will be to allocate responsibility between activities for costs, delays, inferior quality, or other difficulties (Stinchcombe, 1979:61-65; Alchian and Demsetz, 1972). This decoupling principle or team production principle means in particular that highly interdependent activities should not be separated through contracting parts of them, for that separates information flows, authority, and measurement of outcomes between two or more firms.

A derivation from this principle is that activities that have to be performed in series should only be separated among different firms if one is not in a hurry, so that delays (to give a breathing space), inspections, and inventories of partially finished work between stages can serve to buffer interdependencies. Yet we observe that weapons development contracts are nearly always rushed to stay ahead of the Russians, that delays in construction administered by contracts are often the primary determinant of net present value of large capital projects, so such projects are rationally rushed (Moe, et al., 1980, Part I:111, 241), or that airline airframes stand waiting for the delivery of engines from a separate engine supplier at thousands of dollars a day each in interest losses alone (Newhouse, 1982e:46).

Similarly when the system being produced is highly technically interdependent, the quality control determining the reliability of components determines also the reliability of the system. This means that the quality of the work on a subcontracted component determines the effectiveness of another: faulty delivery of hot or cool air through the heating system of a building leads to complaints about the fact that the windows do not open, and unreliable avionics causes a very fast fighter-bomber to fly very fast in the wrong direction. To get the contractor to take responsibility for the performance of the whole system, a client very often has to allow the contractor authority over the components (Scherer, 1964:110-112). Yet we find that such authority is very often administered and set up through contracts.[13]

The central difficulty for contractual arrangements that such technical interdependencies among components create is that the performances in two or more separate contracts are intermixed in such a way that the quality, timeliness, or cost of the separate performances are not separately measurable. This in turn means that it is difficult to establish which contractor was in default when the joint performance was inadequate. Several other common conditions have the same effect on the observability of performances. When performances are difficult to observe, yet hierarchy is also difficult, special provisions may have to be made in the contract to render the performances controllable, which means to simulate a hierarchy by contractual means.

The most obvious problems of observability come when the performance is literally hidden, as the length and composition of piles for a building, the second coat of paint on a three coat paint job, the mean time to failure of a computer or copy machine just being bought, or in international trade the fiscal and monetary policy of the government that backs the currency in which the contract is to be paid.[14]

In the nature of the case a contract for professional services poses great difficulties in performance measurement. One cannot evaluate the quality of a service accurately if one could not have provided it oneself. One may know for example that the rate of cesarian sections in the United States is much higher than it is in other countries where the maternal and fetal-neonate death rates are lower (e.g., the Netherlands or the Scandinavian countries), so there must be excessive prescription of the procedure. Yet an individual mother is not in a position to evaluate the professional advice she receives in her particular case. The extant economic theory predicts that the physician will prescribe the procedure that brings the highest fee, and, since such incentives could be corrected, one hopes it is this rather than incompetence that accounts for the overprescription.[15] Except in very gross cases, defaults in performance of professional contracts are very difficult to prove, and alternative control mechanisms are written into the norms of professional practice rather than into the contract.

In many contractual systems for large scale projects, the client builds a large professional system within its own organization to supervise the administration of the contract. Scherer collected rank data from expert judges separately on the performance of the government team supervising a set of defense contracts and of the contractor. The performances were highly correlated, indicating that client performance and contractor performance are too intermixed to be separately observed.[16]

The ratios of engineers in the client project organization to engineers in the engineering contractor's project organization in the Norwegian North Sea has apparently ranged between one to three and one to seven. Under such conditions there is a large flow of information, consultation, approvals and disapprovals, and the like from the client's engineering crew to the engineer's crew; this means that at each step of the way the client's performance and the engineer's performance are deeply intermixed, and every step on the way to an engineering contractor's default has been approved and/or caused by a client directive. When things go wrong, when the project is delayed or more expensive than planned, there is a flow of recriminations across the boundary nearly as large as the flow of information. In general, such deep intervention makes the contractor's responsibility for defaults very difficult to prove in court.

We see the operation of the same process in reverse when we observe that defense contractors on fixed price contracts tend to refuse to introduce engineering changes, even though they will supposedly be reimbursed for the costs of such changes, because they cannot recoup the full cost of the disruption of production (Scherer, 1964:180,237-8). When the client intervenes with a change order, it is not possible to discriminate exactly the costs attributable the client intervention from the costs normally due to activities the contractor is responsible for.

The general point here is that when elements of hierarchy are built into the contract, by high Defense Department control of contractors, by supervision of the details of engineering work by a large client project crew, or even by an "isolated" engineering change in a fixed price contract, the separability of contractor performance is undermined. Thus hierarchical elements built into the contract tend to undermine the legal obligation of the contractor for the performances specified and to require further reliance on hierarchical devices to adjust to the consequences of poor observability of performances.

Finally we should note that when the contractor is in default, many contracts provide that the client (and sometimes also the surety bonding company) can resume authority over the performances, arrange to have them done by other contractors or by its own work force, and the costs of such substitute performance are an element in determining the legal valuation of the contractor's default. That is, there is substantive hierarchical discretion and activity supervised by the client involved in determining the damages of the default.

Uncertainty and the Requirements for Hierarchy: Future contractual performances under certainty give no difficulty for economic theory nor for the legal theory of contract. But the manufacture of large machines such as airliners or computer systems, of advanced weapons systems, or the building of large capital construction projects, all frequently take place under conditions of *ex ante* shifting and uncertain client specifications, major cost uncertainties that it is rational to adapt to rather than to insure, and *ex post* uncertainty about whether the contractor has indeed done the performances. All of these uncertainties generate pressure to create structures connecting the client with the contractor (and the contractor with any subcontractors) such that adjustive moves can be made authoritative. That is, such uncertainties create the requirement that hierarchical elements be built into the contractual system.

PART 4: ELEMENTS OF HIERARCHY IN CONTRACT CONTENTS

In Part 3 we have shown that the functions for which hierarchies are set up are often necessary to accomplish the client's purposes in contractual relationships. We have also seen, in Part 2, how hierarchies in fact fulfill those functions. The setting can provide some guidance in modifying our Economics 100 or Business Law 100 model of the papaya buying contract to take account of the complexity we find in construction, weapons, airplane, or computer system contracts. We start by taking from our model of hierarchy the elements that we expect to be present when people have to solve hierarchical problems by contractual means.

"Hierarchical elements" in contracts can be described as consisting of five structures: (a) command structures and authority systems, (b) incentive systems, supporting authority systems and also guiding the use of a contractor's discretion by a structure of differential rewards partially isolated from the market, (c) standard operating procedures, which describe routines that involve actions by both contractors and clients, (d) dispute resolution procedures, partially isolated from the court system and from the market, and (e) pricing of variations in performances partially isolated from the market, including especially pricing based on contractor costs. Clearly a structure with relations of command, an incentive system partially isolated from the market, standard operating procedures, internal dispute resolution structures, and subunits whose "price" is determined mainly by costs, is quite near to what we have described above as a typical "hierarchy."

(a) Command Structures and Authority Systems: The naive notion of an authority system is one involving "command," a supervisor selecting an action for a subordinate to carry out. Above the level of foreman of secretary, authority systems rarely depend on command, though an authoritative description of an end to be achieved by an individual is perhaps not so uncommon. At middle management levels and above, revised minutes of committee meetings, or a string of initials approving a proposed budget allocation, or standard operating procedures adopted by the relevant authorities and written into the organizational regulations, or the question by a superior, "And what do you think you (or we) ought to do next?" with its implicit approval, are more common ways of exercising authority.

Authority systems are systems by which flows of information are certified as legitimate or authoritative, so that a person who acts in accordance with them has the risk of being wrong removed from him or her, and laid on the legitimators of the communication (Barnard, 1946:46-83). Thus what we have to look for in contracts are systems for certifying a given communication (other than the contract itself) as authoritative, and therefore as redistributing the risks of being wrong.

An elegant example occurred with the introduction of new x-ray and sonic inspection of steel products. These made possible a much more accurate determination of whether a given piece of steel actually satisfied the standards specified in the contract all the way through, as well as on the surface. Since almost all the increased accuracy was in detecting heretofore undetectable faults, the new devices enabled clients to raise the *de facto* standards for steel. The steel producers argued that the specifications for steel in the contracts extant at the time really incorporated the certifying procedures available when the contracts were signed; the clients argued that hidden defects violated the specifications as much as visible ones, and that inspection procedures not specifically described in the contract were implicitly left at the discretion of the client. (The decisions apparently went against the steel producers in most countries, and now inspection procedures are specified in new contracts.) The legal issue however has clearly, "By what standards is the quality control certification to be taken as legitimate?"

Such quality control systems are common features of contracts, and constitute a clear example of an authority system in Chester Barnard's sense of marking specific communications as authoritative. It is obvious that they distribute the risks of mistakes, since the steel producers were clearly claiming the right to their traditional proportion of mistakes, on the basis of which they had made their bids.

An approvals systems that is more clearly supervisory is that described above for defense contracts and large oil installations, in which a large staff of client engineers reviews and approves plans drawn up by R&D contractors or engineering consultants. The larger the client's engineering organization reviewing the contractor's engineering work, the finer the net of approvals can be. This makes the sequence of steps that have to be approved more dense, so that sketches, drafts, preliminary specifications and drawings, final specifications and drawings, tender documents, technical evaluations of the bidders' replies, technical changes proposed after contract start, and costs for all of these, all have to be approved by the client.

Aside from the extra work involved in creating a document for approval for each intermediate decision, such a fine net of approvals strains out any discretion or originality that the contractor's engineers might have been afflicted with. Such a system makes the client engineer into a supervisor with restrictions on his or her oral and visual contact with the work, thus structuring the incompetence of the supervision and increasing its bureaucratic complexity (see the hearings on this problem in missile programs cited in Scherer, 1964:375-6).

A large number of inspection or "commissioning" provisions have the same general effect. In general the inspection structure set up by the client is not specified in traditional construction contracts, but is assumed according to industry practice. In large capital machinery construction such as refineries or power generating stations a separate commissioning phase is often specified in the contract. At that phase authority is generally reconcentrated in the client's hands, and the engineers or projects managers from the contractor are put at the disposal of the client's supervisor of commissioning to aid in the testing of all equipment. In shipbuilding some part of the inspection and testing is carried out by the classification societies which certify the ship to the marine insurance companies. Since clients do not want ships they cannot insure, and since producing an insurable ship is part of the contractual responsibility of the shipyard, this serves also as an inspection on behalf of the client. It is paid for by the client rather than by the insurance company (Heimer, 1980).

More direct provision for command structures are often written into contracts. For instance, a standard form for subcontracts by an engineering prime contractor contains the language:

PHYSICAL EXPEDITING

When (company name) deems it advisable this order shall be subject to physical expediting by (company name) representatives who shall be granted access to any and all parts of the seller's or sub-supplier's plant involved in the manufacture or processing of this order.

No actual capacity for the expediter to order people around is specifically provided, but authority is clearly being allocated (see Chapter 1).

The provisions about change orders in construction and large engineering project contracts quite often contain language to the effect that the contractor is to accept the orders of a specified person (in England this person, typically called "the Engineer," is employed by the client, and is named early in the contract) on all change orders even when the compensation for the change has not yet been agreed. The command authority of "the Engineer" over contractor personnel is thus established by designating the work to be a change order and not part of the original contract. The original contract however specifies this intermediate hierarchical phase, until the amendment of the original contract by the change order can be agreed on (or arbitrated).

Macaulay reports that in the bad old days, the automobile manufacturer's "regional representative" (the member of the manufacturer's marketing staff who dealt directly with the franchised car dealers) in effect had power to set quotas for sales, for car inventory, for parts orders, for sales and display space, and for other features of the dealer's business conduct not specified in the contract. These came to be points of dispute mainly when they increased costs and investments for the dealer, increased gross volume for the manufacturer, but could decrease profit rates or increase risks for the dealers (Macaulay, 1966). The contract was written to provide that the manufacturer could cancel the franchise unless the dealer's performance was satisfactory to the manufacturer. But this meant that, lacking any other source of judgments of satisfactory performance, that the regional representative could give orders with the sanction of the risk of cancellation. Again the authority structure is not specified in the contract, but the sanctions in the hands of the regional representatives were, and the practice of accepting their judgements created the command authority in practice.

(b) Incentive Systems: By an incentive system we mean a way of measuring or otherwise observing levels of performance of a contractor or of a contractor subunit and allocating differential compensation based on the level of performance, without further recourse directly to the market. An incentive system then is an enclave in the market within which special rules of reward and punishment apply. Of course the broad levels of compensation

tend to be set with an eye to the market, and a compensation system must produce a correspondence between output and costs that is viable in the market. But for example the piece rate systems in most American factories pay less for each additional piece (above the quota that merely earns the guaranteed daily minimum wage) than they do for each piece included in the minimum, which reverses the pattern to be expected on the basis of marginal revenue productivity. The older "Stakhanovite" Soviet incentive systems were closer to the neo-classical ideal.[17] This shows that the piece rates are incentives in a rule-governed enclave, rather than a mere reflection of a market in differential machinist talent.

Actually a normal fixed price forward sale contract creates an incentive system by this definition. For the term of the contract the contractor can sell the client a given quantity at the fixed price, even if it manages to reduce costs during the course of the contract. For the period of the contract, then, the contractor collects the full value of all cost reductions, and none of that addition to net revenue is dissipated by competitive reactions to these new cost possibilities. This superior incentive effect of fixed price contracts is consciously used by the Department of Defense and some large corporate clients as the basis for a policy preferring to let contracts on a fixed price basis. The average profit as a percentage of total sales on fixed price defense contracts runs about three times as much as that on various types of cost-plus contracts (Scherer, 1964:159-60), even though the Department of Defense believes it gets cheaper weapons from them; their superiority as incentive (and competitive) systems thus apparently overrides their offering higher rewards to the contractors.

Once the basic device of building an incentive system into the contract is recognized, it can be extended to a wide variety of substantive measures of performance. In sharecropping and putting-out piecework systems the incentive is based on the quantity of (acceptable) output. The difficulties of such an incentive system in a modern economy have been most fully studied for the Soviet Union (Granick, 1976). In the agency relations much analyzed in the modern economic literature financial outputs provide the measures, which one would not want to do if the workers could eat part of the output before sale (Ross, 1973; Becker and Stigler, 1974). Many construction contracts provide for penalties (liquidated damages) for delays beyond an agreed completion date, and often rewards for early completion. Franchise contracts for sales outlets very generally in effect set up an incentive system to motivate sales efforts and sales enhancing investments by the franchise holder without recourse to competitive bidding for the franchise.

The Department of Defense has experimented with making fees on R&D contracts depend on engineering performance criteria as measured on the resulting weapon. They have mostly discarded the system because contractors successfully argued that if the government had disapproved intermediate proposals that would have resulted in a higher compensation if followed, then the government owed the compensation. Thus the incentive system was incompatible with the degree of detailed authority over the development that the government wanted to retain (see Scherer, 1964:179, quoting USDOD Incentive Contracting Guide at 43). More generally the government's Cost Plus Incentive Fee type of contract tries to create an incentive system partway between that of a fixed price contract and a Cost Plus Fixed Fee contract. As one would expect, it appears that when the risk is higher the contractors force the government to assume greater proportions of the cost overruns (and correspondingly the contractors give up a larger part of the underruns); that is, as one moves toward higher levels of inherent risks and cost uncertainty, one moves toward more hierarchical incentive systems (lower contractor shares in the cost risks)(Scherer, 1964:308).

(c) Standard Operating Procedures: The list of documents required by the operator of an oil field before it will pay a requisition (Stinchcombe, 1974; see Chapter 1 above) is a contractual practice which constrains everyone else to produce the appropriate documents. It provides an orderly way of proceeding in making purchases, a "standard operating procedure." But the companies operating in the standard way producing the standard documents are the consulting engineering firms, the manufacturers and assemblers of machinery, the construction contractors, and so on. It is the power implicit in the right to award contracts

that enables the oil company to set up a standard operating
procedure for a complex of firms involved in supplying goods and
services to them.

The purpose of all these documents being required is only
rarely that the information is needed for some decision by the
client. Instead it is to make sure, as far as one can with documents, that the contractor has followed routines specified by the
client in making purchases, creating a trail of paper for auditing if
necessary, providing documentation in case the regulatory
authorities question a decision, and so on. The information then is
mostly not in the contents of the documents, but in their existence, and what that existence communicates is that standard
operating procedures specified by the client have been followed
by the contractor.

Tenders often require that the bidders on a large project
provide PERT diagrams or other formal schedules with estimated
elapsed time until various project "milestones" are reached.
Associated with this is generally a requirement for reports on the
achievement of the milestones, so that clients can estimate project
completion delays as early as possible. This means in fact that
clients usually intervene to speed up projects that fall behind. The
interventions often legally have the effect of transferring part of
the risk for delays to the client, which is considered to have taken
responsibility for meeting the schedule by taking it (partially)
from the contractor's control. The legal disadvantage of intervening is often suffered for the sake of establishing a standard
operating procedure governing the schedule.

Sometimes the standard routines are established by traditional
practice. For example, the marine insurance contract contains a
"sue and labor" clause which was much more important before
radio communications. It required the policy holder and its agents
(in effect, the captain of the ship) to take whatever legal, physical
and commercial measures were necessary to minimize the loss
after a covered accident. Claims against the party liable for the
damage had to be filed, repairs essential for the safety of the ship
had to be made, perishable cargoes had to be sold, and so on. The
costs were to be borne by the insurer. Such provisions provided
routines for transferring the captain's agency relation to the new

principal which now would suffer the loss. The substantive contents of the obligations were defined by the situation (possible
sources of loss), by the precedents in marine insurance adjudica-
tion, and by traditional requirements for good judgement on the
part of captains (Heimer, 1981:255-260).

(d) Dispute Resolution: The same "Engineer" in English construction contracts who is supposed to administer disputed change
orders is also generally charged with authoritative (interim)
interpretation of the contract in case of a dispute between the
client and the contractor. The ideology here is that the Engineer is
an independent professional who, though employed by the client,
will give an objective interpretation of the contract. And in
England itself this usually works to resolve the dispute – when the
contract language is exported abroad it tends to result in an
interim client dictatorship through the Engineer's agency,
because professional institutions protecting the Engineer's auto-
nomy are not well developed elsewhere.

Many such contracts also specify arbitration in case either the
client or the contractor disagrees with the Engineer's decision.
That is, a hierarchy of nominally independent appeals is specified
within the contract, before the contract is appealed to the courts.

Under pressure from threatened legislation to protect franchised car dealers, car manufacturers developed a hierarchy of
hearings and appeals, programs to help lagging dealers, and
voluntary compensation for dealers who were cancelled (usually
by arranging for a new dealer to buy them out), before applying
the market sanction of looking for an alternative dealer. Since the
legislation was in fact ineffective in protecting dealers, these
procedures were protections for the dealer from the market
judgement by the manufacturer that it could do better elsewhere,
rather than pre-court dispute resolution (Macaulay, 1966). If
these devices applied to unionized workers they would be called
"grievance procedures" and they would be taken as a clear indication of the development of industrial justice with bureaucratiza-
tion (Selznick, Nonet, and Vollmer, 1969; see also Williamson,
1975:30, 73-80).

There are a great many informal equivalents of these formal
hearings involving a contractor and a client. Many of the items of

the agenda of a weekly or monthly meeting between client personnel and contractor personnel are disputes between the two organizations. These can be technical disputes, disputes over what costs will be allowed, disputes about schedules, quality of workmanship, disruption of the client's business, where to put the fill dirt, or disputes about a client's employee who likes "to go over and rattle the contractor's cage a bit." Often the purpose of such meetings is described as "to clarify" the points on the agenda, which avoids naming them as disputes.

(e) Non-Market Pricing: Perhaps the surest indicator that a client intends to change a contract during its life is pricing based on contractor cost. This ordinarily involves complex procedures which supposedly insure that costs are reasonable, such as the list of procurement documents mentioned above, or the complex cost accounting practices required of defense contractors. The general idea of such contracts is that the reward for the competence of the organization, the fee or profit, should be separated from the costs incident upon client change in specifications, client adaptation to cost uncertainties, or client control to secure faithful achievement of unobservables. Hospital services, engineering consultant services, R&D work, change orders in construction contracts, "sue and labor" work of a ship captain in marine insurance, all are usually priced on a cost basis. Cost pricing usually means hierarchy.

Cost pricing though usually means completely leaving the market competitive controls on pricing. When the technology of line of work is not changing too rapidly, the institution of a "quantity surveyor" system, as used in construction in England, becomes possible. The quantity surveyor takes the architectural and engineering drawings of a project and translates them into quantities of technically distinct activities. Thus for example welding pipes together 50 feet in the air is a technically different activity than welding them on the ground and will have a different price. The contractor then bids on the bill of quantities, giving a price to a unit of welding 50 feet up, a price to a unit of welding on the ground, and so on. This pricing system yields the contractor's bid on the contract. For the contract itself, it has the advantages of stating precisely what is included in the contract (the bill of quantities is taken as final), of avoiding many contractor mistakes in reading drawings so the bids are serious, of saving contractor estimating work so that more contractors are willing to bid.

But the contract usually specifies that a reasonable amount of work under change orders will be performed with the same pricing system. The quantity surveyor takes the quantities off the drawings for the change and determines the price. This is not cost pricing *post hoc*, but pricing of work outside the contract by a schedule of prices per unit built into the contract. But presumably the prices per unit reflect the contractor estimate of its minimum costs plus a reasonable profit for the kind of work specified, under competitive pressure. Further, this produces a fixed-price incentive system during the work on the change order, even with hierarchical intervention in the contract by the client. It in effect uses market processes (and some very expensive and time consuming work by a quantity surveyor) to get a market estimate of costs rather than a cost-accounting estimate of costs.

Contract Simulations of Hierarchies: The analysis of typical contract contents in several fields shows that when the extant theory predicts vertical integration, but we do not find vertical integration, we find instead contractual provisions that may be expected to produce the effects of hierarchies. They provide for clients to legitimate communications that will be taken as authoritative by employees of the contractor; they arrange incentive systems by rule partially outside the market; they establish standard operating procedures which involve regular flow of information between the contractor and the client and govern the procedures of the contractor as well as its objectives; they establish rule-governed systems for making fair decisions in case of disputes between the contractor and client without recourse to the courts nor to client choice of another contractor; they price variations in performance by non-market rules, especially by costs or by quantity measurements of outputs.

These provisions very often have a negative effect on the traditional obligations under the contracts. The difficulty of the government setting up an incentive system to get the contractor to do what they later decide they do not want it to do, resulting in governmental liability for the incentive even though the contractor does not satisfy the performance requisites for it, is typical of the legal difficulties one gets into in writing contracts with hierarchical elements in them. The general point is that one cannot require the contractor to do something else than specified in the contract without undermining requirements elsewhere in the contract or accruing liabilities that one would not have had if one had not so required. Much contractual ingenuity has gone into building hierarchical elements into the contracts in these fields in such a way as to leave the legal obligations of both parties clear, but ingenuity does not always satisfy the judge.

PART 5: THEORETICAL CONCLUSION

Our main descriptive conclusions are embedded in Part 4 above entitled "Elements of Hierarchy in Contract Contents." Briefly they are that five elements that make up hierarchies are often found in contractual language, and that they achieve purposes of dealing with uncertainties that rational clients will often want to deal with. The fundamental conditions that call forth such contractual elements are those that ordinarily produce hierarchies in the ordinary sense of that term, and are things that hierarchies arrange themselves to do as well as they can.

In a sense the theoretical conclusion is that the law and the economy can arrange between firms in the market everything they can arrange in the labor market. When stated this way the main proposition is unsurprising and *a priori* quite likely.

It does not follow that there is no use forming a concept of hierarchy with five elements (or some other number), an ideal type concept whose contrasting concept is an ideal-typical market transaction. Such a strategy will be useful only if in fact the various elements cohere empirically. Since in our case they cohere (if at all) in a market subject to competitive evolutionary pressures (Nelson and Winter, 1982), we have to argue that the various elements of hierarchy are functionally related.

We have occasionally noted above various empirical correlations in hierarchical features of contracts: for example the usual non-market pricing of change orders in construction coheres with arrangements for hierarchical command of those changes by the

Engineer. We would have to go through the other nine relation-ships between the five hierarchical elements we have found in contracts to show their empirical relationships as well.

To some degree our analysis of existent corporate hierarchies argues such an empirical correlation. When one is serious about setting up a hierarchy for the long run, one takes out a corporate charter, hires people, sets up an authority system, an incentive system, resolves disputes internally, and the like. The concretiza-tion of all five features in the normal corporate hierarchy there-fore argues in favor of the empirical unity of the concept of hierarchy.

The functional unity of the features of hierarchy is implicitly argued above in Part 3, "Prediction of Performance Require-ments and Performance Measurement." The argument takes the form that all five features of hierarchies (authority systems, incentive systems, standard operating procedures, dispute resolu-tion procedures, and non-market internal pricing) are useful when a client may want to change specifications, when a contractor or a client cannot predict costs very well, or when performances are not easily separately measured.

The end result of this argument, if it is accepted, is actually a continuous dimension between markets (or papaya buying simple contracts) and hierarchies. For example, a normal percentage of the work on a large capital construction project done hierar-chically under change orders is about 20 percent. One could think of such a construction contract then as normally about 20 percent of the way between a pure market sales arrangement and an intra-firm arrangement. Perhaps the normal R&D contract for weapons is 80 percent of the way toward making the engineering department of the contractor into an arsenal development staff, a department of government (Stockfisch, 1973; also see note 6). There is nothing wrong with describing such a dimension along which decision-systems range by its two ends, contract and hierar-chy. It simplifies theoretical discussion.

The continuous nature of the variable from "inside" to "outside" the firm does however make it hard to do empirical work with the dichotomy. When Teece for example gives statistics on what percentages of the distributors, or pipelines, or oil wells, are owned by the refiners, and concludes that the oil industry is not very vertically integrated (Teece, 1976:36, 63-64,96), one wants to tell him to come in out of the rain.

The Williamson hypothesis (Williamson, 1975) can be restated in continuous form in the light of this discussion.[18] Roughly it is that the more the possibility of changing client specifications, the more the cost uncertainty, and the more difficult it is to measure performances, the higher the transaction costs of obtaining performances in the interfirm market rather than the labor market. Whenever these costs are not paid for by compensating advantages of contracting (e.g., due to being a construction client for only a short time, or due to difficulties of R&D performance in government arsenals), we will expect to find hierarchical administration in the everyday sense of that word. We merely add to this some specification of what contracts will tend to look like when the compensating advantages of contracting are high.

Another way to look at these same theoretical conclusions is to ask, "What else besides legally binding performance demands will we expect to find in contracts?" Or, "Why else are things put in contracts besides to establish the right to damages if specific performances are not carried out?" The basic answer we have given is that the additions to contracts serve as the regulations of a formal organization. A corporation has much authoritative "constitutional" writing which is not in the charter or other legal documents, which has the force of law only as long as the real law is not called in. Rule books and memos with enough initials and minutes of the meetings between the production programming department and the shop superintendent serve as such legally unenforceable formal arrangements in hierarchies. In a contractual relation there is no other place to put the list of documents to be submitted with a request for reimbursement, or who is in charge in the interim during a dispute over pricing a change order, or other matters for which one needs a hierarchy, except in the contract.

The normal expectation is that the client and the contractor should agree, formally and in writing, on such matters of joint administrative structure, but that it would ordinarily not be worth anyone's while to go to court over it. We would not be surprised to find halfway through the contract performance a new rule of the client's accounting office demanding a new document before reimbursement (for example, a certification of the exchange rate at which currency was bought to pay the subcontractor), and one would not expect the contractor to sue for damages over such an increase in performances demanded. Putting such things in the contracts has the virtue of explicitness, more than the advantage of legal bindingness.

What usually has to be made binding under such circumstances is the overall control of the incentive system by one of the parties. The nearly hierarchical factual arrangements described by Macaulay (1966) for franchised car dealers were a reflection of the provision that cancellation was reserved to the manufacturer and that the manufacturer allowed a level of profit to the franchise holder which made it worthwhile for the car dealer to tolerate being pushed around.

That is, the function of the legally precarious flow of instructions generated by hierarchical structures built into contracts is to set up a formal organization, a hierarchy, which incorporates elements of the client organization and of the contractor organization into a new unity, under circumstances in which the traditional theory in this field would predict vertical integration.

When two powerful intellectual traditions have built powerful but idealized concepts, such as "market transaction" in economics or "contract" in law, into powerful intellectual systems, the concepts tend to shape perception. Everything appears as either the idealized version or something very different, "hierarchy." It is a great advance to conceive that dichotomy as a variable to be explained, as Coase and his successors have done. But things in the world are hardly ever dichotomies, and they are especially unlikely to be dichotomies when the economy sets a large number of intelligent men and women looking for the intermediate ground. Our argument has been that in many sectors of the economy, such intelligent search for contractual means of creating small hierarchies has been going on for generations.

NOTES

[1] Mansfield apparently does not predict this explicitly. He argues, following Arrow and others, that the private return to the innovating firm will generally be below the social return, because it is difficult to appropriate all the returns from new information (Mansfield, 1977). Hiring a subcontractor to develop new technology results in the subcontractor appropriating the value, as is documented by Frederic M. Scherer (Scherer, 1964:381) for the relations between electronics manufacturers and airframe manufacturers, so subcontracting will rarely be used for R&D. Scherer quotes data showing that, "Only 4% of the four billion dollars in company-sponsored research and development performed during 1959 was contracted to outside organizations; the rest was performed in-house" (Scherer, 1964:372). It follows that R&D should be integrated to facilitate appropriation. The assumption that private firms never contract for R&D is implicit in the methods of Mansfield, et al., (1977). See also Teece (1981) where amounts of in-house R&D in coal gassification and oil shale by oil companies are predicted on the basis of a theory of appropriability of returns.

[2] Scherer (1964:165,178) compares civilian in-house R&D with weapons development contracts.

[3] See Alchian and Demsetz (1972), Newhouse (1982). On the general inter-penetration of clients and suppliers, and the conditions which produce it, see Reve and Johansen (1982).

[4] Simon (1957:183-195). Williamson's argument that more than authority – specifically the capacity to audit performances and incentive systems based on statuses and promotions – is required to make a hierarchy work is based on an analysis of Simon's paper (Williamson, 1975).

[5] Scherer (1964:145-6). Note that the theory that predicts when hierarchy rather than markets will be used argues on the basis of competitive pressures on efficiency. These competitive arguments do not apply to governments, except perhaps in the long run in warlike periods. The explanation of why the American government does not develop its weapons in government arsenals, does not deliver Medicare and Medicaid through a National Health Service or through county, military, and veterans' hospitals, and does not build its own public buildings, must be found in political history. Governments which do all these things with hierarchies show every evidence of being viable in the modern world, and in the medical case infant mortality statistics suggest they are more effective. Since we are here mainly interested in how hierarchies can be built with contracts, we will avoid trying to explain why the government uses contracts when the economic arguments suggest hierarchies would be more efficient. Perhaps government hierarchies are less efficient for special reasons, especially in the United States.

[6] See Scherer (1964:108-9); also Kidder (1981:121-2). For a similar problem in software design, see Allman and Stonebreaker (1982), where it is estimated that "Perhaps only a third of the total effort is required to get a large system to the stage where we can make it work."

[7] Alchian and Demsetz (1972) define "manage" as "renegotiate with," which makes the same point.

[8] Scherer (1964:308). Returns on contracts by type of risk sharing for cost uncertainty is given in Scherer (1964:159); the dependence of contractor willingness to share the risks of cost uncertainty on the amount of uncertainty is documented in Scherer (1964:226).

[9] Page (1976). See also Moe, et al.(1980:324, 329) for the cost of having to recruit and train an unexpectedly large number of new workers on a project.

[10] Three bids is a rough estimate based on miscellaneous sources on the construction industry in several countries.

[11] Compare the reasoning behind the provision of Danish law that contractors assume the risks of cost uncertainties unknown to the clients: ". . . the contractor will in many cases be in a better position than the client for limiting the impact of the (cost) uncertainties and can by virtue of his professional knowledge estimate the risk in advance to some degree." My translation from Kreiner (1976:127).

[12] See Klein, Crawford, and Alchian (1978); on opportunities to "renegotiate" the terms of construction contracts under way, see Kreiner (1976:119). The ability to change the terms of a contract already in existence due to bargaining advantages developed during execution implies that "repeated play" short term contracts also would not solve the problems involved. This is why Klein and others predict vertical integration in these circumstances.

[13] See Scherer (1964:111). Western Electric insisted that components for missiles be shipped to them for measurement and testing, before being sent to missile sites for assembly, even though the components were being made on contracts between the suppliers and the government; and some prime contractors accepted a zero profit override to have component suppliers be subcontractors rather than to contract with the government so the suppliers would report to and coordinate with them. Both facts indicate subcontracts with hierarchical elements.

[14] Kreiner (1976:91-119) has a good account of the variety of things that are hard for a client to observe in construction contracting.

[15] "Second, while it is possible to conceive the fee as being directly functionally dependent on the act [of the agent, rather than being dependent on the outcome – as in fee for service agency relations rather than a typical sales agency relation] the theory loses much of its interest [because the agent by assumption will choose the act which is paid most], forcing a particular act."(Ross, 1973) Physicians have less trouble conceiving of the interest of such fee for service arrangements than do economists.

[16] Scherer (1964:99) reports an r-square of .862. This is not in agreement with the figure given in Peck and Scherer (1962), reporting on the same study. The r of .903 reported there gives an r-square of. 815. Either one is extremely high and both show that contractor performance cannot be distinguished from client performance.

[17] David Granick suggests that this Soviet practice resulted in greater than proportional increases in average wages with increased productivity. Periodic campaigns to revise the incentive pay scales reduced this creep (Granick, 1954:83-85, 245). For a comparison of Hungarian and American machine shop incentive systems, see Burawoy, (1979). On incentive systems as characteristic of hierarchy, see Williamson (1975:145) and Stinchcombe (1974:123-150).

[18] Williamson has gone some way toward restating his main hypothesis in continuous form in Williamson (1979).

CHAPTER 3

SUBSTITUTES FOR EXPERIENCE-BASED INFORMATION

THE CASE OF OFFSHORE OIL INSURANCE IN THE NORTH SEA*

Carol A. Heimer

Marine underwriting has been said to be "the intelligent application of the experiences of the past to the expectations of the future." The same has been said of horseracing. Underwriters, however, lack the benefit of stud books when faced with a first-of-a-kind risk (Oxford, 1965:285).

Introduction

This is a paper about the functional equivalents of stud books.

Even in information-based industries like insurance, people are not really paralyzed by information shortages. Though underwriters may have little information about the likelihood of someone catching the Loch Ness monster in the year during which a liquor company offered a reward (Borch, 1976, uses Bayesian statistics to estimate what the underwriters *really* thought the odds were, given how they spread the risk), or about the odds of an actor's eyebrows growing back improperly after being shaved off for a filmed burning at the stake (Oliver Reed in *The Devils*), or about the likelihood of an earthquake destroying a given fixed oil installation in the North Sea, they still are able to provide insurance coverage in such cases.

But if the technology and organizational structure of an enterprise (an insurance company in this case) have been designed on the assumption that a particular sort of information will be available, then modifications will be required when crucial pieces of information cannot be obtained. Presumably these adaptations to information shortages will be patterned rather than random. That is, in this case, we may find that insurers will consistently make one sort of modification. Rather than using the full range of alternative techniques or information they will always adapt in one or two ways only. The purpose of this research, then, is to determine how insurers calculate when there is a shortage of information of the sort they customarily use.

I have chosen to study this question by examining the insurance of the Norwegian sector of the North Sea oil business because this case is an extreme example of a fairly common problem. In the case of the oil projects and installations in the North Sea, insurers are confronted with a shortage of information at the same time as they have a strong incentive to act anyway. They cannot do quite what they usually do because their technology is a technology based on experiential information. One knows what premium to charge for auto insurance because one knows the odds of experiencing a loss of a particular size. But one cannot know how likely it is that one of the oil production platforms in the North Sea will suddenly crumble and sink into the sea. So insurers have to figure out what to do about not knowing. They have to decide what to substitute for the sort of information they are used to using. They might decide to use a different kind of information, they might decide to limit their coverage, they might decide to make the clients pay for the shortage of information (this is the traditional justification for profits outside the insurance business, anyway – the entrepreneur is being paid for taking the risk), or whatnot. But presumably these decisions about what to substitute for the usual information are not random ones and by seeing what substitutions were made in this case and why, we can learn a bit about how people actually use information and how they make decisions in the very common cases where information is incomplete but not entirely inadequate.

The paper will be laid out as follows. I will begin by providing some essential background on oil insurance, explaining insurance technology, and saying what information insurers therefore need to make decisions. Then I will discuss what insurers might be able to substitute for experience-based information. Next I will turn to the two cases I studied, the insurance of mobile rigs and the insurance of fixed installations. Because they are less expensive, more numerous, and more homogeneous than fixed installations, finding acceptable information for decision making has been easier in the insurance of mobile rigs than in the insurance of fixed installations. Finally, I analyze three of the main features of such decision making. I argue that when insurers lack the information they customarily use, they try to limit their own ignorance and the ignorance of their policyholders by requiring certifications and feasibility studies, they pay as much attention to the social sufficiency of information as to its technical sufficiency, and they use scarce information to reformulate complex unanswerable questions into simpler ones that can be answered.

Background on Oil Insurance

Though people often speak and write as if this were the case, oil insurance is not really a single kind of insurance. Many diverse sorts of insurance contracts covering a broad spectrum of risks and many kinds of policyholders are included under the rubric of oil insurance. Property insurance contracts (covering everything from drilling rigs to fixed installations to smaller boats and pieces of equipment) are by and large taken out with hull insurers, while liability coverages (including obligations arising from contracts and subcontracts between various companies working in the North Sea, as well as obligations to uninvolved third parties) are often carried by P and I (standing for protection and indemnity) clubs. In this paper I will be concerned only with property insurance, though the same sorts of questions could easily be asked about liability insurance. And although there are many different sorts of policyholders (including small consulting firms, construction companies, suppliers of various sorts, and rig owners as well as oil companies of varying sizes), I discuss specifically only insurance contracts covering the risks of rig owners and of groups of oil companies that own and operate the fixed installations.

Because the Norwegian oil activity is *offshore* the insurance coverages are given by marine insurers and the insurance contracts therefore follow many marine insurance traditions. This means, among other things, that maritime authorities, classification societies (Det norske Veritas, the Norwegian classification society, plays a quasi-official role in certifying that vessels are up to standard but also acts as a consultant in technical and safety questions in the design, construction, and maintenance of vessels, offshore installations, and so on) and marine consulting firms play important roles in oil insurance. It also means that the foreign (especially British) marine insurers are more important participants in Norwegian offshore oil insurance than are domestic (or foreign) "land" (or "non-marine") insurers. (See the beginning of Lund, 1978, for a discussion of marine and land insurance markets.) Of course there are many organizations specializing in issues related to oil activities (such as the Norwegian Petroleum Directorate and numerous consulting firms) who play important roles as well. The point is simply that the insurance of oil activities is linked to the insurance world through the marine insurers and that the experts and techniques normally used by marine insurers therefore loom larger than they would without this particular mediating link between oil policyholders and the rest of the insurance world.

Another important factor to keep in mind is the staggering quantities involved in the North Sea, whether one is talking about tons of concrete or steel, hours of engineering work, or dollars of investment. Of course, it is primarily the dollars invested that trouble the insurers. The problem is that the fixed installations are so valuable that the insurance companies have a great deal of difficulty finding enough insurance coverage. (In insurance circles, this is called a "capacity" problem.) This means that the fixed installations are often underinsured (that is, the insured value is considerably less than the cost of replacing the installation if it should be completely lost and often less than the original cost of constructing it), that the insurance is carried with a group of insurers rather than with just one, and also that reinsurance is extremely important. Reinsurance is essentially insurance coverage of a part of an insurance contract. That is, when insurers reinsure their contracts, what they are doing is taking out further insurance contracts with other insurance companies to cover the possibility of large losses. When an insurance company is very unsure what its loss experience will be in a particular case and when the values involved are very large, then reinsurance is crucial. This reliance on reinsurance and the practice of forming panels to provide the first insurance coverage together imply that the contracts between insurers will be especially important in oil insurance. An insurer who wishes to participate in oil insurance must first of all be embedded in the relevant network and, secondly, must respect the views of the other insurers. This in turn has important implications for adaptations to information shortages, as will be discussed below.

An insurance contract includes coverage for losses caused in particular ways, up to specified limits, and under certain circumstances. Some of these decisions about insurance coverage are negotiated at the time the contract is made while others are made in advance by groups of insurers and other concerned parties. These standardized portions of the contract are called the insurance conditions; the insurance conditions include statements about what perils (causes of loss) are excluded, definitions of relevant terms (what a drilling rig is, for example), lists of the objects insured, rules about deductibles, warranty clauses about approvals and feasibility studies, and so on. In addition to these standardized portions, there are also individualized portions that include the insured value, the limits on individual accidents, the rate to be charged for the coverage, the time limits of the coverage, extra coverages, and so on. The line between standardized and individual parts of the contract is somewhat fluid both in the sense that a policyholder sometimes can modify the standardized portions through negotiation or by adding further coverages and also in the sense that the proportion of the contract that is standardized varies from one kind of insurance to another. (There are more standardized items in the insurance of mobile rigs, for example, than in the insurance of fixed installations, or at least there is more flexibility about what standard clauses are included.)

So part of the reason that oil insurance is interesting is that there are more decisions that have to be made since it is a relatively new field. In oil insurance it is not just a matter of taking a pre-existing policy form and filling in the details about any given individual object; instead the insurers, their clients, and other interested parties (such as the government) are still engaged in the process of deciding which insurance conditions are appropriate, how to calculate the appropriate premiums, and so on.

In general, though, a potential policyholder approaches a broker or insurer (brokers are not much used in Norway) who arranges the insurance contract. The policyholder gives information about the object insured, says generally what sort of coverage is desired, and of course pays the premium, reports losses, and provides evidence that the object is kept up to the standard required by the relevant authorities. The insurer (or panel of insurers) is the one primarily responsible for arranging the conditions of the insurance contract, for setting the premium rate or adjusting a scale that already exists, for finding other insurers to participate in providing coverage, and for getting appropriate reinsurance. How much of this is worked out by which party varies by the type of insurance involved and by whether or not conditions have already been worked out for that particular kind of coverage.

The information for this report comes largely from a series of interviews with insurers, insurance managers in oil companies, and people associated in various capacities with consulting firms and with Det norske Veritas. Supplementary information comes from internal documents and reports given to me by these people, annual reports of companies, government publications, conference papers, newspaper and periodical accounts, and a few books and academic journals.

Pooling and the Insurance Mechanism

Insurance is a risk management technique that decreases the economic consequences of a loss for any one individual or firm at any one point in time by pooling the losses so that all of the policyholders experience small losses (commonly called premiums) all of the time but no one ever experiences a disastrous loss. Losses can be pooled in three different ways. Either the losses of a *group of similar insured units* can be pooled, or the losses of a single unit (or of a very few units) can be pooled over *time*, or the losses can be pooled over a *group of insurers*. Insurers commonly use two or three of these techniques in insuring any given policyholder, especially if the amount at stake is large. The more accurately losses can be predicted, the less important pooling becomes.

When the units are quite small (that is, when the payments in case of loss are small) and when there are many of them, it is very common to pool losses over insured units. This is the main form of pooling used in auto insurance, life insurance, and some kinds of fire insurance.

But when the units are large and/or when there are very few similar units in the universe, then it is more common to pool losses over time. Part of the reason for this is that the owners of the large units are likely to insist that their units are unique, that their loss prevention efforts are more productive, that their equipment is better, or that for some reason they are less likely than other policyholders to suffer losses and therefore should not be forced to subsidize inferior policyholders by being grouped with them. (So, for example, fire insurance in the U.S. is divided into "class risks" which includes residences and "special risks" which includes factories, large stores, and so on.) In these cases, then, an insurance company is really a fancy sort of bank in which the policyholders deposit money at regular intervals and from which they withdraw funds when they have accidents. Another way to think of this (a way popular among Norwegian shippers and marine insurers) is to think of insurance as a method for "leveling and liquidity" (see Tronstad, 1979:7.14). The insurance company pays for losses, large or small, when they occur but charges the premiums at regular intervals so that the policyholder does not experience large fluctuations in its needs for liquid resources. This formulation makes it clear that pooling is over the life of the firm (or of the individual object insured) rather than over a group of similar units. The policyholder pays for its own losses but on an installment plan.

One of the important differences between a bank and an insurance company is that even when losses are mainly pooled over time they can still be pooled over units or over insurers, as well, so that when there are big disasters the profits from one line of insurance in a single company can help cover the losses from another line of insurance, or the profits from the premiums of one policyholder can help cover the losses of another policyholder, or the profits of one insurance company can help cover the losses of another insurance company.

The last possibility, pooling losses over a group of insurance companies is usually arranged through reinsurance. The importance of reinsurance varies with the size of the potential losses. Reinsurance is considerably more important when a company is insuring large risks than when it is insuring small risks, and there is therefore a strong connection between pooling over time and pooling over insurers. Of course, pooling over insurers is really just pooling over policyholders at a different level.

This discussion of pooling illustrates several very important points about insurance, and I will take up each of these issues in turn: (1) the interdependence of insurers because of the ultimate pooling of the losses and profits of various insurance companies through reinsurance agreements, (2) the importance of determining which units are similar and how far they are similar so that one can decide at what point their losses should be pooled, (3) the importance of time and of a large universe of similar units to the success of the insurance mechanism.

First let us note that in the case of insurance in the North Sea oil projects, pooling is a very serious problem. The individual objects being insured are extremely valuable so the insurance values (the amount an insurance company might have to pay out in the case of a disastrous loss) are very high. This already makes it difficult to pool over several units. What automobile owner would like the thought of helping to cover the losses on the two billion dollar Statfjord B platform (this was its value in 1980) with his or her auto insurance premiums? But there is also a great deal of variability among the various items being insured in the North Sea, so the possible universe for any one kind of insurance is very small. This is already true for mobile rigs (there were about five

hundred of them in the world in 1980) but is even more true for
the fixed installations. Some fields produce the petroleum products from mobile units, but most have fixed installations. These
installations may be constructed of steel or concrete and vary
greatly in size and design. There also is a great deal of variation in
how many platforms are used for each set of wells. For these
reasons it is very difficult to pool over similar insured units in the
North Sea oil projects, though this is more possible for mobile rigs
than for fixed installations.

But it is also difficult to pool over time. This is partly because
very little time has elapsed since the beginning of the oil activities
in the North Sea (the first discoveries of oil were in the 1960s) but
also because, for insurance purposes, this time period has to be
subdivided into several phases. The insurance requirements during the exploration phase are very different than the insurance
requirements during the construction phase and these, in turn, are
very different than the insurance requirements of the production
phase. So the time period over which one can pool losses for any
one unit is really very short. But this problem is even worse than it
sounds because the period when pooling over time is the most
difficult is at the very beginning. This is because the insurance
premium is supposed, over the long run, to cover both small
losses (particular average losses) and the big disasters (total losses
or constructive total losses). Over the long run the insurance
company accumulates some surplus (over the amount that covers
the small losses) to cover big disasters. But at the beginning of any
insurance contract, there is no surplus to cover a disaster. And of
course if the disaster is really big there will be no time period after
the disaster to recoup the loss in small increments through insurance premiums. The brief way to state this is that pooling over
time works best when there is some time to pool over and
especially when the time being pooled over is time that has
already passed. These luxuries are not available in the insurance
of the North Sea oil projects.

I have already mentioned that it is difficult to pool over units in
the North Sea partly because there are so few units available but
also because there are large variations between units. An additional reason why this is difficult is that in order to justify pooling

over units, one has to have some notion about how these units are similar. The idea is that there are only supposed to be loss-irrelevant differences between the units pooled over, so that the fact that a loss occurs to one unit and not to another will be a matter of accident or chance. The point is that insurers cannot justify making one unit subsidize another's defective machinery, faulty design, sloppy workmanship, careless crew, or daredevil managers. But in order to group the various units being insured into appropriate categories, then, one needs a great deal of information or a well-developed and defensible theory about the main causes of loss. This generally requires a great deal of experience with losses to those sorts of units and this, of course, is not available in the North Sea.

But in some senses this is irrelevant when we are talking about the insurance of the fixed installations, at least. In these cases the insurance values are sometimes up over a billion dollars and it really does not matter whether the insurance companies can pool over time or over similar units because it would take so long to recover from a really disastrous loss even with these sorts of pooling. In this case, then, the most relevant sort of pooling occurs between the insurance companies themselves and this occurs primarily through reinsurance contracts. The insurance contract on these installations is never with a single insurer but with a group, so the risk is already spread around a bit, but besides this each of the insurers passes on a substantial portion of the risk (up to about 90%) to still other insurers. So an initial insurer will have to cover a small proportion of the loss and then will be compensated for part of this by a reinsurer (who may in turn have reinsured part of its reinsurance, though this process is not repeated often because the premium has a slice taken out of it at each step).

One of the most important implications of this emphasis on reinsurance is that the already conservative insurance companies are forced to be even more conservative. In effect it is not possible to insure a fixed installation in the North Sea unless the insurance contract is acceptable to the insurance community as a whole since quite a large proportion of the major insurers end up getting involved in it in one way or another. This is not true when insurance values are smaller because a single insurance company can cover the maximum loss, should it occur, when the value is small. But when many insurance companies have to participate both in the insurance itself and in the reinsurance, then the insurance contract has to be acceptable to all of them. And there is very little room for maneuvering when it is hard to get the coverage under any circumstances.

From the discussion in this section, it should be clear that more of the insurance technology described above is applicable to the insurance of mobile rigs than is applicable to the insurance of fixed installations. As is summarized in the table, only one of the four methods can be used in the insurance of fixed installations while all of them can be used to one degree or another in the insurance of mobile drilling rigs.

Table 3.1: The Applicability of Insurance Technology to Insurance of Mobile Rigs and Fixed Installations.

Insurance Technique	Mobile Drilling Rigs	Fixed Installations
(1) Accurate prediction of losses	increasingly possible	currently impossible
(2) Pooling over similar units	increasingly possible	currently impossible
(3) Pooling over time	possible	currently impossible
(4) Pooling over insurers (reinsurance)	possible	possible

Information Requirements of Insurance

Insurers need very specific sorts of information. They need to know how often they can expect their policyholders to experience monetary losses of various magnitudes. They need to know, for example, how often they can expect a $2 million loss on a jackup rig, whether such a loss can be expected more or less frequently if the rig is a semisubmersible, and whether the loss would occur substantially less often if certain causes of loss, such as accidents during relocation from one work site to another, were excluded. So insurers need information about the relation between the size of the losses, the frequency of losses of various sizes, the characteristics of the objects insured, and the causes of losses. With this sort of information an insurer can calculate how much to charge the policyholder per unit (dollar usually) of coverage. The premium actually charged is then the product of this charge per unit (rate) and the total number of units of coverage. If the rate has been calculated properly, the insurer should receive enough premium to cover the losses and the administrative expenses, and should have some profit left over. Since chance plays an important role in the timing of losses, the insurance company should come out ahead part of the time and behind part of the time, but this should balance out over many policyholders, many lines of insurance, many years, and many insurance companies.

There are two rather different ways in which insurers could collect and process the information necessary to set rates and to formulate insurance conditions. Insurers could either collect and statistically analyze information or they could accumulate and assess experience. The difference that I have in mind has to do both with the form in which evidence is collected and also with the use to which this evidence is put. When one collects information, one gathers data about a series of variables (such as tonnage, safety equipment, quality of steel, training of the crew, etc.) that can be analyzed separately to determine their individual effects on loss experience. When one accumulates experience, one is more likely to end up with data about the loss experience of whole units (such as ships or rigs). This information about whole units could, of course, be transformed into information about variables and their relation to loss experience, but the point is that one is not *naturally* inclined to do this sort of analysis.

Instead of leading to statistical knowledge about causal relations, accumulated experience is more likely to lead to good judgment. When one collects and analyzes information, one may be more likely to know which differences between jackups and semisubmersibles account for the different loss experiences, but if one accumulates experience one will still know that the loss experiences of these two kinds of rigs are different and one may also know a lot of detailed information about individual policyholders. Since insurers are in the business of compensating for losses rather than designing better rigs, they do not usually need this more refined knowledge of causal relations.

This distinction between collecting and analyzing information and accumulating and assessing experience obviously represents the two extremes and what insurers really do falls somewhere in between. But there are also variations among insurers and, in general, marine insurers (and therefore oil insurers) are more likely than life insurers or fire insurers to base their decisions on judgment rather than on statistics. This is partly a matter of differences in traditions and partly because there is more variation in exposures in marine insurance than in some other lines. (See Greene, 1973:668 for a discussion of the role of underwriting judgment in marine insurance compared with other lines.)

Though in general it may not matter very much whether insurers base their rating and underwriting decisions on statistical analyses of information or on judgments based on experience, there are some cases in which this tradition makes a great deal of difference. In particular, when insurers are faced with the problem of setting rates in new fields, they have no accumulated experience to make judgments with. In insuring first-of-a-kind risks, it is probably easier to find substitutes for statistical information than for experience.

In the next section I will discuss the sorts of substitute information that tend to be available about the North Sea oil business. Oil insurers have for the most part not chosen to use this substitute information and in the rest of the paper I will analyze what insurers substitute for experience and why substitutes for experience and substitutes for statistical information are not interchangeable.

Created Information as an Alternative to Experience

Though insurers may be accustomed to using information derived from loss experiences in very similar situations, there are many other kinds of information available that insurers could substitute when they do not have any experience. In this section I will describe some other kinds of information that insurers could choose to use. In later sections when I discuss the choices insurers have actually made it will be clear what the rejected alternatives were.

Though it is true that there is a shortage of *experience* (that is, information based on events which have taken place in that particular setting or one very like it and that have involved objects nearly identical to the ones currently being insured), there is no shortage of other kinds of information. This other information is not information that simply accumulates, like experience, but instead is *created*. Presumably insurers could either create information themselves or require that the policyholders, or consultants hired by the policyholders, create the information for them. Of course much of this information would then have to be transformed into a form usable by the insurers, but this is certainly not an impossible task.

There are many ways in which information about the probabilities of losses of various sorts and of varying magnitudes is created. First, one can create *experimental or simulated* information by doing laboratory research or computer simulations. Both computer simulations and laboratory experiments are used to study the patterns of waves and the effects of waves of various heights (see, for example, Aagaard and Besse, 1973). Simulations also are used to estimate the effects of oil spills (see, for example, Donovan and Owen, 1977). And, of course, there is a lot of testing of equipment that produces information about failure rates and so on. (See, for example, NOROIL, 1980b:34, on the testing for fire resistance of the gratings on walkways.)

A second possibility is to create what one might call *synthetic information* by piecing together information from actual experiences that in one way or another resemble the North Sea oil situation. For example, one might piece together information about the oil production platforms in the Gulf of Mexico and information about the differences between shipping experiences in the North Sea and the Gulf of Mexico. In this way one might develop a formula for predicting North Sea experiences from Gulf of Mexico experiences. Presumably one could also do this for pollution damage from oil spills. That is, one could take the information about the long-term effects to the Louisiana coastline and adjust these for differences between Louisiana (see, for example, St. Amant, 1972) and North Sea marine conditions, marine life, wave patterns, and so on. Or one might want to piece together information about loss experiences of drilling rigs and information about the different stresses on accommodation rigs so that one would have some idea about how the loss experiences of converted drilling rigs would be different than the loss experiences of either accommodation rigs originally designed to be stationary or of drilling rigs used for the purposes for which they were originally designed.

Analytic information created by such techniques as risk analysis is a third possibility. Using fault trees (which identify failures leading up to a critical event) or event trees (which identify the event chains leading up to unwanted consequences), one can decompose the causes of critical events or the consequences of critical events and in this way determine the probabilities of various events or of the loss consequences of particular events. Risk analyses are often carried out by various parties in the North Sea oil business. Governmental regulations require risk analyses at early stages in the design of the platforms. Organizations like Det norske Veritas and smaller consulting firms also regularly use these techniques (see, for example, Det norske Veritas, 1977 and 1978; Tveit, Myklatun, Bohler, and Vesterhaug, 1980; and Donovan and Owen, 1977). Descriptions of design accidents provide the same sort of information but for a specified set of critical events (see the Norwegian Petroleum Directorate, 1979). A somewhat related technique, reliability analysis, uses probabilistic methods to compare the reliability of different types of structures according to design codes, materials, load types, and structural elements (see, for example, Fjeld, 1978, and Moses and Stahl, 1979).

Information also can be collected as experience is accumulated. Such information is usually collected by insurers only when losses occur, but one could also collect information about factors known to increase or decrease the likelihood of losses. This *pre-loss information* could then be used to modify predictions about the likelihood of losses. In effect, then, this is a sort of continuous, pre-loss form of what insurers call experience rating. This kind of information could be collected from instruments installed on the structures or during inspections. At present when inspections are carried out the information is used primarily to indicate what repairs are needed. But there is no reason why it could not also be used to modify risk assessments for insurance purposes. Non-destructive testing is gaining importance as an inspection technique in the North Sea because so much of the equipment that needs to be inspected is located underwater or is likely to have flaws not easily visible to the human eye (see NOROIL, 1980a:32). Norwegian Petroleum Directorate regulations include some requirements about data-collecting instruments on the offshore structures (Norwegian Petroleum Directorate, 1978).

Finally, risk assessments can be based on *expert advice*. Political risks, for example, are sometimes assessed by consulting a group of experts (such as economists, political scientists, experts on international relations, historians, sociologists, and businessmen) about the political and economic conditions in a particular country. These opinions are then fed into a computer program that combines them to produce estimates of the probabilities of a group of undesirable political events (such as sudden expropriation or domestic price controls). (On this subject see Gebelein, Pearson, and Silbergh, 1978.)

To say that there is a lot of relevant information available and that insurers could have even more of it created if they chose to do so is not to say that this information is all that easy for insurers to use. There are several reasons why this information is often quite difficult to use. First there is the question of completeness. Insurers have very little use for even a good estimate of the probability of civil disorder or of the strength of a deck leg unless these can somehow be combined with other calculations to give an overall assessment of political risks or of platform strength, or whatever. An insurer needs a more or less complete picture of the risks, so all of these pieces of information must be added together and added together without too much redundancy (so that the probabilities of a deck leg collapsing do not get added in both when one is using information about strength and when one is using the information generated by a simulation of the effects of waves).

A second problem is that these pieces of information have to be translated into a common language. The probability of civil disorder and the strength of deck legs have to be transformed into estimates of the probabilities of economic losses of various magnitudes. These problems of summing probabilities and of translating information into estimates of economic losses are more difficult with some kinds of information than with others. Risk analyses, for example, are probably easier for insurers to use than are the pieces of information collected during inspections.

Not all kinds of information are equally reliable, and the need to assess the reliability and applicability of these various forms of information presents a third problem. Risk analysis, for example, is unable to take into consideration the effects of human adaptation (which may make things better or worse) during a chain of events. It is also unable to treat continuous variables so components must be depicted as performing perfectly or failing completely and the effects of degraded performance cannot be taken into account. And expert advice may be very misleading either because of the way that one combines the advice of several experts or because the estimates of the experts are really just subjective probabilities and therefore biased in the same ways that other judgments are (see Tversky and Kahneman, 1974, for a discussion of biases in judgment). A simulation may give inaccurate information either because one's model or theory was a bad one (see Aagaard and Besse, 1973, for examples of conflicting results from different models) or because one's input values were inappropriate. Each of these forms of information has its drawbacks and insurers would not only need to be aware of these limitations but also to compensate for them. These difficulties alone might go a long way toward explaining why insurers for the most part have not used these alternative kinds of information.

Insurance of Mobile Rigs

One case about which quite a bit of information is available is mobile rigs. Mobile drilling rigs have existed since the 1940s when they were first used in the Gulf of Mexico, so there is a fairly extensive body of information about them. But the existing information about mobile rigs is not really very useful for two reasons. First, there are quite significant differences among mobile rigs so what we know from the loss experiences of the rigs in the 1950s does not tell us much about what we can expect from modern rigs. The differences are large enough that people in the oil business speak of first and second generation rigs. Besides the differences between first and second generation rigs there are many differences among second generation rigs themselves. There are important differences in design having to do with whether or not they are self-propelled, how heavy they are, whether they rest on the ground or float in the water, and so on. Second generation rigs also differ in function (drilling, accommodation, construction) and some rigs designed for one function are converted and used for a completely different function.

Another reason that the information available on mobile rigs is not so very useful is that the North Sea conditions are more severe than the sea conditions in other places where the mobile rigs have been used. So if we know how many losses we can expect for a particular kind of rig in the Gulf of Mexico, this does not necessarily mean that we would expect the same loss experience in the North Sea. There may be hurricanes from time to time in the Gulf of Mexico, but the North Sea is always cold, almost always has high waves, and so on.

When oil activities first began in the Norwegian North Sea, Norwegian marine insurers decided that they wanted to get into insuring these operations. One of the main motives for this decision (aside from the obvious one of profits) was that their customers were now coming to them with new insurance problems. If the Norwegian insurers did not provide the insurance coverage that their traditional customers were requesting it was entirely possible that these people (mostly shippers) would not only take their oil insurance business elsewhere but would take their marine insurance business elsewhere as well. It was not just the promise of new business but also the threat of losing old business that inspired Norwegian marine insurers to offer oil insurance.

At this time insurance for mobile rigs was available only on the London market. When insurers talk about markets it is sometimes a bit difficult to find out exactly what they mean. Sometimes they do mean something rather amorphous, like the market that economists speak of, but sometimes they mean something quite specific. In this case the "London market" means two brokerage firms, Sedgwick Forbes and Bland Payne (the two later merged) and a committee of six "leading underwriters." According to Norwegian insurers, the expertise and contacts were all located in this group of people and it was literally impossible to insure a mobile rig except through this group of people. (Mobile rigs are not nearly so expensive as fixed installations – in 1980 their values range from about $15 or $20 million to above $70 or $80 million with most running about $40 million. But this is still a large enough value so that an insurance company has to worry about reinsurance and therefore connections and reputation are important.) Given the Norwegian insurers' dependence on the London market for expertise and reinsurance, they could not themselves underwrite the insurance of mobile rigs without the blessing of the British insurers.

The Norwegian insurers formed a pool, the Norwegian Oil Risk Pool, to insure mobile rigs. (See Hesselmann, n.d., for information on the Pool.) This Pool negotiated with the London insurers about the conditions for reinsurance and for transmitting information and contacts to the Norwegians. Apparently the British were aware that other insurers were going to try to take over part of the oil insurance business and decided that they would lose less business if they were cooperative than if they refused to help the newcomers. The British agreed to help the Norwegians if the Norwegians would use the British rates and the British conditions and give a fixed proportion of the reinsurance business to the British market. In return the Norwegian Oil Risk Pool got contacts, expertise, reinsurance, and a 12% fleet discount on the London rates.

The Norwegian Oil Risk Pool was formed by eleven companies. The agreement was that the Pool would be the insurer and that a certain part of the commission would go to the company producing the business while the rest of the commission would be split among the member companies according to the degree of their participation in the Pool. Member companies participated in all policies according to the extent of their participation in the Pool as a whole. An additional requirement was made of the policyholders; they were required to place the entire insurance with the Pool. The main reason for this was that the Pool recognized that it was in a fairly strong position in being able to offer the insurance but that if it took only a piece of the insurance the policyholder could easily get others to take a piece. If this happened then there would be more price competition and the rates would fall, something that insurers are desperately afraid of in the early phases when they are unsure what the rate really should be.

When the insurers say that they were using the London rates, it is not really clear what this means, except that they had very little control. But it turns out that various discounts were given so it was not quite the London rate that was being charged. The Pool began by giving the London rate less the 12% fleet discount but were also able to give a further discount on the administrative expense portion (because they were able to keep this work and therefore the corresponding portion of the premium within the Pool). The London rate seems not to have been terribly complicated – it was simply a fixed percentage of the value of the rig. The rig owner would state the value of the rig and then the insurers would charge a fixed proportion of that for insurance coverage. Of course it is not quite this simple because rates varied according to what kind of rig was being insured.

But after a few years, the Norwegian insurers in the Oil Risk Pool abandoned the London rate. It is not clear whether they had agreed to use the London rate only for a few years or whether they could abandon it because they could now get reinsurance elsewhere, having now acquired some expertise and contacts. Most likely the agreement to abandon the London rate was negotiated with the Londoners during the annual meetings.

The Norwegian underwriters chose to use a more complex rating scheme. First they had to decide whether or not to have separate categories for different kinds of rigs. That is, they had to decide whether or not to pool the losses for all rigs together or to pool them in separate subcategories. It was obvious from the start that there would be a separate category for jackups (drilling rigs which rest on the sea bottom while drilling) but it was not clear whether or not there would be any further subdivisions between the various kinds of semisubmersibles. One of the main questions was whether a self-propelled rig was less exposed to losses than one that had to be moved by other vessels. During the discussion of this question, the Deep Sea Driller was lost. A self-propelled semisubmersible, it was lost apparently because it could not steer very well. Insurers took this as evidence that rigs might actually be safer when being moved by more manageable vessels (like tugs) and therefore decided that there was no reason to offer a lower rate to the owners of rigs that were self propelled.

There was also some question about whether some designs were so much better than other designs that they should be given a lower rate. This was apparently a difficult decision and led to a series of meetings with Veritas. Veritas had earlier reviewed the design of semisubmersible rigs in connection with its work with Aker in designing the H3. Ultimately it was decided that all semisubmersibles should be grouped together.

A second question had to do with the total loss portion of the premium and the particular average portion. (The terms "total loss" and "particular average" are used in marine insurance to refer respectively to the case in which the insured object is sufficiently damaged, by covered perils, so as to be of only trivial value and the case in which the insured object sustains smaller damages by covered perils.) It was quite clear that the total loss portion should be a percentage of the insured value. But it was less obvious how one should calculate the particular average portion. A $20 million rig does not have many fewer $10,000 accidents than a $65 million rig, so it is not really fair to charge the policyholders a rate that varies directly with the value of the rig. The usual procedure in marine insurance is to have the total loss portion vary with the insured value and to have the partial loss portion vary with tonnage. The Norwegian Oil Risk Pool considered this possibility, but since there were significant variations in tonnage by design and since tonnage was not really related to anything that would make a rig more or less likely to have a small accident, this rule did not make sense. A further argument against using tonnage was that the Pool had already decided not to charge different rates for different designs and a rate based on tonnage would in effect reverse this decision. So the insurers had to come up with another alternative.

After several sessions of brainstorming they decided to tie the particular average rate to the value. There would be a fixed particular average premium for rigs valued at $20 million or less and an additional premium would be charged for each million dollars of value above this. But the size of this additional premium would decline with each increase in value. So the premium for the particular average portion did increase with the value of the rig but at a decreasing rate.

The insurers were obviously a bit nervous about this deviation from marine tradition, and they have kept careful records which they review annually to see if the loss records indicate that this decision was appropriate or if they should change to another system. Up to 1980 the loss records indicate that the decision to peg the particular average portion of the premium to the insured value in the manner described above was appropriate.

But rates are not set only on the basis of loss experience or expectation about loss experiences. Competition is also important. The general tendency is to calculate what rate one really believes is appropriate (in the case of the Norwegian Oil Risk Pool, by making up the scales of insurance rates for jackup and other rigs of various values) and then to give a discount on the scale (or charge an extra premium) to bring it into line with the market conditions. In spite of the fact that the loss experiences indicate that the scale is none too high, insurers are offering ever lower rates because the competition is stiffer.

The competition has become stiffer because the market capacity has increased as more and more insurers become willing to enter the offshore market. When more insurers are willing to cover a particular kind of risk then a policyholder can get pieces of the risk covered by different insurers and this sort of fragmentation leads to strong competition. In 1980, the Norwegian Oil Risk Pool was losing business because it was unwilling to give much lower rates. Part of the business was being lost to foreign insurers, some of them receiving business from Norwegian brokers, while part of it was being lost to other Norwegian insurers who were not members of the Oil Risk Pool.

Insurance of Fixed Installations

The evidence about the insurance of fixed installation is considerably less complete, partly because there are still very few of them (only 14 fixed production platforms operational by 1979 or 1980 in the Norwegian sector of the North Sea with 7 more projected by 1982; 23 fixed production platforms operational by 1979 or so in the British sector with 17 more projected by 1982), and there are important differences even among these few (for example there are steel and concrete production structures; there are other fixed installations like storage tanks and pump stations in addition to the production platforms; and there are from time to time also some floating production platforms), and partly because a higher proportion of the insurance work for these installations is done in London and therefore cannot be studied very easily from Norway. Norwegian insurers do participate in the insurance of fixed installations; they used to participate mostly as reinsurers but their role is growing and they now are represented on the panels that arrange the insurance contracts.

There are really two sorts of property insurance coverages for fixed installations, the insurance of the construction period and the insurance of the production period. (Presumably there will later be insurance of the dismantling phase as well.) Unlike with mobile rigs, the premium rates for the property insurance for fixed installations are not calculated all at once (and then adjusted if necessary) but instead are calculated on an individual basis. Further, the rate is not a simple function of the insured value. The insured value is generally a good measure of the likelihood of large losses in the range of that upper limit. For example, all other things being equal, one will be much more likely to have $50,000 losses on a house valued at $300,000 than on one valued at $50,000. But since the owners of the fixed installations often cannot get insurance to cover the entire value of the installation, insured value is often almost as much a measure of the market capacity as of the likelihood of large losses. Without this problem, it still would be inappropriate to have the premium be a *simple* function of the value because the value of the installation changes constantly during the construction phase and also because the risks are very different at different points in time. The variation in the risks is due both to increasing concentration of the value as the pieces of the platform are assembled and to variation in the danger of different operations.

So though it is certainly possible to state the premium as a percentage of the final insured value (in the case for which I saw calculations, the premium for the entire construction phase of a concrete platform was about 4.95% of the final insured value while the premium for the entire construction phase of a steel platform was about 3.8% of the final value), this is a bit misleading because the final premium is really a composite of many separately calculated premiums covering different pieces of the final platform and different operations carried out on these components. Some of these premiums are calculated on an annual basis while others are calculated for a single event.

For example, the insurance premium for a large concrete platform during the construction phase might include the following components of approximately the following sizes: about 3.7% of the total premium might cover the concrete construction, about 7.4% the towing of the concrete to the location for mating with the deck, about 11.0% the construction of the deck, about 2.8% the structure as a whole while awaiting tow-out, about 35.0% the tow to the field (about 7.4% of which might be an excess cover for total loss), about 30.3% the completion of the platform on the site, about 2.8% liability cover, about 1.1% a terrorist cover, and about 6.1% for drilling perils.

The premium for the insurance of the construction phase for a steel platform might be allocated a bit differently: about 4.7% of the total insurance premium for the construction phase might be to cover the jacket while it was being built; about 2.3% the construction of the support frame; about 5.6% the construction of the deck modules and equipment; about 18.6% the towing, positioning, and submerging of the jacket; about 23.3% the transport of the support frame and various equipment; about 3.7% non-material investments and site preparations; and about 41.9% the securing of the structure to the sea bottom and the completion of the installation.

Notice that in both cases the portion of the premium covering towing and other transportation is very large but that more of the premium covers completion after towing for the steel platform than for the concrete platform. Of course it is rather difficult to compare the premiums except as a total proportion of the final insured value since the components are so different. But it is still astonishing to find that about 40% of an insurance premium covering perhaps 3 to 3 1/2 years of construction is due to risks concentrated in a few days of travel and towing.

These calculations of the component premiums are based on very different kinds of information and therefore vary a good deal in their precision. Insurers apparently begin with the development master schedule for the construction phase. This is a time chart showing what components are expected to be constructed during what time periods, when they are to be joined to other components, when production is expected to begin and so on. With this chart an insurer can calculate the value of the installation or its components at various points in time.

After having calculated this buildup in values, the insurer must then calculate the probabilities for losses to these values. In some cases these calculations are fairly straightforward extensions of calculations that insurers have made before; in other cases they are completely new. For example, one could argue that the construction of a concrete structure at the shipyard is really not so much different than building anything else out of concrete at that shipyard except, of course, that it is bigger. But insurers know how to adjust for size if that is really all that is involved. One simply applies rates for construction of various sorts to these large values (or heavy weights, if one calculates insurance per ton of concrete rather than per dollar of value) to come up with a premium. I would guess that the insurance rates for pre-tow-out construction are about what one would find in other industries (about .5% of the insurance value at that point per year for the construction of the concrete structure, about .75% per year for the construction of the deck for a concrete platform, about .75% per year for the construction of a steel jacket, about .6% per year for the construction of the support frame, and about .75% per year for the construction of the deck modules and other equipment). So insurers are fairly confident that their loss experiences in these areas will not deviate too much from their expectations.

But there are other calculations about which they are quite unsure. For example, no one knows very much about how to calculate the probabilities of losses due to accidents in mating the deck and concrete structure. There are lots of unknown parameters here and, in the words of one insurer, these scare the insurers stiff. In these cases the insurers talk to classification society personnel, to engineers at the oil and construction companies, and to consultants, but they still end up with a guess. In the case of towing, the big unknown is the weather, and this is a factor about which it is very difficult to calculate, especially in the North Sea.

Another difficulty has to do with the build up in value as the structure nears completion and the concentration of these values in fewer locations. This obviously is part of why towing is so hazardous. This concentration of values in one or two locations also increases the possibility of indirect damage should an accident occur to one part of the installation. But except for the large premium for towing and the additional excess premium for the possibility of a total loss during towing, there seems to be no explicit consideration of this problem. It is true, though, that the premium rate for platform completion after towing is 1.5% (of the final value) per annum which is higher than the rate for earlier construction work, but this could be because construction at sea is more hazardous than construction on land rather than because there is more possibility of an accident damaging contiguous areas or equipment.

But if the insurance rates for the construction phase are often straightforward extensions of calculations for construction or for maritime activities, this is less often the case in the insurance of the production phase. The premiums for the operating phase average between about 1.75% and 1.9% (of the insurance value) per annum. Here again there is a great deal of variation in how precise the different parts of the calculation are; one insurer acknowledged that there is a great deal of guesswork involved and said that some portions of the calculation are sufficiently obvious that one could program them but that other portions are much more a matter of juggling relevant variables in one's head.

With a premium of 2% (and no profits or operating expenses), 50 years of loss free operation (or one year of loss-free operation for 50 platforms of the same size) would be required to build up enough premium to cover one total loss. The loss ratio (losses to premiums) is currently about 70% so no reserves are being accumulated. Under these circumstances and with the concentration (in 1980) of perhaps $20 billion worth of platforms and equipment in a few square kilometers of the North Sea, one can see why insurers all over the world might react nervously if one talked about earthquakes in the North Sea. (The earthquake coverage exclusion is often excluded from these policies; that is, earthquake is covered.)

At least in the insurance of the production phase, the ingenuity of the insurers seems to have gone more into the solution of the capacity problem than into the accurate calculation of the risks. The main solution the insurers have devised is to reduce the number of intermediate links in the insurance and reinsurance chain. When insurers (and reinsurers) accept a contract and then pass on most of the risk to another party through a reinsurance contract and when this happens several times, the premium ends up being split between many parties and capacity is wasted because companies are asked to give coverage at quite low rates. But if one breaks the insurance into layers and gets direct participation in these layers rather than indirect participation through complex reinsurance agreements, one is able to get the same group of insurers to provide more coverage. Insurers are then being paid for providing coverage. When insurers take only a very small proportion of the insurance and pass the rest on, they are in effect being paid for administrative work rather than insurance. One of the main ways to get more direct participation is to make up a broker panel with direct connections to various national markets. Instead of all of the coverage being filtered through the London market, then, some goes directly to the U.S. and some to Scandinavia and West Germany.

The insurance of fixed installations is rather different than the insurance of mobile rigs, then, partly because the capacity problem is more important for fixed installations and partly because there are so few of them, they vary so widely among themselves, and there is so little experience (even from other settings) that insurers are forced to make more calculations and to make them for each new insurance contract. This means that the insurers do use many different kinds of information. But because this sort of insurance is so new to Norway, it is difficult to predict exactly how and when insurers will use this information, and when they will simply raise the premiums to compensate for the extra uncertainty or spread the risk among more insurers so that no one will lose too badly if the calculations are wrong.

Insofar as there is experience-based information, the London insurers would be the ones who would have it and they are the ones mainly responsible for setting the rates for fixed installations at the present time.

Limiting Ignorance

In spite of the fact that the oil activities in the North Sea are relatively new, there is a lot of relevant information available. Some of this is information that has existed for years (e.g., information about weather patterns, about the experience of fishermen and shippers in the North Sea, and about oil activities elsewhere), while some of it is information that has been generated specifically to solve problems encountered in the exploitation of the oil resources of the North Sea (e.g., the reports written as part of the Safety Offshore Program (SPS), the research done by Veritas and others on underwater inspection, the investigations following the Bravo blowout and the capsizing of the Kielland). But though there is a lot of information available, it is not the sort of information that insurers are in the habit of using. In this case, the insurers have two choices: (1) *they* can learn to use this information by developing new expertise or (2) they can require that their *policyholders* develop and use the expertise. Insurers have for the most part opted for the second course of action.

Insurers can make sure that they do not lose money either by correctly estimating the odds of loss and then charging premiums large enough to cover these expected losses (and to provide a profit on top) or alternatively they can guess at the odds of loss and then do whatever they can to keep the losses down. In effect, this strategy of trying to prevent losses is a strategy of trying to eliminate or avoid the most disastrous losses. We would expect to see such loss prevention efforts under the following conditions: (1) when there is not very much information and when appropriate information is costly to acquire and process, (2) when there are especially large concentrations of losses in certain time periods or in particular operations, and (3) when conditions are changing fairly rapidly so that one does not want to be stuck with a standard which is invalidated by new information. I will discuss each of these situations in turn, providing evidence from specific cases of insurance in the North Sea.

Notice that part of what an insurer is doing is making the policyholder pay for the acquisition of information and for the transformation of this information into a form usable by an insurance company. Insurance companies use almost exclusively information about loss experiences. It would be quite possible for them to build up their staffs by adding people who could do risk analyses and who could tell them whether the steel on the platforms was corroding faster than had been estimated and whether this significantly increased the probability of accidents. But these experts would very shortly be superfluous since loss experience would mount up and insurers would use this in preference to the estimates based on the probabilities of failures of various components. So part of the reason that insurers do not want to acquire the expertise is that the expertise would only be useful for a short period of time.

A second reason that insurers do not want to acquire the expertise themselves is that the information such experts could provide would have to be transformed into estimates of the odds of various kinds of failures and of the likely sizes and costs of such failures. Besides the problem of generating information, then, there would be the problem of transforming the information into the premium rates. This effort would also only be needed for a short period of time.

But a third reason that insurers do not want to acquire the expertise themselves is that they would then have to charge a higher premium to pay for the new staff and new training and this premium would have to be fixed *before* anyone could reasonably estimate how much extra expense was involved. The fees paid to Noble Denton (a British consulting firm especially known for its expertise in towing) or Det norske Veritas for feasibility studies and certifications are in effect extra insurance premiums, but by requiring a separate negotiation with another party, the insurance company has more leverage than if it itself negotiated with the policyholder. The payment of the "premium" to Noble Denton is a condition for the validity of the rest of the insurance but this "premium" is not fixed before the insurance contract is signed and may therefore vary with changes in the amount of information that must be acquired and with changes in the cost of generating this information. So the insurance company gets the policyholder to agree to purchase, for an unspecified sum, information indicating that the object insured or the operation being performed is as safe as can reasonably be expected.

And, of course, this information may be more costly to acquire because of intermediate steps indicating that the object or operation could be safer (and therefore requiring modifications and repairs). So policyholders are agreeing to pay an unspecified amount for a good which they will be required to purchase and about whose characteristics they will have very little say. Very few policyholders would agree to buy insurance coverage this way, but when they already have a sunk cost (the insurance premium) and when the insurance company itself has little control over the requirements of the certifying/consulting organization and does not itself receive direct financial benefits and when this is a condition for insurance coverage, then many policyholders will agree to this arrangement.

The information generated by these consulting organizations and classification societies is in a form that is usable by the insurance companies. The insurance companies do not do any further calculations with this information. They simply make such certifications and studies a requirement for the validity of the insurance contract. This then is a case in which the insurance companies have chosen to simplify the question. (Simplification of questions as a general strategy is discussed in a later section.) The question is no longer whether or not the odds of loss rise when the corrosion rate is greater than assumed before, or whether the towing operation is more hazardous than had been anticipated, but simply whether or not the component or operation is as safe as can reasonably be expected. If so, then the insurance coverage at the rate charged will be valid; if not, then in order to get the insurance coverage, the policyholder must do whatever the third party says to bring its operation up to the level of safety that can be expected. An alternative not usually discussed would be to allow the policyholder to pay an additional premium to keep the coverage without meeting the standard. But when insurers do not really know what the odds of losses are, they would be extremely reluctant to accept this alternative since it is always possible that they have already grossly underestimated the odds of loss and since reinsurers would be reluctant to accept such an arrangement.

Even when there is very little experience-based information available, some facts stand out. In the case of the North Sea oil exploitation, these facts have to do with the concentration of risks in certain areas. The single most dangerous phase of the construction period is the towing operation. And the single most important cause of loss to mobile rigs is bad weather. If one wanted to concentrate loss prevention effort where it would be most effective, then, one would require the consultation of experts about towing operations and about weather conditions during towing and during the moving of mobile rigs. It is certainly possible to hire experts during other phases, and the policyholders often do, but if one wants to concentrate effort where the potential losses are greatest, then one will concentrate on these areas. Of course part of the reason that the towing procedures are so dangerous is that the possibility of a total loss is higher during this phase. During many of the other operations the probabilities of total losses are quite small while the probabilities of small losses (particular average losses) are relatively high. Part of the reason that the odds of a total loss are high during towing is that the cause of loss is something that acts on the whole rather than on a piece of the object. (It is hard to imagine only a piece of a steel jacket sinking.) If any part of it is lost, the whole is lost.

But another part of the reason for the increase in the odds of a total loss is that over the course of the construction project the values involved are becoming ever more concentrated. At first, the objects involved are spread over various workshops but as the installation gets closer to completion the objects are assembled into ever larger pieces, so that if something happens to one piece, more associated or contiguous pieces are likely to be affected later in the construction period than earlier in the construction period. Another way of saying this is to describe it as an increase in the interdependence of the parts or an increase in the proportion of "failures" which are "common cause failures." If one towed the pieces out earlier in the construction phase, towing would not be so dangerous because whatever was lost during any given towing operation would not be so valuable. Towing is always dangerous but it is more dangerous when one is towing something very valuable.

What this suggests is that requirements of inspections, certifications, feasibility studies, and so on will increase not only when the operations involved are dangerous (probabilities of loss high) but also when the values at stake are high. So certifications are more likely to be required when the operation is hazardous, when the high probability is one of total losses rather than of particular average losses, and when values that have risen are concentrated so that losing one part means losing others. What is crucial is not just the nature of the operation involved but the combination of this with certain traits of the object on which the hazardous operation is performed.

The final reason for requiring inspections, certifications, and feasibility studies is that they build flexibility into the insurance contract. The less certain the situation – that is, the newer that type of situation – the more need for this sort of flexibility. Since an insurance contract would be a lot less useful to the policyholders if there were continual change in coverage or in premium rates, flexibility cannot be built into the contract there. But at the same time it is unfair, and perhaps impossible, to make the insurer bear the entire burden of the ignorance that goes with a new field. One way around this problem is to have the coverage and rate be constant but to have a third party responsible for seeing that the policyholder really does take account of new information, maintain the object insured, and use proper procedures. It is particularly important that the policyholder respond to information indicating that the risks were higher than had previously been thought or that the risks lie in a different area than imagined.

In the case of an accident such as the capsizing of the Kielland, then, the first response is not to cancel the insurance policies, to exclude certain perils, or to raise insurance premiums, but instead for the classification societies to require another round of inspections. Though the insurance companies themselves make no move in the case of such an accident, there are insurance implications to the actions of the classification societies. If an owner refused to have its rig inspected, for example, its insurance would cease to be valid since the classification society could withdraw its approval and notify the insurance company that it had done so. But this is a rather curious set of relations. Though it is clear what the insurance company gains by giving control of this certification process to a third party – flexibility in requirements, easier negotiations with the policyholder, information in a form easily used by the insurers – it is also clear that the insurers lose something by relinquishing control.

In particular it is entirely possible that the classification societies or consulting firms might not always act as the insurers might wish. This set of relations evolved mainly at a time when the classification societies were owned by the insurers (or at least by some insurers) and were dependent on them for business. In the early days of Det norske Veritas, the main business of DnV was classing the ships sent to it by the insurers. If the classification societies did not respect the wishes and look out for the interests of the insurers they would lose customers and ultimately go out of business.

But it is not so clear that this would be the case these days. As the classification societies grew, they also diversified. Their customers now include not just the insurance companies (mostly indirectly through the owners, of course), but also the policyholders themselves. Organizations like Veritas depend not only on the good will of the insurers but also on the good will of the owners of ships, oil rigs or oil installations since these companies themselves hire classification societies to provide feasibility studies, consulting services, design assistance, and so on, even when they are not required either by insurance companies or by governmental authorities.

I am not suggesting that the classification societies will not be interested in maintaining their credibility with the insurance companies; I am suggesting that these relations are now considerably more complex than they used to be because of a shift in the relative weight of insurance companies and others as purchasers of classification society services. The flexibility that an insurance company gets in what it will ultimately require of its customers carries a price tag. Requiring certifications and feasibility studies does provide flexibility, it is true, but the insurers do not have much control over what use is ultimately made of this leeway.

There are then several important advantages to this arrangement in which the insurance contract requires feasibility studies and certifications by outside organizations:

(1) The insurance company gets information in a form which is easily usable. Instead of having to figure out the implications either for the size of the loss or for the likelihood of the loss of any given fact uncovered in a study, insurers have only to declare the contract valid or invalid. Insurers get binary information that is put to a predetermined use.

(2) The insurance company gets the policyholder to make use of the more detailed information. If the losses might be bigger than had earlier been anticipated, the policyholder must take remedial action. This is the best use of information as far as the insurers are concerned *unless* the information is *experience* information that can be used to predict losses.

(3) This arrangement is quite flexible because it, unlike the insurance premium and contract, is an agreement about the acquisition of sufficient information more or less regardless of price. It is a bargain about an absolute and if this becomes more expensive, then the policyholder still has to comply or else lose the investment in the insurance contract (both some portion of the premium already paid, and the labor required to negotiate it).

(4) The insurance company is spared the expense and trouble of acquiring expertise that it would only use for a short period of

time, and the expertise is concentrated in organizations used by many insurers.

(5) The policyholder is in effect forced to pay a higher premium than it might otherwise be willing to pay and also forced to pay for others to acquire information. Instead of insurers subsidizing technological development, insurers force policyholders to do this.

(6) Though there is certainly no guarantee that all of the relevant information will be generated, or that all of the mistakes will be caught and corrected, or that the classification societies will enforce stricter standards after accidents, this arrangement substantially increases the chance of these things happening. These contractual arrangements are intended to make the policyholder consult experts at crucial times and follow their advice. This agreement limits losses by limiting the role of ignorance in causing losses.

Choosing Which Information to Use

It is quite often the case that there are several ways that one can know any single fact. One can, for example tell which direction is north with a compass, by the stars, by where the sun is rising or setting, by the relation between familiar landmarks, by which direction the wind is blowing, by the direction of shadows at particular times of day, and so on. Similarly there are numerous ways of telling what time of day it is, of checking whether one has done a mathematical problem correctly, of telling where the fox is when one goes on a hunt, of telling whether a woman is pregnant, and so on.

But though there are multiple indicators available, some indicators are used more commonly than others. Most people tell time by looking at clocks or watches (or by calling the time number on the telephone these days), everyone in Chicago knows which direction is east because that is towards the lake, and most people follow the hounds to find the fox. But though people tend to converge in their use of one or two indicators, this is mostly a matter of habit and each individual can choose freely which indicator to use since in these cases no one else has to accept the validity of that indicator. One of the main reasons that people can choose freely which indicator to use is that in many cases the action that follows from knowing the fact is an action that is carried out alone and does not require the cooperation of others. If one is going to leave for the store at 4:30 in order to get there before it closes at 5:00 one does not need anyone else to agree that looking at one's clock is a good way to know when it is 4:30. But if one is supposed to meet one's spouse at the airport at 5:00 then there may be some discussion about whether or not the watches are synchronized and how to remember to leave on time.

Many actions cannot be carried out by a single actor but instead require concerted action and in such cases the evidence has to be convincing to enough actors to get the job done. An extreme example is the case of a criminal trial before a jury in a political system that requires unanimity to convict. In this case the problem is to provide evidence that both convinces all of the jurors and is also of the sort that previous generations of judges, lawyers, legislators, and laymen have agreed is admissible. There may be several pieces of evidence about whether the accused has committed the crime; some of these may be ruled irrelevant or inadmissible by the judge; different pieces of evidence may be differently convincing to individual jurors. It is possible to imagine an even more complex situation, at least as far as the question of information use is concerned, and that is the case in which the jurors would not only be required to agree on the question of guilt but also to agree on which piece of information was decisive evidence of guilt.

So the point is that, when people must agree, two criteria must be used to choose which information to use. When a single actor is needed to implement a decision, then the question is only which piece of information he or she will accept as evidence of the fact that needs to be demonstrated. But when several actors are required to carry out the decision, then the problem is not so much to get evidence to answer the question but to get *information that everyone concerned will agree is evidence*. That is, the information needs to be *socially sufficient* as well as *technically sufficient*, and the two are to some degree independent so that socially sufficient information need not be technically sufficient and vice versa. As long as everyone agrees to act as if the king's new clothes are splendid, it may not matter that he is naked. The question of technical sufficiency is always a social matter, too, but it is still a bit different to ask what makes information acceptable to one person than to ask what makes information acceptable to *all* of the people.

There is substantial variation between lines of insurance in the degree to which the insurance contract requires agreement among several insurers. In lines such as auto insurance where the sums involved are relatively small, the insurer can calculate rates however it wishes and can employ whatever indicators of insurability it wants. (This is not quite true, of course, since legal systems often regulate insurance and require that insurance schedules not be discriminatory – that is that people be charged according to the likelihood of loss rather than some groups subsidizing others. And in countries or states where rates are closely regulated, insurers may have very little flexibility.) But when the objects insured are of high value and there are few similar objects to pool together, an insurer is very much dependent on reinsurance and has to use information acceptable to the other insurers.

This was clearly the case when the Norwegian Oil Risk Pool was formed. Though Norwegian insurers may not have had much idea about how to set the rates at that time and were therefore relatively content to accept British rates, they were unhappy with the British insurance conditions from the very start. But as long as they were completely dependent on the British for reinsurance, they had to use these conditions. As their dependence decreased, they began to substitute their ways of doing things for the British ways. The set of insurance conditions was altered first (in 1974-75), but changes in the rating scheme followed shortly thereafter (around 1977).

Disagreements about the acceptability of information are especially clear in the disputes about who is acceptable as a warranty surveyor. The insurance policies require certifications of various sorts. Most of the statements about such matters are rather vague: they say that the insurance contract is not valid unless the insured has met all of the governmental requirements and acquired all of the necessary certificates. But there are other points in the contract at which other requirements (independent of governmental regulations) are added by the insurance companies.

The main example of this is the stipulation that a specified organization must be consulted about towing. The recognized expert on towing operations is the British firm Noble Denton. But there are many other companies that know *something* about towing and it is not obvious why the insurers should continue to name Noble Denton as the only acceptable certifying organization for tows. Norwegian insurance companies, in particular, thought that their policyholders should be given a choice between Noble Denton and Det norske Veritas. If Norwegians were not dependent on British reinsurance, they could simply have named Det norske Veritas (or whomever they chose) as the appropriate warranty surveyor.

But when several actors have to agree on such matters there is a very strong pressure to rely on tradition and also to use firms with international reputations. This is rather like Schelling's (1960:54-58) problem of how to decide where to meet in New York City. If you have forgotten to discuss the problem, you will very likely go to the information booth in Grand Central Station. But this problem of tacit coordination is considerably more complex when several cultures overlap. The obvious warranty surveyor for a Norwegian insurer may not be the obvious warranty surveyor for a British insurer. And this problem is exacerbated by the fact that these insurers are entering a new field. While there might be a cross-cultural tradition in marine insurance to help bridge the gap between Norwegian and British insurers, such a common set of traditions does not exist in the insurance of the offshore oil projects. In addition, the traditions from marine insurance may not be entirely appropriate for offshore oil. Though Noble Denton might know a great deal about towing it is possible that another company that has a great deal of knowledge about oil construction might be more able than Noble Denton to imagine what could go wrong in towing a steel jacket. So it is not *obvious* in a case of partial information which piece of information one should choose. But when many people have to agree on a single decision, they are likely to decide on the basis of their common experiences. The blind spots are in some senses predetermined.

Another reason that these negotiations between Norwegian and British insurers might be particularly delicate has to do with recent changes in Norwegian marine insurance conditions. Since the Norwegians revised their marine insurance codes in the 1960s, they are now very different (and, most think, better – see, for example, United Nations Conference on Trade and Development, 1978, and Wilmot, 1975) than the British marine conditions. So when insurers decide to build the offshore oil insurance conditions from the marine conditions, there is no longer any common set of marine conditions to function as the groundwork. But because of the strength of the British insurers, the Norwegians were, temporarily at least, forced to accept the British marine framework as the starting point for offshore oil insurance. They abandoned this framework for drilling rigs as soon as this was feasible, but it is not possible to abandon it in the insurance of the fixed installations.

From the Norwegian point of view, technical superiority was sacrificed to the social requirements of the bargaining or coordination problem. Two factors stand out here: the constraints introduced by the need for an agreement between two parties operating in different legal and cultural systems, and the difference in power between these two parties that make it more likely that the predispositions of one of them will prevail.

There is, then, a very strong tendency to follow traditions, whether or not these traditions are relevant. Traditions have several different functions in the relations between insurers in the North Sea. Tradition is, first, a starting point. One almost never starts from scratch; instead one builds on the knowledge and experiences one already has. Traditions are scrapped only when they can clearly be shown to be inadequate. When the Norwegian Oil Risk Pool was developing its premium scales it had to find a new way to calculate the particular average portion since this could not be based on tonnage. But the first thought of this group of insurers was to use tonnage as they always had. Similarly one does not design a new set of conditions for each new kind of insurance, and a classification society does not develop a new set of rules for each new object. Instead one adapts the old conditions or rules to the new situation, only altering what is clearly inappropriate and only when that becomes painfully obvious. One does not begin by asking what is required in this new situation; instead one begins by asking how this situation is different than situations previously encountered.

But part of the reason that one uses tradition as a starting point is that many people have to agree on where to start. The second function of tradition, then, is to provide a standard, a common set of experiences that help the various actors orient themselves to each other. Even if they do not quite approve of the tradition, all of the insurers know what it is. Even if Norwegians would prefer to start from Norwegian marine conditions, they know what the British marine conditions are; even if one has a different view of the competence of Noble Denton compared with Norwegian consulting firms, one still knows that Noble Denton is the internationally recognized expert in certain fields and that one at least has to make a case for substituting another company for it.

But tradition is more than this. It is also a set of expertises. So part of the reason that insurers are so much opposed to using risk analysis is that they are trained to use actuarial tables, not to look at fault trees. They know what the weaknesses of actuarial tables are and where one has to be careful and add information from the scuttlebutt about the sailors from one country or the shipowners from another or the engineers from a third, but they do not know where supplementary information is required when using other techniques or how to splice this supplementary information together with the formal information.

What all of this boils down to is that the more the insurance is dependent on reinsurance (that is, the more there is a capacity problem), the less room for innovations and the less room for careful consideration of where tradition is applicable and where it should be abandoned.

Turning Complex Decisions into Simpler Ones

Ultimately an insurer has to decide which potential policyholders to insure against which causes of loss (perils) under which conditions for what insured values and for what premiums. This is a rather complicated set of decisions, and depending on how one approaches the problem, it could lead to lengthy tables of insured objects by covered perils by conditions of coverage by insured value by premium. Mostly insurers do not use such tables but instead make a series of piecemeal decisions (that end up being fairly complex in themselves). So the first use of information in a case like this is for the purpose of posing the questions sensibly. In many cases this is a matter of turning a complex question into a far simpler one. When there is an information shortage, this principle is crucial – the most efficient use of the scarce information is for posing the question. Though it is rather difficult to imagine how one could get the information necessary to fill in all of the cells of the tables described above, it is far easier to imagine how one might use more incomplete information to answer a series of simpler questions about which perils to exclude, which objects to group together, and so on.

This process of simplifying decisions often involves several discrete steps. The first step is often to figure out what information one would ideally wish to have. In effect this is a matter of realizing that ultimately one would like to be able to consult the sort of table described above. Then one must decide which dimensions of the table can be separated from which other dimensions. Of course each decision about coverage is tied to a corresponding decision about a rate and a type of insured object. But some other kinds of decisions, such as about which objects to group together, what limits to place on coverage, and which perils to exclude, can be made almost completely independently of decisions on premiums (though of course they have significant implications for other decisions which *are* related to premiums). The second step, then, is to decide which decision can be broken off and made independently.

The third step is to transform these individual decisions into answerable questions. In many cases one transforms unanswerable questions into answerable ones by changing them into questions requiring simple yes/no responses. For example, one does not ask how to group the various objects but instead asks whether to classify drilling rigs as ships and whether to group semisubmersible rigs and jackup rigs together.

Simplifying complex decisions is mostly a matter of deciding whether or not one has the information necessary to fill in the cells of the complex tables and if not how one can sensibly separate the questions and transform them into answerable questions. This is, in practice, a rather confusing process because important information is contained both in the *cells* of the tables and in the *system of categories* of the tables. (For example, one can know both that the weather losses are x times higher in the North Sea than in the Gulf of Mexico – information contained in the cells – and also that weather is a relevant condition to consider and that the North Sea and Gulf of Mexico have very different weather conditions – information contained in the system of categories.)

In the rest of this section I will discuss some of the important decisions that insurers have had to make in providing insurance coverage in the North Sea and will point out the ways in which they have simplified complex questions so that they were answerable with the information available.

How to Group Policyholders: The question of how to categorize the units being insured is fundamental. The insurer has to decide how similar to or different from the units it has traditionally insured this new unit is. The question of whether or not a drilling rig is a ship sounds silly (and some rather ludicrous discussions are cited in Summerskill, 1979) but the answer to this question determines whether the usual exclusions apply, whether the proper authorities are the shipping classification societies and the maritime governmental bodies (though this question of jurisdiction is partly decided by the governments in question), and whether one can look for reinsurance in the land market. One important example of this in oil insurance is the question of whether the limitations on liability for ships also apply to mobile rigs which are often classified as ships. In deciding whether or not a drilling rig is a ship, then, one is deciding which traditions to build on and, unfortunately, which ones to neglect.

This question of whether or not the new object is to be classified as being the same thing as the old object is for the most part not decided by insurance companies. Instead it is decided mostly by classification societies (there are also some court cases on crucial questions, such as whether the limits on liability will apply) and then mostly on a piecemeal basis. One does not decide once and for all that a drilling rig is or is not a ship. Instead one decides whether the rules about the F-class apply as they are or have to be modified. Some of the modifications in existing rules come about before the classification society ever has to class a drilling rig (or whatever new object it is), through the work of committees set up to assess future projects of the classification society, and some of them arise when the accident experiences of the new object indicate that the old rules apparently do not fit it so very well. These accident records may be assessed either when someone notices that there have been too many of a particular kind of accident or when the work of a division is reviewed (internally) annually or when some major accident occurs and the classification society makes an investigation to see how it happened.

But there are dangers in this piecemeal way of determining whether a drilling rig is a ship. For instance, safety regulations come about as a result of modifications of old safety regulations rather than as a result of a systematic review of the functions and corresponding safety requirements of the new object. An organization like Veritas may stress the strength of the steel without bothering to check whether the real point of vulnerability has anything to do with the strength of steel.

The insurer not only has to decide whether these new units are the same as old ones but also whether the new ones are all alike or must be differentiated among themselves. For example, the insurer must decide whether a jackup rig is significantly different from a semisubmersible or not. The criterion for "significantly different" is whether the loss experience (per unit of value, or per ton, or whatever) is different. In making this sort of decision, the insurers do use many different kinds of information.

Though they prefer to use loss experience, when this is unavailable they will use other sorts of evidence. In making the decision to separate jackups from semisubmersibles but not to differentiate self-propelled semisubmersibles from others, the Norwegian Oil Risk Pool consulted Det norske Veritas. But it is unclear whether they simply asked Veritas' opinion or whether they asked for all of the information and then assessed it themselves. It is clear, though, that the insurers made this decision separately from other related decisions that they had to make at the same time. So the question of whether to compute the particular average component of the premium on the basis of tonnage was considered separately, though a decision to use tonnage would in effect have been a decision to have subcategories of semisubmersibles.

Limits on Liability: Another way to simplify a complex question is to limit the sums of money involved. This solution is used in nuclear energy in the U.S. (the Price Anderson Act limits the liability of the energy companies and the government for losses due to nuclear accidents), has been used in marine insurance (there is a convention rule limiting the liability of a shipowner), and is now used to some degree in oil insurance. But there are several ways to limit liability. Liability can be limited by law so that a policyholder does not have to pay more than a specified sum, or it can be limited by contract. This latter solution is very common in the North Sea oil business. For example, an oil company may begin by insisting that a contractor has unlimited liability and end up agreeing that the contractor's liability is for no more than $2 million. While it is rather difficult to get insurance for an unlimited quantity, it is much easier to get insurance for $2 million. Because of the difficulties of calculating in cases of unlimited liability, insurance companies often limit the quantities themselves. Many insurance contracts limit liability for each accident, for a particular kind of loss, or for a calendar year. They then do not have to bother calculating about the small but still meaningful possibility of having to pay out $2 billion (the value of the largest platforms).

Limits on Validity: Just as there is very little information about the conditions under which $2 billion losses occur, so there is also very little information about what kinds of losses are likely to occur to a vessel that does not maintain its standard. Part of the reason that insurance contracts are not valid when the standard is not maintained is simply that the insurers do not have much loss experience from such ships. Even if a particular rule were irrelevant to loss experience insurers would not know this (if the rule had been in existence for a while) and so it is sensible for them to refuse to consider the insurance valid under those conditions.

Excluded Perils: One can ask the question about which perils to cover in several different ways. One can list covered perils, one can have an all-risk policy in which everything is covered, or one can have a policy that excludes only named perils. If one wants to pose the question simply, of course the all-risk policy is most sensible. But there are always certain dangers that loom large and so insurers tend to exclude those which have potentially disastrous effects. A policyholder can usually opt for this coverage for an extra sum. Insurers used to list the covered perils but this led to a lot of court cases about what exactly the list meant and also to insurers charging excessively high premiums (because there was a lot of duplication of coverage when one simply added up the list of perils, and it was unclear how to exclude the intersection of the coverages until experience had accumulated).

Modifying Decision Rules in Insurance Rating and Underwriting: From experience one may know that the closest grocery store still stocks last year's potatoes in July, only erratically carries shrimp and frozen whale meat, and has fresh bread only on certain days. Initially these seem like serious inconveniences but once one learns the idiosyncracies of the local stores, one can formulate a series of rules for shopping behavior and the inconvenience becomes trivial. One in effect develops a series of shopping lists which automatically pop into one's head in appropriate situations: while I am downtown I should go to the fish market for shrimp, as long as I am in the neighborhood I should buy some yogurt, this store has cheaper canned tomatoes so I should pick some up even if we are not out yet.

But when one moves to a new neighborhood one discovers that this set of store-specific shopping lists is no longer very useful and that instead of being able to summon from memory an appropriate list, one has to go through the store looking for each individual item and checking its quality. Because by now one has forgotten *why* one had all those store-specific lists, one forgets to make sure that the vegetables are fresh before buying them and one's spouse may not even know that one brand of corn muffin mix is superior to another since the rule had only to do with buying corn muffins in a particular store.

This experience of having to adjust shopping habits to a new neighborhood shows two things: (1) that a set of habits (in this case a set of shop-specific lists) may have to be transformed into a long series of simple decisions (whether to buy a particular item in a particular store), and (2) that when knowledge is stored in habits it is less accessible for analysis (so one may forget why one had several shopping lists).

Decision rules become similarly obsolete in insurance when conditions change or when insurers begin to cover a new sort of object. Before discussing in a general way why this problem occurs and what conditions exacerbate it, I will go through a rather elaborate and partly fictitious example.

Many of the decision rules that insurers use are based on the classes established by the classification societies. Very often a vessel is required to maintain its class in order for the insurance contract to be valid, but in some cases there are also special classes and discounts are associated with the attainment of such classes. In order to have a particular class, a ship has to meet a series of standards (called "rules"). So a class designation is really just a sort of composite variable. A ship which has a particular class is one which has met the specified requirements and therefore has a particular set of characteristics.

In 1956 Det norske Veritas developed an F-class for ships that met closely specified requirements having to do with fire protection. (The development of the F-class is discussed in Barlaup, 1964:121-128). These rules were designed to eliminate conditions that led to fires, to prevent the spread of fires to other parts of the ship, and to improve the chances of putting out fires. Meeting this series of requirements (that is, having a particular set of characteristics) qualified the ship for the F-class.

If insurance companies were to give discounts for meeting the F-class requirements, they would base this decision on information indicating that there were substantial differences in loss experiences between F-class ships and all others. But they would not examine the question of whether it was reasonable to give a discount for meeting only some of the requirements for the F-class. That is, insurance companies would treat the F-class requirements as a single variable rather than as a series of variables, and would collect evidence about F and not-F rather than about the effects of individual safety features like lifeboats, CO_2 fire extinguishers, special exhaust systems, and so on. (Of course having a class based on this set of features would make it more likely that these features would tend to coincide empirically since the policyholders would get the class discount only if they met *all* of the requirements. The partition of ships into F and not-F is more sensible when one can in effect force ships from intermediate categories into these two.)

Now assume that the insurers began to offer coverage for a new sort of object such as a drilling rig, and also assume that the insurers and classification societies are quite feeble-minded (which they are not). The insurers would then continue to give the F-class discount to drilling rigs which met the specified requirements and the classification society would continue to require the same things in order to get the F-class.

There are several reasons why these actions would be inappropriate. First, when the rules for the F-class were formulated there may have been many differences between ships which met the requirements for the F-class and those which did not. Among a new set of objects there might be fewer differences between F and not-F objects. This could happen, for example, if certain features became standard equipment. In such a case the relation between F and not-F would be different for ships than for other objects like drilling rigs because not-F drilling rigs were more like F drilling rigs than not-F ships were like F ships. If insurers had been giving F class ships a 10% discount from the normal ship rate, they might then want to give F-class drilling rigs a smaller discount from the normal drilling rig rate. (Of course this sort of convergence between the F and not-F categories could also occur in ships if new ships were built with some of the F-class features as standard equipment. According to Barlaup (1964:128) many ships not qualifying for the F-class did adopt some of the F-class features.)

A second reason that it might be unreasonable to use the ship F-class rules in classing drilling rigs or any other new object has to do with the individual requirements. It may well be that the factors that reduce fire losses in one kind of object do not enhance safety in another. Though one might need rules about the construction of engine rooms and the location of storage tanks on an oil tanker, one might need rules about an entirely different set of items (like equipment to deal with explosions and blowouts) if one were concerned with fire safety on drilling rigs. And even when items from one list appear on the other, there might be minor modifications. For example, rescue vessels can be expected to reach oil rigs working fairly close to shore in a much shorter period of time than they can be expected to reach tankers farther from shore. If a fire wall must keep the temperature in an area adjacent to the fire low enough to keep the crew from roasting, then the requirement for a drilling rig might be that the fire wall should maintain the temperature below this level for 4 hours while the required time period might be much longer for a tanker.

But unless one retains a sense of the logic behind the rules one is unable to alter the rules so that they are appropriate to new circumstances. One has to be able to break the composite variable (F-class) into its components (the individual rules) and to examine each of these components to see if it is appropriate to the new situation.

In the example discussed above, the insurers and the classification society know exactly what requirements are associated with each class. That is, they know what series of characteristics is summarized by each class designation. Because the corresponding insurance decision rule (to give a discount for meeting and maintaining certain standards) is based on a composite classification scheme (the various classes) whose individual components (the rules) are *known*, the insurers (and the classification society) know how to adjust the decision rule when a new object comes along.

But many of the decision rules used by insurers are instead summaries of countless experience-based underwriting judgments. Instead of classification society engineers deciding that a particular combination traits would produce favorable loss experience and combining these traits into rules for a class, the categories are ones that have occurred "naturally." Unfortunately this means that one is less likely to know which individual differences between the objects in different categories actually produce the difference in loss experience and which individual differences are only spuriously related. (Of course even when one has designed the system of categories one is unlikely to know the exact contribution of each individual characteristic.) Marine insurers adjust their rates with the nationality of the vessels, political conditions, season, general economic trends, and so on. But it would be difficult to say exactly which traits associated with Norwegian ownership, for example, might produce a lower loss experience. Presumably a superior loss record for Norwegian ships might be due to any number of factors such as the experience and training of the crew, the effects of the work environment laws, good design and construction, careful maintenance, and so on. Norwegian ownership of ships may indeed coincide with a series of traits that jointly produce lower losses, but Norwegian ownership of drilling rigs may not coincide with such traits and Norwegian ownership of ships apparently did not always (and may not in the future) coincide with these particular traits. (Around the turn of the century Norwegian ships had a very bad reputation.)

One of the main problems with experience-based decision rules, then, is that before one can adjust the rule to a new situation one has to figure out what factors *account for* the lower (or higher) loss experience on which the insurance discount (or additional premium) is based. Until some sort of change occurs the ratemaker or underwriter does not really care *why* Norwegian-owned vessels have fewer losses. But if insurers have to decide whether to give a discount to Norwegian-owned drilling rigs they must determine whether Norwegian ownership will imply lower losses here as well. If this decision is to be based on more than a guess, insurers will have to determine which traits associated with Norwegian ownership of ships account for the favorable experience and then see if these same traits coincide with Norwegian ownership of drilling rigs.

But when one thinks of the individual traits only as a composite and makes decisions about this complex of traits, then the knowledge behind the decision rule is less easily transferred to new situations in which the complex of characteristics may not occur. That is, when the knowledge is stored in complex habits (or decision rules) that have evolved from countless individual decisions, then the knowledge will be less available for analysis and less transferrable when the situation changes. If the decision rules are instead based on statistical analyses and on the experiences of categories that were designed (rather than occurring naturally), one is more likely to know which traits of the various groups are the relevant ones and the decision rules are therefore easier to adjust.

I have argued that the decision rules used in insurance are often based on *groups of distinctions* between objects, and that when insurers have to make decisions about new sorts of objects they often have to decompose these composite variables into their component variables since different composites may occur (naturally) or be required (have to be designed) to form the basis of decision rules. This problem is even worse when the decision rules are ones that grew out of experience with naturally occurring composite variables than when the decision rules are based on artificial composite variables. When one is working with these naturally occurring composite variables it is not so obvious what the components are, so it is harder to make an equivalent decision rule about a new object.

In concluding this subsection I should mention that although Veritas did indeed design a set of rules for the F-class, insurers did not give discounts to shippers who met the F-class requirements. Their argument was that there was no evidence at the time they were formulated that these rules would necessarily lead to a superior loss experience. Veritas was eager for the insurance companies to give a discount to customers who met the requirements for the F-class because this would be a way of paying them back for the extra equipment, maintenance, and inspection costs. Apparently the F-class rules did lead to a superior loss record since they later became the standard requirements.

Paired Comparisons in Underwriting and Ratemaking: In most of the cases I have discussed above, insurers transform complex questions into ones requiring only binary information. But this is a lot more difficult to do when one is fixing a rate. Rates are necessarily continuous rather than categorical. One cannot decide to charge some policyholders 2% and others 5% and to have no possible rates in between. Instead one has to charge one policyholder 3.4%, another 4.1%, and still another 2.7%. But one can make decisions about rates either by figuring out a series of decision rules (an additional premium for one characteristic, a discount for another) or one can make the decision in a more intuitive and individualized way by comparing a policyholder with those who were charged rates in the neighborhood of the rate it should be charged and then continuing to compare it with individual policyholders until one finds the two whose rates are just above and just below what it should be charged. In effect, then, the underwriter is asking a long series of yes/no questions (is policyholder x's loss record better than policyholder y's?) and then adding them up (and weighting some questions more heavily than others) to come up with a decision about what rate is appropriate for a particular insurance coverage for a specified object and policyholder.

This sort of procedure is possible only if one does not have to write down the rates and justify them to a lot of customers and government officials. From descriptions of the activities of the London underwriters one can infer that they might well use this sort of procedure. Such a procedure is possible only if one is willing and able to keep a lot of very detailed information in one's head and if one is quite adept at comparing policyholders on a series of dimensions and then somehow making a decision from these comparisons.

Conclusion

Ignorance is not bliss when one is aware of one's ignorance and still has to act on the basis of the incomplete or inadequate information. Given the difficulties of making decisions with inadequate information, of defending these decisions and marshaling support for them, and of facing the consequences of poorly grounded decisions, one might expect that ignorance would lead to paralysis. But this seems not to be the case. People quite commonly encounter situations in which their information is inadequate and they manage to act anyway. Such situations occur whenever one has to apply general knowledge to specific cases and learns that there is a great deal of variation about the mean. Young doctors encounter this sort of ignorance, as do new parents who have read all of the baby books, or workers beginning on-the-job training after a formal education.

But information is also inadequate when a person encounters a new or changing situation. The available information is always inadequate when a factory starts to make a new product, when a person begins a new job, when a person moves to a new city, or when a disaster occurs and the environment is radically altered. That is, information is likely to seem inadequate whenever one encounters natural variation within the general category about which one has information or when there is a variation because of change. Between these two, a great deal of human experience is included.

But though it is obvious that people do continue to make decisions and to carry them out in these circumstances, it is less clear *how* they manage to do this. What this paper has been about, then, is how people make decisions and carry out their plans when they do not have the information they have usually used in making these particular decisions. In short, it has been about what one can substitute for information and about what kinds of information are substitutable for one another under what conditions.

In this paper I have argued that insurers, like other people and organizations, continue to make decisions and to act even when they do not have the information that they customarily use to make these decisions. I have also argued that the shortage of the information customarily used does not lead insurers to employ whatever is available but instead to use particular kinds of substitutes. Which substitutes are chosen depends partly on the nature of the information originally used, so insurers who normally use experience-based information do not substitute radically different sorts of information that would have to be transformed before they could be used by insurance personnel. Insurers often require certifications and feasibility studies partly because these produce information that is easy for *insurers* to use by forcing policy holders, certification societies and consultants to process the more complex data. Further, substitutions depend on the function of the information, so when insurers have to act in concert they also have to agree that the information on which their action is based is valid and appropriate. Finally, when insurers have to make complex decisions, they must often simplify these decisions to fit the available information. One of the first uses of information is as a basis for deciding how to rework old decision rules to fit new situations.

NOTE

* I would like to thank Nicolas Wilmot for his enthusiasm about this project and for getting me started interviewing before I thought I was ready, Terry Boswell for chasing down articles on risk assessment in the offshore oil business, and the people I interviewed for so willingly providing information and helpful suggestions.

CHAPTER 4

AUTHORITY AND THE MANAGEMENT OF ENGINEERING ON LARGE PROJECTS*

Arthur L. Stinchcombe

Introduction

To build refineries, nuclear power plants, spacecraft, or oil platforms on the continental shelf requires a great deal of engineering.[1] The engineering work changes during the course of the project, emphasizing conceptual design or feasibility studies first, then procurement of major manufactured machinery, then detailed engineering of structures, instrumentation, piping and connections, and finally testing, commissioning, and producing the final drawings and documentation for maintenance and operation.

The size of the engineering job means that one will probably have several organizations involved: at least one client, one or more engineering consultant firms, and fabrication and construction contractors. The changes in the volume and nature of engineering work during the project, and the fact that one does engineering for a given project only for a few years, means that the main project organizations are temporary and are constantly changing form as the project develops.

But these background facts mean that authority and responsibility are constantly being created and destroyed, separated and combined, and routinized, formalized, or ignored to deal with an emergency. The social structures in the industry have to be arranged to set up and tear down project organizations efficiently in order to do the engineering properly, on time, and within budget.

This paper has two purposes. The first is simply to describe how some organizations in the Norwegian North Sea translate legal ownership rights and contractual relationships into a temporary and manipulable operating authority structure to get the engineering decisions on oil platforms made, and then to get these translated into contracts for fabricators and construction firms. There is surprisingly little in the organizational literature on "matrix organization" or "project management" describing exactly how people tell when they have been authorized (or perhaps commanded) to do something. The answer is that the structure of authorization varies quite a lot, depending on the organizational philosophy of the client, on the type of decision being taken, on the phase of the project, and on the tendency of such temporary organizations to malfunction.

The second purpose is to describe some pathologies of such organizations, and to go a little distance toward understanding the causes of such pathologies. If the first part of the essay describes how the organizational gears in the North Sea are formed, the second part describes some imperfections in the manufacture of such gears and the kinds of sand that can get in them.

The descriptive part of the paper has three major subsections. The first is on the "large structure" of interorganizational relations: why the client so often has final authority, the ways the relations to engineering consultant firms can be arranged, who has contracts with fabrication and construction firms under various arrangements, and who is responsible to the government for what. Then we focus more specifically on the nature of engineering work and what this implies for the authority system. Engineers provide "decision support": first they estimate and outline the costs and benefits of a given technical decision so that its feasibility and economic profitability may be estimated (conceptual engineering), thus supporting the client's decision on whether to go ahead or not. Then they specify in detail what implementing such a decision will involve (detailed engineering and fabrication or construction monitoring). Then they describe what such an implementation means for maintenance and operation of the plant (preparation of manuals, as-built drawings, and commissioning). But this means that the final output of the engineering firm is a proposed decision for the client to take. This dependence of engineering performance on client approval of the proposed decisions creates many of the distinctive problems of authority in large capital projects.

The second descriptive section describes variations in the authority pattern within this overall large structure. When fabrication and construction are to be done by outside firms, as is typical in the North Sea, the output of the engineer-client decision system is a procurement contract or a construction contract. If the client (the oil field operator in this case) enters into direct contracts for procurement and construction, the level of client intervention must increase as proposals come near to becoming contracts. The authority system then must be different in procurement and contracting activities than in design activities. If the engineering consultant enters into the contracts in its own name (the "turnkey project" system), procurement still occupies a different place from design, though the details of this difference are different. As the project moves into the fabrication and construction phase, authority has to move to the sites where the work is being done. Thus there is temporal reorganization of the authority system, and "closeout" of engineering design work and the creation of site crews is a crucial reorganizing process. The authority system also varies with special circumstances, which may for example call for creating committees in which several organizations are represented for particular types of decisions.

The third descriptive section moves to a still more microscopic level, and describes how particular communications receive (or do not receive) the stamp as "authoritative," as "instructions" to be acted on or implemented, and how the other "information" communications in the organization are related to these authoritative ones. We will find that due to time pressures and the clumsy structure of formal approvals, much action is actually based on "information" rather than on authorized "instructions." But this in turn makes the helterskelter, shifting organization of authority relations in project work a real problem, because unless engineers know to whom they are responsible and what person or structure will finally approve their work, they do not know whose "information" they can use as a reliable predictor of a future "instruction."

The final section on poorly manufactured gears in the organizational mechanism and the sand in the gearbox is a somewhat disorganized mixture. Let me here just list the main topics: (1) Disagreements among authorities, (2) Dealing with constant change of organization, or "the liability of newness" of organizations, (3) Non-performance of authorities due to incompetence or irresponsibility, (4) The growth of useless routines or "bureaucracy," (5) Misclassification of the importance of decisions, especially treating the non-routine as routine and vice versa, and (6) Cultural differences in the interpretation of employee rights.

The Large Structure of Interorganizational Relations

Ownership and Contracting Strategies as Determinants of Structure: The crucial actor who sets up the authority system in the North Sea is the "operator" of the oil field, an oil company which takes responsibility for the development of the field. Formally this operator acts as an agent for an owner group, a set of oil companies and other investors who have a concession and a landing permit for an oil field and who derive from this the authority of "owners." The conditions under which the operator holds this agency vary somewhat between fields, and certainly between countries, and the conditions under which the concessions of an oil field are made are generally much more restrictive in Norway than in the United States or Great Britain.

Mostly we will not be concerned here with this "political" part of the authority system which ends up making the operator responsible for most day-to-day decisions, except to note that it is partly a matter of Norwegian public policy to encourage operators to use contracted Norwegian engineering expertise and to let procurement and construction contracts to Norwegian firms. Hence the mixture of organizations that make up the construction project is in part a reflection of the ultimate authority of the Norwegian state over the oil on the continental shelf, as manifested in the state's public policy on Norwegian participation in building the platforms.

The operator is then the client in most of the contracts let in the North Sea, and in particular is the client of the engineering consultant contract. It is decision support for the operating oil company that the engineering consultant provides – whenever the engineering consultant takes a decision on its own or lets a contract on its own, it is because it has been delegated the authority to do so by the operator. This authority of the client is pervasive, so that for example clients whose company language is English will cause all negotiations of contracts to be done in English, will cause a preference throughout the project for secretaries whose native language is English, will cause the standards specified in specifications to be the American Petroleum Institute's standards, and so on.[2] Conversely, when the Norwegian Petroleum Directorate wants to make someone with clear authority responsible, for example, for following quality control regulations, it will choose the operator.

In the North Sea these clients supervise the work of engineering consultants quite closely. The ratio projected by Statoil between Statoil hours dedicated to project management and the hours of the engineering consultant is about 1 to 3 (at the peak manning of the project it is about 1 to 5; Statoil, 1982). It appears that other operators have worked with ratios of between 1 to 5 and 1 to 7. This is roughly the same ratio of supervision as one finds in the engineering organizations themselves or in engineering done by companies for their own production processes, so the addition of client supervision apparently roughly doubles the supervisory person hours that are ordinarily required for engineering work.

The ratio of supervisors to working engineers required within the engineering consultant is not reduced by any substantial amount (many practical engineers assert that the amount of administration within the engineering firm is actually increased by having to deal with the extra people assigned in the client organization), so that, for example, roughly an eighth of the project costs in the consultant are for "administration" narrowly defined (office services, personnel, and the like), and lead engineers and disciplinary supervisors are required in the consultant's own organization. (Part of the differences between Statoil and the other operators in the ratio of its managers to engineering consultants is that Statoil plans to leave the detailed engineering to contractors rather than have the engineering contractor do so much of it, which decreases the number of consultant personnel for the same volume of work.)

This topheavy structure of supervision is partly due to the inherent difficulties of management through subcontracting. The basic trouble with subcontracting is that before an invoice is submitted or a product delivered to another organization, it has to be certified and inspected and approved in the submitting organization as ready to base a legal claim to reimbursement on, and has to be examined and certified and investigated by the client to make sure they are not paying more than they ought to. Much of this certification work is done much more informally in other industries when it is a matter of communications or deliveries from one department of a firm to another. Estimates of the extra costs of building by subcontract rather than by direct hire run to 10 or 15 percent, and most of this extra cost is administrative cost. Extra administration naturally requires more administrators and supervisors.

For example, a considerable task for the engineering consultant toward the end of the engineering phase is to translate the data about machinery of vendors into appropriate form for maintenance and operations manuals, for quality control documentation in case the regulatory authority want to look at it, and for the capital accounting records for depreciation purposes. This is final certification of the operating system for the client. For another example, the engineering consultant will insist that the extra engineering work that comes from the fact that the client has changed its mind about what it wants to be translated into approved change orders, so that the extra will not appear in the business discussions as inefficiency of the engineer. Both these extra certification requirements add administrative person hours to the engineering work.

Further difficulties due to the requirements that interorganizational transactions be more carefully certified show up in the accounting system. When the engineering consultant is hired on a cost-reimbursable basis, all its costs have to be accounted for in such a way that they can be approved for reimbursement – it is hard to get a client to approve "petty cash" reimbursements of small things or "general administrative expenses," which might slip by a cost accountant within a firm. So the cost accounts for cost-reimbursable contracts have to be much more carefully done.

During the early days one has to get the approvals system, the routing of various types of documents and the points at which they will be approved, approved by the client. One cannot create a project organization as one goes along, as one might do with direct hire projects, because one may set it up so that the client never gets to approve actions that it wanted to have a say in. Approvals of approvals systems sounds like laying bureaucracy on top of bureaucracy, but it is central to operating with several organizations in a combined project organization.

Much of the appearance of excessive "bureaucracy" in project organizations in the North Sea is actually a consequence of *non* bureaucratic administration. Because contracts require certification before payment, extra work is created because the project organization is set up through the market rather than through an integrated bureaucracy. This overall dominance of the operator as the client of all the contracts for the engineering can be used to generate different structures of authority relations in the overall project organization. There seem to be three main variables that make up the "contracting strategy" of operators that affect the role of the engineering consultant: (1) the degree to which the client itself keeps responsibility for supervising engineering work rather than contracting this supervision out to the engineering consultant: this distinguishes the "Engineering Main Contractor" role of the engineering consultant with low client supervision from the "Project Services Contractor" or "Project Management Consultant" role with higher client supervision; (2) the degree to which the client itself enters into the contracts with the suppliers and the construction firms versus letting the engineering consultant enter into those contracts: this distinguishes "turnkey projects" in which engineering consultants enter into the contracts from all the strategies in which the engineers serve a truly consultant role; and (3) the degree to which the detailed engineering work is contracted out to the fabricators and construction firms versus being done by the engineering consultant: this distinguishes the "Project

Services Contractor" role for the engineering consultant from the "Project Management Consultant" role.

A fourth variable cuts across these distinctions in shaping the authority relation between the client and the engineering consultant: how far the contract for engineering services is embedded in a fixed price contract (as e.g., when detailed engineering of generators or turbines is included in a fixed-price procurement contract for these, or when a "turnkey project" is let on a fixed-price basis) versus being let on a cost reimbursable basis. To overstate the difference, the client must embed its supervision of engineering on a fixed price contract in the original specifications, while it can continue to alter the specifications and to supervise in detail and to require detailed cost documentation when it has a cost-reimbursable contract. In general the amount of supervision involved in having 1/7 to 1/3 as many people in the client dedicated to the project as are employed by the engineering consultant is incompatible with a fixed-price engineering contract.

A fifth variable is involved as a practical matter in determining the actual authority structure of the project system, though it is more an engineering matter than a matter of contracting strategy. The larger the size and complexity of a component (e.g., the deck and modules are complex, generators and turbines are complex, computer installations are often complex, all in the sense of the amount of engineering work and the number of technical and economic decisions that have to be especially made for that component on a tailor-made basis): (a) the larger will be the fabricator's or construction firm's engineering crew, (b) the larger will be the site crew controlling the work on behalf of the client, and (c) the larger the volume of exchange of information or special contracts on problems as they come up, and the greater the specialization of communication by subparts of the project. All this leads to a much more detailed information and control system involving the engineering consultant firm, the client and the fabricator or construction firm. This systematic variation in the complexity of the authority system embedded in a contract with the size and complexity of the contract can result in a tangle of authorities and an explosive growth of bureaucratic difficulties if not well managed.

Aside from matters of contract strategy, the structure of contracts itself can create extra difficulties with particular types of technical problems. For example, suppose one firm outside Norway is designing the drilling equipment for a platform and has a contract directly with the operator. They propose to change something which has implications for weight or requires extra power supply or something, and which consequently entails coordinating this change with a different subcontractor. The formal line of authority that has to be traversed may be from the drilling contractor to the operator to the engineering consultant and back to the operator again and finally to the deck contractor (or generator contractor) (perhaps via the engineering consultant again) then the reaction may have to travel back through all the same spokes of the wheel of which the operator is the hub.

The actual technical adjustments may be relevant to one or two engineers each in the drilling design contractor and the deck contractor, who could clear up the technical matter in a 15 minute telephone conversation confirmed by telex. The general point is that the actual structure of contracts will happen to make the authority system for a particular technical problem much more complex than it need be, regardless of the general strategy of the operator in working out the structure of contracts.

Given these general provisions on the structure of contractual relationships, there is still a further variable in the *content* of those relations, depending on what is delegated across a given contractual link between organizations. For example, over time Statoil seems to have developed both more competence and more willingness to intervene in its role of major owner (on behalf of the Norwegian state) with decisions that most owner groups usually leave up to the operator. At various times Norwegian news media have described rumors about operators taking a tough position on some technical or economic question (e.g., not wanting to inject water to maintain pressure and increase recovery, or not wanting to build the third platform in a field as a copy of a very expensive second platform). In recent years these rumors have pointed out that the operation is now confronted with the possibility that the major owner in the owner group might take over the operator role itself. So the exact powers that are delegated to the operator may shift over time, as for example, with increased competence of Statoil to take over as operator.

Similarly, the operator oil company has to delegate authority to the project task force it sets up for a particular construction project; but the actual degree of delegation varies from company to company, and some companies end up requiring engineering consultant personnel to wait for approval for a given trivial action to come from the United States.[3] In addition to these complexities within the owner group and between them and their contractors, the Norwegian government's delegation of operative responsibility to oil companies and their contractors is conditional, and varies over time as the objectives and possibilities of the government change. The Norwegian Petroleum Directorate intervenes in technical decisions, and its technical opinions have changed over time; the Ministry of Oil and Energy and the *Storting* put different conditions on permits to land gas and oil at different times; media exposure with heavy political consequences is a continuing risk for the owners and operators. Consequently, the first delegation of oil development from the government as land-owner to the oil companies as concessionaires and operators is problematic and shifting, and the consequences of government regulation penetrate to the details of engineering work. One often gets explanations from working engineers of a complex documentation system that it is required by the Norwegian Petroleum Directorate or by the Ministry (Stinchcombe, 1980).

The Nature of Engineering Work as a Determinant of Structure: The nature of the engineering task, to provide the client with the materials for making decisions about the technical features of a piece of capital equipment or a capital installation, implies that the engineer supplies a lot of decision material to the client. The engineer has to organize its own internal flow of work and paper so as to produce an adequately described technical solution for the client. Such a proposed decision must satisfy various economic and productivity requirements of the client, in such a form that the client can effectively buy the equipment and can let the fabricating and construction contracts.

Obviously the engineer will want to know ahead of time whether the lines along which it is working will produce an acceptable final decision before investing many engineering person hours in it. But the usual form of these preliminary "requests for instruction" by the engineer is that *the engineer develops a document* which *the client reviews and approves.* In this situation what one needs to specify is not so much what communication from the client is an "instruction," as what document from the engineer is a "request for an approval."

To decide on an appropriate supervision strategy for the client's project organization then is actually, to a large extent, to specify which intermediate documents the engineer should produce for approval. For example, when one platform is supposed to be a fairly close copy of another, but with some modifications, one needs to be able to produce partial copies of drawings of the unchanged parts of the previous platform (which will not have to undergo as much scrutiny before approval), and add the drawings of the changed parts, clearly labeled for closer attention by the client. One has to invent a system for copying parts of drawings, in such a form that changes can be made, and invent a system for labeling them and keeping track of which parts are new, which old. This is because the client has no reason to approve things again that they have already approved. It shows clearly how the shape and content of the documents are determined by the requirement to provide information for client decisions – the information for actually building the changed structure would not require the labeling of which parts had been changed, but would only require the final correct drawing.

Thus the nature of the authority system that bears on the engineering consultant is shaped not only by the broad structure of interorganizational relations as described above, but by the peculiarity that the product of the engineer is a proposed decision by the client. In the case of turnkey projects, the client from the beginning delegates almost all such decisions to the engineering organization, but turnkey organization has been rare in Norwegian offshore development. Many senior Norwegian engineers got their experience in the shipbuilding industry, which has always been mainly organized on a turnkey basis. They often complain about oversupervision by the client.

Authority Variations within the Project

Closeness of Control: The client has various reasons to control some parts of project work more closely than other parts. First, some parts are more corruptible than others. Capital procurement and construction contracting are known in many countries as functions vulnerable to bribery, discrimination against some classes of suppliers, and favoritism. The time sheets of an engineering consultant on a cost-plus or labor-rates contract are notoriously subject to errors, almost always to the client's disadvantage. Procedures of certification and verification grow fastest around the accounting office, and auditing is concentrated there, because money is of interest to so many people. Since the client ultimately bears the cost of all corruption of procurement, overcharging on time sheets, or misapplication of money (except on fixed price turnkey projects, where the engineer bears those costs), the client may want to control highly corruptible activities such as procurement, contracts, records of cost-plus contractors, and accounting more closely than other activities.

Second, the operator and the owner group are legally liable under the contracts they enter into. The owners generally require that they review all large contracts recommended by their agent, the operator, and it is common corporate practice to have all contracts reviewed by a responsible officer before they are signed on behalf of the corporation. This in turn means that the documents that constitute the contract must be acceptable to the committee of the owners or to the operator's treasurer (or to their designated staff), as well as to various committees or supervisors of the operator's engineers.

Thus the point at which the engineering proposal is about to be turned into a legal obligation, putting the operator's and owner group's assets at risk, is always a point of special authority structures. This is also true when it is the operator's agent, the engineering consultant, rather than the operator's own engineers, which recommends a contract. It is not only the corruptibility of procurement and contracts that results in their close supervision; it is also the fact that these are points of the legal assumption of risk by the operator and the owner group, and corporate organization always requires special review at these points.

Third, various activities are specified as the operator's responsibility by government regulation. Quality control and safety are leading examples. The operator has to show the authorities that its supervision of these activities is sufficient to cause them to conform to regulations.

Finally, the operator understands that the scheduling of arrival of certain procurements or of certain engineering documents is crucial, so generally directs its own efforts to checking up on those key activities. A weekly update on schedules of procurement and delivery of crucial items may be discussed in a meeting between the engineering consultant and the client, or the client may have a free hand to tell the documents control people to send copies of any given document anyplace they think it wise. This special authority arrangement is because deliveries of procurements and documents are crucial to the overall progress of the project, and one would not want some trivial bureaucratic snag to keep them from happening on time.

There are many symptoms of the points of close supervision for a given project. The most extreme control is, of course, when the client explicitly excludes contracting or procurement or systems programming for the platform control system or other activities from the engineering consultant's activities and runs them directly under its own authority.

A second clue is the distribution of workers in the client's project supervisory workforce. If, for example, most of the mechanical engineering work on a given project is industry standard (or a copy of a previous project), there may be very few mechanical engineers and a great many accountants and bookkeepers in the operator's project workforce. The mechanical features of several million kroner of procurement may be approved by one person, while it takes several to manage a much smaller quantity of travel vouchers.

A third sign of close attention is the practice of clients approving "key personnel" in the engineering consultant's organization by name (for most positions the client may specify only a job description and a salary range). One may find that only middle managers need to be approved by name in the engineering sections, but approval by name is required for buyers (i.e., people without subordinates) in procurement.

Sometimes one sees evidence of the client being willing to pay costs to increase control. For example, if engineers have knowledge of comparative prices as well as technical descriptions in evaluating bids, they may be able to judge whether a substantial technical advantage of one bid is worth a small increase in price. If the client specifies that engineers, who are not under such close supervision as procurement or contracts people, cannot have knowledge of prices, but can only transmit a judgement of "technically acceptable" or "not technically acceptable," then they are sacrificing rationality in such tradeoffs between technical and commercial advantages. This then is a symptom of closer control of procurement than of engineering, and of being willing to pay a cost for such control.

Finally, which communications need special approval is often a symptom of where there is especially close control. If every telex has to have a number issued and recorded before being sent, and if people actually get into trouble for not following this formality, then whatever is on telex is evidently closely controlled. If meetings with vendors always have to be in English so that client representatives can attend, then vendor meetings are closely controlled.

Closeout and Site Crews: There is a constant geographical reorganization of activities in building a large capital project. In marine projects, design engineering is largely done in a centralized location (or in a few locations), fabrication of machines and construction of modules or subassemblies at numerous sites on land or in protected waters, and final assembly, hookup, and commissioning out at sea on the shelf. Further, a different set of organizations is involved at each site, and the complexity and centrality of the activities done there will require different degrees of control. The authority system therefore has to be reorganized geographically as the project progresses. From the point of view of the engineering consultant's design organization, this reorganization involves "closing out" their project, and creating new "site crews" that are differently composed and differently organized.

"Closeout" is the process of finishing all the steps on each item of work, such as putting together all the documents and information from the vendor into a vendor data book for a given machine, getting the final construction drawings approved and sent to the appropriate site, closing the files on procurements in the accounting office, sending workers off to their home organizations with all their papers and accounts in order, organizing routines for the sites so that they can eventually produce the "as built" drawings for operator maintenance and operations personnel in a uniform way, getting the X rays of all the seams into an appropriate file for regulatory authorities to check quality standards.

The general purpose of closeout is to turn over all items, drawings, documents, accounts, and so on, to the new authorities in a "clean" form, without dangling ends. All files finally closed should be in form so that they can be audited or reviewed as necessary, and so that they can be understood by third parties who may need to use them later without having telephone access to the person who wrote them. When there are remaining difficulties, those must be described exactly enough so that the new authorities at the site can see what they still have to do.

The job of site crews is to enforce the contract for fabrication or construction in respect to the quality of work and materials, schedule, documentation, and, where relevant, budget, or to help negotiate changes in that contract when it becomes necessary. There are numerous compromises to be made and judgements to be weighed. One has to work out an observation and inspection scheme to identify places where the contractor or supplier may try to cut costs by cutting quality (Kreiner, 1976; also Reve and Levitt, 1983). In general, the site crews are therefore much more under the control of the contracting party (the operator in most cases in the Norwegian North Sea), are much smaller than the design crew for the same unit, and need to be made up of people with broad experience of construction or manufacturing processes. Often working at sites involves receiving special allowances for working away from home, and is a concentrated source of practical experience, so the jobs on site crews are often much sought after. As usual, the distribution of sought after opportunities among the work force tends to lead to closer control by higher authorities, to prevent development of little empires distributing privileges lower down.

Many of the symptoms of closer client control mentioned above are also therefore features of site authority systems. Site crews are often administered directly by the client instead of by the engineering consultant, site crew members are often approved by name rather than by job description by the client, close communication on schedule is generally maintained with the site crew, and authorizations of communications have special procedures for site crews. These controls tend to take on a more complex form when the activities at the site are more complex. For example, when detailed engineering is part of the construction contract, there are likely to be more approvals for site work than when the site receives already approved detailed drawings.

Site experience is one of the main ways that feedback about what works in a given technical area or about what problems should be solved on future projects gets back to the engineering consultant in construction work. Manufacturers of capital equipment who have less tailor-made products get feedback from repeat customers and from company maintenance personnel who are sent out when there is trouble. This feedback can be incorporated in design modifications of a new generation of the capital equipment.

This valuable site experience happens less frequently on very large projects because the projects take so long. And because of the dominance of the client in this part of the process, the experience accrues most rapidly in the operator's staff rather than in the engineering consultant firm's. The requirement for broad experience on site crews tends to mean that those with the most experience get the most valuable feedback, increasing the inequality in competence between experienced and inexperienced people. In particular, valuable site experience in the Norwegian North Sea tends to accrue disproportionately to experienced foreigners, who also disproportionately collect the extra allowances paid to site crews.

In the commissioning phase, the final testing and the beginning of operations, the authority system is again reorganized, and in general the authority of the client grows still more. This is where the claims, if any, against their contractors and suppliers will have to be documented and negotiated.

Thus when the construction and fabrication work is delegated through contracts and subcontracts to sites, the client's control of the engineering and management work is tightened. Then total authority is reconcentrated in the operator's hands in the commissioning phase. This overall adjustment of the authority goes at different speeds and takes on a different structure at different geographic sites, making the authority system of the project an ever-changing kaleidoscope.

Variation by Special Arrangement: Superimposed on this gross variation of authority systems across functions and over time and space is a never-ending stream of temporary readjustments to meet particular problems. An especially prominent form of this is a committee made up of representatives of various organizations to solve a particular problem. As in a legislature, individual pieces of authority – votes or the right to initial a proposal before it is final – are dissolved into committee authority. The decision of the committee, at least if it is consensual, then commits all the relevant authorities to the collective decision.

These committees tend to cluster at the same general points where we have noticed closer client control. There are more multi-organization committees in evaluating bids than in other activities; new committees are formed at closeout time to get the last tag ends of files arranged; the administration of a complex contract may create not only a site crew that acts as a committee, but a committee to supervise the site crew in the project organization or in the base organization; when approvals for engineering work reach a high volume, a weekly or biweekly meeting of engineering discipline supervisors from the consultant may take place with engineers and managers from the client to deal with outstanding problems; the layers upon layers of joint ventures often found in the North Sea have corresponding layers upon layers of periodic joint venture policymaking committee meetings; the bidders on a procurement contract themselves form committees to prepare a bid, which may turn into a project team if they win the contract.

These *ad hoc* committees have life spans that vary from one meeting to whole phases of the project. The authority of the committee is vague around the edges, since the committee is normally set up to deal with a single central set of issues and *whatever* decisions may be entailed by those issues. The population and growth rate of decision-making committees involving several organizations in a given area of decision is the best evidence of where the authority system is growing and changing at a given time. When managers complain that they have to spend all their time in continual committee meetings without clear agendas, it is a symptom that the authority system has got out of hand, so that everything is an emergency.

A similar symptom of a shifting and problematic authority system is the creation of positions as "coordinator" (or sometimes "project engineer," where there is no defined project of which he or she is engineer) with relatively undefined places in the system of routines. Such coordinators often do not know what they should coordinate, and the people who are supposed to communicate through them (to be coordinated) often communicate directly instead. They may therefore serve more as symptoms of authority problems than as solutions for them.

The general point here is that a hurriedly constructed authority system which starts to be dismantled as soon as it is built always has holes in it, through which important matters fall. The constant invention of new temporary authority structures, such as committees or coordinators or project engineers, is an attempt to plug these holes.

On Variations in Authority Systems within the Project: One has not finished describing the relations among the major actors in a North Sea project when one has described general organizational philosophy and contracting strategy of the major actors. The reason is that authority has to bear on specific activities, and different project activities are of different levels of concern to the client. Some activities are more corruptible, some redistribute legal risks, some are more crucial to project success. These activities therefore require special authority structures. Furthermore, activities vary dramatically over the life of the project, from conceptual engineering and feasibility studies, to detailed engineering, to fabrication and construction, to testing and commissioning. Each of these requires a different authority system. In particular, the closeout of engineering and movement to the construction and fabrication sites is a major reorganization of the authority system. And finally, the relations among organizations and the detailed structure of authority changes from day to day depending on the situation, with residual client authority used to create committees for special problems and to appoint temporary authorities with general "coordinator" responsibilities. The broad structure of interorganizational relations, as reflected in project organization or contracting philosophy, does not therefore predict very well at all what the authority structure governing a particular activity at a particular time will be.

Authority Structure and the Flow of Information and Instructions

The above authority structures are "static" from the point of view of individual actions and communications, although we have pointed out how these static structures change over the course of the project. We want now to look at how these static structures are related to the flow of communications that have the character of "instructions," of authorizing an action to be taken. Perhaps the central practical problem for an authority system in a shifting environment such as large capital projects is to make it clear in every case whether a given communication is "information" or "an instruction."

In engineering work a good deal of information has to be exchanged that is technically necessary for making decisions – so that the design of the fittings in one part of the engineer will correspond to the size designed into the tubes by another part, for example. A good deal of commercial and administrative information also has to flow, without that information being of itself instruction for a particular person to pursue this or that objective with these and those resources. Accountants, for example, keep informational cost figures as well as submit invoices which are instructions to pay.

In order to work properly a system of authoritative communication therefore has to have reliable signs attached to communications to show how far they are to be taken as authoritative, as reliable bases for action, as "instructions." The point is that an approved "instruction" clearly assigns the risk of a wrong decision to the person or other authority structure who issued the instruction, while a verbal "opinion" does not necessarily mean that the client organization is assuming the risk of a wrong decision. The working engineer receiving an instruction verbally therefore is motivated to redistribute the risk. The time taken to try to establish verbal opinions (e.g., from someone who works for the client) as instructions is a cost which one ordinarily does not have to pay in other kinds of organizations. Because verbal instructions from one's superior are in general clearly authorized, the superior does assume the risk of a mistake, and one is "instructed" only by one's supervisor, and only "informed" by others. But since exactly who in the client organization is a given working engineer's superior is not usually well defined, which verbal instructions from the client are authoritative is not very clear.[4]

If we look at the authority system from the point of view of a young engineer just breaking into the business, he or she has to find out what will be finally acceptable to the client in order to do the work assigned. The rational strategy is to collect information about what will be accepted as quickly and cheaply as possible. One wants to use other young colleagues in one's discipline as much as possible to get a tentative reputable solution to a problem, before going to senior colleagues, wants to refine the solution using senior colleagues' advice before going to one's superior, to check with the crucial working engineers in other disciplines before sending it around to other disciplines for formal comment, to check with the client's disciplinary engineer before sending it through the Project Director for client approval, and so on. One would not want to send all one's mistakes to the client's Project Manager.

In general the cost of getting information to improve one's engineering proposals increases with the authoritativeness of that information. Thus the young engineer is well advised to make a great deal of use of questioning colleagues, as little use as possible of sending things through formal channels, until the proposal is improved as much as possible. But what an "improvement" is is a better bet about what will be finally formally approved. Of course one cannot carry the minimization of the use of authority so far that one's work never gets done.

From the point of view of the working engineer, then, the authority system is a sort of map which tells him or her the probable technical value of information from various sources and the authoritativeness of the judgement of his work that comes from those sources. The map of technical value is largely a map of the engineering disciplines, involving the specialty of the possible source, the source's experience, the degree to which the sources's assignment makes him or her conversant with the particular problem, (formal or informal) judgements of competence, and the like. The map of authoritativeness is some combination of the source's formal rank and formal assignment of responsibility for tasks, whether the source is employed by the client or by the consultant, and the source's informal standing as a person to be listened to in serious matters or something of a lightweight.

One wants to use sources of high technical value and low authoritativeness when one is unsure of oneself, sources of high authoritativeness when one wants one's work to be judged as finished. The movement of engineering solutions from one state to the other is the individual *use* of the authority system.[5] Rational use of the authority system as a map of course varies with general engineering experience, familiarity with the philosophy and proce- dures of a particular project or client, one's own position of authority, and so on, so that people of high general experience, much familiarity with the client and high authority do not need to try so hard to use low-cost sources of advice.

The fact that the informal communications are part of the same system as the formal approvals (rather than, for example, an intrusion of "friendship" into work relations where it does not belong) is indicated by the fact that the formal and informal are tied together by individuals' strategies for getting their work done in acceptable form. For example, there is much invention of half- formal communications, ways of showing that a communication is "sort of authorized." Perhaps the lowest level of these is the notation in an engineer's diary that he or she talked to so-and-so in the client organization about a certain problem, and so-and-so said thus-and-such. This helps the engineer to remind the client that his proposal is not outrageous (even if perhaps unacceptable later on), because it was previously informally approved by so-

and-so on a given date. So-and-so is probably gone by now, so the approval is no longer valid, but the risk of unacceptability is somewhat redistributed by the diary note.

Minutes of meetings, circulated, with a note that unless one hears objections one will act on them, move informal meeting conversations to a slightly more formal, more "approved," level. A memo to the client saying what was agreed is a more formal "request for approval," but comes long before the formal submission of bid documents for final client use in a contract.

These inventions of semi-formal procedures show the strategy of increasing the degree of approval of a particular proposal gradually, and so gradually redistributing the risk of being wrong (or of having the client think one is wrong, which is perhaps worse than being wrong) and firming up the grounds on which one is working toward the final solution.

But there are a number of specific features of the organizational situation of oil companies working in the North Sea that create special problems in distinguishing "information" from "instructions." The chief one has to do with the high degree of time pressure, which in turn derives from the very high cost of delays (Stinchcombe, 1980; and Moe, 1980). Time pressure means that very often one has to act on preliminary verbal "information" while waiting for the formal approval of the final "instruction." To take an elementary but common example, the approval by the client of a "manpower approval request" to extend someone's position for a few weeks to complete the work may take two or three months, and not come back approved until the extra weeks have run out and the work is all done. The working engineer has to develop a finely tuned sense of whether the person who issues an urgent verbal instruction probably can make it stick – i.e., whether in effect it is an authoritative "instruction" rather than a tentative opinion.

Sand in the Organizational Gears

Disagreements among Authorities: The sketch of the authority system in large capital projects that we have given above rests on the fiction of the unity of the client, the unity of the engineering consultant, and the unity of the fabricators and construction firms. But firms are made up of people who may disagree. Our presumption above was that once the proper procedure is gone through, there will be one and only one decision recommended and approved. In some ways this is a tautology, since the course (or courses) of action actually followed has (or have) been, in some sense, decided upon. But disagreements among authorities are routine, and organizations can follow contradictory lines of action simultaneously.[6] Both halves of such contradictions can enter the approvals process for particular decisions.

The contradictions can arise in many ways: from competing ambitions of managers, from different outlooks of engineers versus procurement or accounting people, from different national traditions in labor relations, from differences in technical judgement between the engineer in charge when the specifications were drafted and approved and the one in charge later when the contract is being finally negotiated or even later when change orders are being written. They can also arise because of other difficulties in the authority system to be described below, such as the incompetence of a given person in the client to draft a clear instruction free of contradictions, or failure by people in the client to follow their own rules about consulting all concerned departments before giving an approval.

Because the evolution of an approval (through the strategy of an individual engineer as described above) develops over time, preliminary opinions or tentative approvals may differ from the final decisions. This is why it is so important for an engineer to keep a diary and to send memos about his conferences with engineers in the client. Thus even when there is a clear way to get a final resolution of contradictory opinions, some waste of time and effort is created by working on the basis of intermediate tentative approvals which are later decided to have been wrong. When the press of time requires the engineer to act on an informal approval, which then has been embodied in bid documents before it is disapproved, the cost of contradictory opinions can be substantial.

The probability of contradictory instructions (or tentative instructions) is increased in project work because the procedures are constructed in a hurry, because they are executed by people with short average tenure who are recruited from many backgrounds, and because they change as project tasks change. If one asks in an interview late in the project who one's superior was during the project, one may get quite a long list of people who have held the superior's position, or a long list of positions held by the interviewee, each with different superiors. Sometimes an interviewee will say, "I'm not sure whether I belong to that group [and have that superior] any more." The exact degree of responsibility of a temporary boss for the performance of his subordinates tends to be unclear. This uncertainty of supervision means that the procedures have to bear more of the work of resolving disputes and contradictions – the hierarchy is the standard way of resolving disputes, so an uncertain hierarchy increases the number of unresolved disputes.

In addition, the procedures themselves in a hastily constructed organization may not reflect a unified philosophy of organization which tells how to achieve consensus. Since engineers in the ordinary course of events disagree about what is the most strategic solution, a unified philosophy of how to resolve engineering disputes – that would ordinarily be found in the engineering section of an industrial firm – is required for smooth functioning of an approvals system.

The Liability of Newness: But the problem with the newness of project organizational structures is not only disagreement; it is also confusion. The central source of efficiency in organization is routine (Nelson and Winter, 1982). One chief advantage of routines is that they can be improved, and the improvement stays there to become a human capital advantage to the organization. For example, roughly speaking, the second airplane of a given model produced by a given firm costs about 27 percent less than the first, the fourth about 27 percent less than the second, the eighth about 27 percent less than the fourth, and so on. Similarly, an engineering firm can engineer the second in a series of platforms more cheaply than the first, and they look very efficient indeed by the third. This is called a "learning curve," but actually represents the improvement of routines over time.[7]

We see several kinds of adaptation to this fact in offshore

engineering work. Thus it may pay an offshore operator to organize its field development so that engineering the second platform is started just as work on the first one runs down, and is done by the same engineering company. Late in a project it may pay to appoint a relatively inexperienced person from within the project to a high vacancy, rather than a more experienced person who does not know the project routines. People introduced into a project often comment that much of their work for the first months is learning the routines of the project. If a manager or lead engineer is appointed from outside the project, it is wise to make sure he or she has the same secretary as the predecessor, to teach the newcomer the job. (Sometimes it is wise to appoint the secretary to the job instead of hiring a new executive.) Extra work should usually be assigned to the organization currently working on the project, and construction contracts in many countries oblige the contractor to do the extra work that may develop (e.g., at cost plus a fixed percentage). Functioning crews should be moved to sites as design engineering comes to an end, rather than picking out the best individuals from various places. It may be wise to leave a supervisor position open rather than to disturb a crew that works well with a new boss. In many ways practical engineers show they understand the advantages of "a going concern."[8]

But such devices to use routines to reduce the liability of newness are often impossible on any given project at any particular time. And when things are not routine, they are emergencies. The confusion value of not having done a thing before, the cost of running everything as an emergency, is roughly 27 percent. As the organization gets run in, its efficiency improves rapidly and it runs cooler.

One of the chief challenges of an engineering consultant is to try to build the efficiency of routines that work into the consultant organization, so that it does not disappear as each project is dismantled. The modern device for trying to do this is to embody project routines and experience in computer programs for administering future projects.

Non-Performance of Authorities: The formal plan for routing of a form of various approvals assumes that people will uniformly do their jobs. But in interviewing people about their work on projects or reading about project administration troubles one gets comments like, "[My superior] has been a good deal in Monaco," or "I came back from vacation to find [my superior] had not answered my memos that were up to three weeks old," or "I've seen vendors' drawings that my sixteen-year-old son would be ashamed of," or "You have to check people's time sheets with the calendar (to see whether what they reported is possible)," or "The letter came back typed with a 'value' controlling the flow in the pipe," or "[The client's official] sent this letter with insane instructions on contract strategy with the sentence, 'Please indicate immediately your agreement with this position.' "

One of the ways that routines improve over time is that people find ways of going around non-functioning links in the network. Incompetence, nonfeasance in office, paranoia, timidity and fear of doing something in a new way, misunderstanding of instructions, a new operator causing a computer error wiping out half of the distribution list for a particular set of documents, all can cause a theoretically perfect authoritative routine not to function. In an organization that is thoroughly run in, the non-functioning links will have bypasses built around them. An organization has to be a machine that will still function when one takes out a random 10 percent of the parts. The more crucial any particular link is in the approvals system, the more it matters whether it malfunctions, and whether when it does there is a well-developed bypass.

The Growth of Useless Routines or Bureaucracy: At interest rates in the region of 10-15 percent and investments in a platform on the order of a couple of billion dollars (or 12 milliard kroner), a day delay in getting into production may cost on the order of three-quarters of a million dollars. While delays in engineering are cheaper than delays in commissioning or in drilling (because not as much has been invested by that time, and the delays slow down *both* the investment *and* the returns), speed in decision making is a central determinant of economic productivity. The complexity of decision making produced by close supervision by the client that introduces useless routines and superfluous approvals can therefore be very expensive.

Concretely useless routine takes the forms of: long lines of communication passing through steps of officials not concerned with the substance of the decision, successive delays at each step in an approvals process, urgent meetings to take a decision to which the wrong people have been invited (or to which the right people could not make it), meetings with unclear agendas where a half dozen people have a half dozen different ideas about what should be discussed and decided, or a careful complex review process adequate to the purchase of a mainframe computer applied to the purchase of ash trays or the approval of a travel voucher.

In each of these cases we have a communications process that is much more expensive than it need be, that takes time to inform people who do not want to know, that spends more to make a decision than any possible savings there would be in making the perfect decision, or that wastes the precious resource of an earlier production start for trivial benefits. If a telex has to have an internal registration number for filing before it is sent out, and the clerk in charge of issuing such numbers goes home at 5:00, an important telex message can be delayed until the clerk comes in in the morning. It is hard to row with such bureaucratic weeds on the oars.

One source of such red tape is that each person in the client project organization is a possible inventor of organizational complexity for the consultant. Each can call for one more person to be informed, one more initial on a document, one more urgent meeting, one more meeting because he or she is confused, one more urgent update on a particular matter, in time for a report to his or her central office that will never be read, one more check of whether the Norwegian bid for ashtrays is really competitive.

One also stretches lines of communication in trying to solve the "information versus instructions" problem. When one specifies only a few legitimate contact points between the client and the engineer (in the extreme, one might specify that all instructions and requests for approval go through a Project Director on the client's side and a Project Manager on the engineer's side), then one specifies that the official channel will be a long ways up and a long ways back down (then back up and down again), and that all practical communications will have to take unofficial shortcuts.

Legitimacy of the approvals system is in conflict with speed of the communications system.

Those special committee meetings and special coordinators or project engineers that cluster around crucial difficult points in the communications system, as described above, also create extra communications. A person who is supposed to coordinate has to get communications from all those who are supposed to be coordinated, and send to all of them. Coordinators and "project engineers" complain of being forgotten when the communications go through the shortest path, though as one of them commented, at least if the coordinators are forgotten they cannot be blamed for any mistakes.

Another source of much of the flow of paper is the passion for project planning, with the accompanying pressure to get a centralized overview of the project details. It is now thought that sufficient data have to flow to project schedule control to direct expediting work toward the right vendors and extra man-months of engineering work to the right disciplines. Sufficient data have to flow to project accounting to project cash flows for a few months, to optimize borrowing and lending. Many different sorts of higher managerial problems are better solved if a correct overview of the project is available and updated.

The overall problem is one of the relation between the centralized aggregate "managerial" information and decentralized detailed "action information." Responsibility for the actual development of specifications may be delegated to the relevant specialized engineer, but Documents Control and Quality Assurance may both need to know from him or her what documents are to be required of the vendor, project scheduling what the schedule of the delivery of the units is projected to be, the engineering manager may need to know which parts of the specifications are changes from the previous platform to obtain engineering approval from the client, project cost control may need periodic updates (getting more and more certain) of projected costs. The buyer in procurement who takes over from the engineer may have actual control of negotiations, yet need to supply the same variety of constantly updated information to all the same centralized data bases.

The availability of computers with efficient data base management systems has probably increased the demand for updates of data from the operating levels. While the need for information for the action decisions may remain at the level of discipline engineer or buyer, the accuracy of the aggregate overview requires that as much as possible of the information available in the head of the person at the base level be transferred to the computer.

These centralized systems themselves have several sources. Quality control documents in orderly and well-indexed form are required by the regulatory authorities, and many of the other aggregate level reports have their direct or indirect causes in similar requirements of "auditability." In the revealing accounting phrase, for auditability one needs to create "a trail of paper." The aggregate level reports may be worth their cost in data collection efforts by making higher level decisions (and higher level remedial action in case of deviations) more rational. And at least they make higher level managers happier. It is built into the system that data collection and data entry costs are a burden on the decentralized centers of "engineering" decisions, and their benefits are better reports by various higher managers. There are therefore systematic variations between levels in evaluations of these centralized data systems, with lower levels complaining of excess bureaucracy and higher levels being proud of their new computerized reports and their modern use of the computer for planning.

Treating the Non-Routine as Routine and Vice Versa: When one procures a turbine and generator system or a computer system, the engineers, programmers, and maintenance people have to exchange a great deal of technical information with the vendors. Because some such systems may have long lead times, they may have to be procured before project routines are well established. In procuring structural steel, the engineer sends the specifications in standard form to purchasing, then forgets about it unless there is an engineering change or a mistake in his or her calculations. The procurement process for rotating equipment or computer systems makes extensive use of engineering input throughout the process; that for structural steel makes little use of engineering once the specifications are approved.

This contrast in the complexity of procurement in its turn requires a different system of routines for the two cases. One ordinarily signs a maintenance contract with the vendors of computers, but builds up one's own maintenance program for less complex equipment. One can expect the formal requirements trying to secure the sole authority of the buyer over procurements to create irritations among rotating equipment engineers, but satisfaction at having the job finished among structural steel engineers. And this in turn will tend to create a routine of continuous consultation between the buyer and the rotating equipment engineers, a routine without consultation for structural steel.

The key to making such a system of differentiated routines work is a correct classification of instances by their complexity, by the number of component decisions that make up the total decision process. Some such classifications will be built into the professional experience of the relevant people. A good rotating equipment engineer will be used to visiting generator plants, while a good structural steel engineer may never have been inside a rolling mill. Some of it is built into classification routines of a project, such as a rule that all contracts above a certain money figure will be reviewed by the owner group.

But such professional and bureaucratic routines sometimes misclassify instances as complex when they are really simple, or as simple when they are complex. The routines which are based on the theory of complete buyer authority after specifications have been approved, which for example try to create an "arms length" relationship between the consultant's engineers and the vendor's engineers, try to treat technically complex procurements as if they were simple. Conversely, treating the procurement of an expensive lifeboat (ordinarily procured in the way machines or "turnkey projects" are procured) as more complex than a less expensive tailor-made fire detection instrumentation and control system may underestimate the uncertainty of the system procurement. The first is a case of treating the non-routine as routine, to preserve a generally valuable unity in negotiations; the second involves treating the routine as non-routine to preserve the generally correct notion that more expensive procurements are more crucial.

Over time a system of routines tends to develop an appropriate classification system for decisions by pressure from the people responsible for decisions – they complain if an important matter is treated as routine, or if a routine matter is treated as if it were an emergency. But since project organizations are usually new, and since it is harder to change organizational routines when the client has to approve all routines, this evolutionary process has generally not gone as far in project work as in manufacturing firms. Professional judgement often has to substitute for working routines, and misclassified decisions have to be treated with special arrangements outside the routines.

Employee Rights: In general all sorts of employee rights make organizations harder to operate, at least in the short run. Vacations or sick leaves mean that positions have to be filled by deputies. The right to go home after eight hours may interrupt a meeting whose agenda was badly planned or which took a bit longer than planned. The right to be an engineer and be assigned only engineering work may make it hard to find a good deputy for a draftsman who gets sick. The right to refuse an assignment in a different geographic area makes it hard to fill out site crews.

The history of labor relations in different countries, or in different industries within a country, or in different firms within an industry, produces different customs about how to weigh employee rights versus organizational efficiency. In some Japanese companies employees simply do not take their vacations year after year – this is rare in Norwegian companies. Texas is perhaps halfway between Japan and Norway in this respect. In general the customs deposited by the history of labor relations are different in the places of origin of American oil companies than they are in Europe generally, and than they are in Norway in particular. Much of the sand in the gears of project organizations in the North Sea may be due to the systematic production of lowered morale by managers ignoring rights that their subordinates feel entitled not to have ignored.

NOTES

* The data on which this study is based come from many different sources. The most important sources were about 30 interviews with people from several different engineering companies working on several projects in the Norwegian North Sea. I have also used general and specialized press and journal sources for news on the industry, some internal memoranda from various projects, and informal conversations with colleagues at Industriøkonomisk Institutt.

1 Large research and development tasks have many of the same organizational problems as large capital construction projects, for the same reasons. (See Frederic M. Scherer, 1964; Marschak, 1967; Newhouse, 1982; and Brooks, 1975).

2 The way interdependence among organizations leads to traditionalism in the standards of what information is authoritative throughout an industry is studied in the Norwegian insurance industry in Heimer (1981).

3 Anything that might get into the newspaper generally has to be approved by top corporate headquarters, for example. Why people in Tulsa or New Jersey are especially good judges of Norwegian media strategies is not very clear.

4 Statoil's guide (Statoil, 1982) does try to specify, for each engineer hired from the consultant, who in Statoil is his or her superior. The relation of the Statoil superior to the person's superior within the consultant organization is not very clear. There is perhaps some inherent dilemma here, so that clarity about interorganizational arrangements of authority decreases clarity about authority within organizations.

5 See Blau (1963:Part II) for the detailed study of individual strategies in using authority systems in an enforcement agency.

6 For example, in Stortingsmelding (1979-80) the government simultaneously urges that contracts for deliveries be entered on a purely business basis and that Norwegian suppliers win 75 percent to the bids (paragraph 4.4.2) and it backs up the 75 percent figure by urging the government to base concessions policy on the operator successfully meeting the goals for Norwegian suppliers (paragraph 3.3.2, point e). Clearly, the implicit contradiction between using purely business criteria and awarding a fixed percentage (or higher) to Norwegian bidders had gone through many stages of approval before being printed as proposed government policy. The present government also urges contracts to be awarded on a purely business basis and is also dismayed when it looks as if a big contract will go to a yard abroad.

7 For airplane manufacture see Newhouse (1982:19-21, 25). See for learning curves in weapons production Scherer (1964:120-121).

8 See Commons (1924:Chapter 5) for the development of the idea of the defensibility of the "going concern value" of a firm in law.

CHAPTER 5

ORGANIZATIONAL AND INDIVIDUAL CONTROL OF CAREER DEVELOPMENT IN ENGINEERING PROJECT WORK*

Carol A. Heimer

When social scientists write careers, they are usually concerned either with the outcomes for different categories of people (e.g., social mobility studies) or with models that might explain certain facets of the career history (e.g., vacancy chains). But even in longitudinal studies of careers, one gets little sense of how the purposeful actions of individuals and organizations are combined with chance events in the evolution of a career. No doubt each of these factors plays a role in a career history, but the social science literature tells us little about when chance, individual action, organizational action, and market forces will be more or less important and why. Such questions should be of interest not only to social scientists but also to organizations that try to structure the careers of their employees and to individuals who try to make the best of situations in which their fates are only partly under their control.

From the social science literature, we can abstract two broad kinds of theories of career development, which we might call the organizational model and the market model. In the organizational model (e.g., in Piore, 1975), management arranges a series of ranks, a promotion policy, training and apprenticeship programs, and so forth. The result is a series of ranks and experiences that occupy the whole working life of an employee. In the market model (e.g., in Becker, 1975, or Mincer, 1974), which might also be called the human capital model, pay and/or rank of the individual is dependent on his or her marginal productivity, and people invest in developing their competences because they are rewarded with higher rank and salary for making such investments. Individuals sell their competences on an open market, and the model assumes that a person would get more or less the same pay in another organization. A working life, under the market model, is a series of maximizing moves into positions where one can exploit one's human capital better.

The theoretical controversy about market versus organizational models of career development highlights a central issue in the literature on career development and social mobility. The key question in this controversy is "who controls people's careers?" A strategic way to answer such a question is to turn the central issue into a variable or series of variables that may vary from situation to situation, from occupation to occupation, and from employer to employer. The point is not to choose between the organizational and market models, but instead to see in what cases individuals will have control over their careers and will try to develop their human capital and move from one organization to another to increase their income, in what situations employing organizations will control careers by offering wages that are high enough to keep employees from looking for alternatives, and what difference this will make for the development patterns of individual employees or categories of employees.

I am going to try to show how organizational structure and human action combine to produce the career patterns of different categories of workers. While human capital theorists (see Becker, 1975, and Mincer, 1974; or see Blaug, 1974, for a survey of the field) write as if career development were primarily a matter of will, I will largely be taking individual intentions as given and asking how the individual's capacity for human capital development is constrained by organizational policies and larger forces. When careers take place in organizations, the rewards for individual investment in training or education are largely controlled by the organization. If a person is in a truncated career line, as most women are, for example, he or she can surely invest in developing human capital, but this hardly guarantees that the organization will reward that investment.

At the same time, I will be arguing that individuals are self-conscious, active molders of their own fates. Some people make investments when others do not; some groups of individuals work together to modify organizational policy so that their investments will yield larger returns.

A career, then, is the result of a complex interaction between organizational policies, collective action, individual choice, and chance. But individual outcomes and actions are constrained by the larger framework. These larger influences show up not only in differential payoffs and differences in efforts to get ahead, but also in people's expectations about how they should be treated and what they see as "natural" outcomes for people like them.

Attempts to control career development are, then, first, attempts to encourage investment that will increase returns to individuals, organizations, or even societies, and, secondly, attempts to appropriate the returns from such investment.

In this paper my purpose will be to address this question of control over career development. I will argue that no one controls a career as such, but that career development depends on a series of factors some of which facilitate individual control and others of which facilitate organizational control. After describing these factors and discussing their relation to career development, I will argue that project work is a strategic place to study the issue of control over career development because control over careers is especially problematic in these settings. Next I will describe my data and compare the careers of engineers, managers, and clerical workers in engineering consulting projects in the offshore oil business in the Norwegian North Sea.

Components of Career Development

When we talk about control over a career we are really talking about control over a series of elements that determine whether a person's abilities are developed, whether such development is noted and recorded, and whether the person has access to information about jobs and potential employers have access to information about him or her. Neither organizations nor individual employees nor markets control careers. Rather, they control and manipulate resources that make careers possible. We need, then, to decompose control over careers into this set of variables and to discuss each of these in turn for engineering, managerial, and clerical careers.

Aside from raw ability, which is determined before people embark on their careers, advance in a career depends on the following six factors:

> the availability of appropriate jobs;
> access to information about jobs;
> the arrangement of jobs into a clear sequence;
> tasks or training that enhance ability;
> the collection of information about the individual's ability,
>   education, experience, and progress; and
> the dissemination of such information.

Without jobs, careers cannot develop. If there is no opportunity for combat, military careers suffer. When the population of college students begins to shrink, the careers of academics suffer. Long periods of unemployment have important effects on the career development of those who experience it, and cohorts of individuals who come into the work force at a time of high unemployment are marked by this experience for the rest of their working lives. There are many possible explanations for this, including employers turning for new hires to the groups of people just graduating from school rather than to those who missed their chance a year or two earlier, lack of information to distinguish between those who were unemployed because of undesirable personal characteristics from those who were unemployed because of the general economic situation, and decay in networks that might be able to help one find a job or to give potential employers information about one's abilities (Granovetter, 1983:25-26).

Jobs can also be temporary or permanent, and work can be arranged by subcontract so that the job is really located in another firm. Both of these will have implications for career development. Individuals do not plan to advance in temporary jobs and employers will not be especially concerned with the development of employees hired only temporarily or on subcontract from another firm. But an important implication is that such practices may make it possible to offer job security and career advances to some categories of workers at the expense of others. In universities, faculty members who have tenure or are in tenure-track positions are able to spend their time doing research at least partly because others are hired in temporary positions and given heavy teaching loads. In some senses, then, jobs are not "available" for careers if they are temporary jobs.[1]

But even when there are permanent jobs available, some people are more likely to have access to information about those jobs than are other people. Jobs in personnel departments give employees access to information about positions in their own organizations. Jobs that require people to meet with employees of other organizations (e.g., with consultants, vendors, customers, inspectors, or competitors) provide information about employment opportunities elsewhere. People who are involved in professional networks are more likely to have friends in other organizations who can tell them about jobs there.

The arrangement of jobs into a sequence is important because it allows an employee to plan for career development. When such a sequence exists, the employee can see which tasks are important training for later jobs, what education is usually considered appropriate for such a career, and how long one is expected to remain at each level. An employee on a career ladder can request help from the organization in getting appropriate education or training and can push for promotion when he or she has spent more than the usual amount of time at a particular level or has secured the requisite education or experience.

A hierarchy of positions thus provides a basis for negotiation between employee and employer about career development. When career paths are less sharply defined, there will be considerably more ambiguity about which qualifications are really appropriate for any given job and it will be harder both for employees to prepare for any particular position that they might like to occupy and to insist that they are credible candidates for such positions. Clear career paths thus increase employee control over careers, though of course employer organizations can always raise the requirements for a position and foil employee plans.

In addition there are variations in the extent to which people have access to training or education that will prepare them for jobs that they might like to have. Some jobs involve a lot of routine work done over and over and therefore provide little opportunity to learn skills that will lead to promotion. Other jobs, because they involve a lot of contact with a direct superior who must be out of town frequently, provide opportunities to train for higher positions by taking over some of the work of a superior on a temporary basis. Working alone usually means that a person has less opportunity either to see what others are doing (and so will lack the information to decide whether he or she would like these jobs) or to get casual instruction in how other people's jobs are done. Some jobs are more divisible than others so that a person can start with a small piece of the job and gradually take over more and more parts of it as his or her competence increases.

And there are educational requirements for some occupations, and people vary a good deal in their likelihood of being able to meet such requirements. Certain kinds of careers, for example as an engineer or other professional, are pretty much ruled out if a person has not already gotten the education by the time he or she starts in an organization. A person does not (nowadays) get on-the-job training to become an engineer or doctor, and it is also extremely uncommon to take evening courses to prepare for an engineering or medical career. Further, women do not usually go back to school to become engineers or physicians, partly because of the requirement for demonstrable proficiency in mathematics or a good background in the sciences in order to be able to qualify for such education. When part-time schooling will qualify one for career advances, there are still differences in people's abilities to get such training. People without children are more likely to be able to manage the combination of school and work, and men are more likely to be able to persuade their wives to assume a disproportionate share of the childcare burden than vice versa.

There are also large variations in the extent to which information about an employee's abilities, training, and experience are collected and made available to others. Difficult tasks are rather like tests in school. Students or employees can demonstrate their mastery by doing well. But if such tests are never given, then there is no information about whether the student or employee has mastered some skill or has some desirable ability.[2] Rosenbaum, 1981, argues that early winners are given additional challenges and opportunities. Those not perceived as winners are not given the chance to take these harder "tests."

Even if the "tests" are given, records of scores are not always kept. If no one cares whether someone does well on some test then no one will bother to note the results. Further, if a particular job is not thought of as a step in a career, the tasks involved in the job are unlikely to be ranked by their difficulty and this will make it hard to tell whether the incumbent is progressing or to record what progress has been made.

Vague job descriptions, for example, mean that it will be difficult to say what the employee has been doing (unless the boss pays close attention) and hard for the employee to claim any particular experience that might qualify him or her for further positions. (Pfeffer, 1977:566, argues that productivity evaluation is more difficult in staff than line positions. Presumably this is partly because of vague job descriptions.) When a particular job is not linked to others it is more difficult for an employee to demonstrate that there is any continuity between the tasks involved in various jobs and to claim that he or she has already been doing 3/4 of the tasks involved in the higher-ranked occupation. Well-established ladders stress the continuity between jobs, while the absence of connections on organization charts stresses the discontinuity between positions.

Even when information about an individual's abilities and experience is collected, it must still be disseminated. Many of the contacts that make it possible for an employee to get information about job openings also make it possible to disseminate information about his or her talents. As Granovetter (1983:17) points out, situations that bring a person into contact with others for long enough for them to learn about whether he or she is a good prospect and which then widely distribute those with this information are situations in which people are likely to have opportunities to move.

In thinking about the diffusion of information it is important to remember that those people who are the repositories of information about jobs and about potential incumbents of those jobs are not in the business of keeping detailed notes on all of the people they come into contact with. This means that much of the information is based on guess work, the lack of negative reports, gossip about superlative performances, prejudices about what is really involved in some particular job and what a person with a given educational background and career history is qualified to do, and assessments of the prejudices of employers about who is qualified for what, of co-workers about who they would be compatible with, and of applicants about what they might like to do.

"Statistical discrimination" is an important feature of such systems. Potential employers will not investigate to see whether or not some secretary has really been doing the boss's job and so is qualified for his position – they know that in general this is not what secretaries do and that is enough. Further, women and men are often recruited in different ways and that means that people will continue to assume that men usually have one kind of background and women another. Though they will be right about the average man or woman, such use of averages will work to the advantage of men who are recruited the way women are and to the disadvantage of especially talented women or of women who come through the channels used by most men.

The same sort of filtering of information will mean that women will usually find out about "women's jobs" and men about "men's jobs." Even when men and women are members of the same network, their informal contacts are structured differently. Attending the same party, a woman will be more likely to end up chatting with the wife of the company president while a man will talk to the president himself. But even if they both talk to the executive's wife, the woman will learn about secretarial jobs while the man will hear about professional and administrative openings. Granovetter's (1983:23-24 and 38) observation that the kinds of jobs one has information about depend on one's class and ethnicity also holds true for other ascriptive (and some achieved) characteristics.[3] Lackeys find out about lackey jobs partly because they mainly come into contact with other lackeys but also because whomever they come into contact with gives them information about lackey jobs.

If these factors contribute to career development, then we need to ask how variations in them come about and how this enhances or decreases the control that individuals or organizations have over careers. In the next section I will argue that project work is a strategic place to study these questions. Then I will discuss the careers of engineers, managers, and clerical workers in terms of these variables. Both engineers and their employers try to plan and control engineers' careers. Control is encouraged by the high rewards for engineering careers and facilitated by the relatively easy assessment of engineering talent. It is considerably harder to judge whether a young administrator will blossom into a good manager, but both organizations and individuals invest heavily in managerial and administrative careers. Not surprisingly, we will see that organizations invest more resources in the careers of engineers and managers than in those of clerical workers. But this lack of organizational investment also decreases the control of clerical workers themselves since they cannot easily plan careers when organizations do not agree to reward individual investments.

The Organization of Project Work and Control of Careers

Projects are a strategic site for research on career development because project work makes organizational control of careers a central concern of both employers and employees. To show why the control of careers is problematic in project work, I will outline the organization of project work in the Norwegian engineering consulting companies I studied. These were companies working on several different oil projects in the Norwegian North Sea.

When I say that work is organized on a project basis, what I mean is that there will be a dedicated crew of people who, in this case, do the engineering work (actually about half engineering and half document processing) for a given oil production platform. There are, then, really three organizations involved in the project work. First, there is the client organization, usually an oil company that is the "operator" for the field and manages the engineering and construction work on behalf of the consortium of oil companies that have rights in the oil field. The client organization specifies what work is to be done, sets up the contracts to get the work done, approves the work once it is done, and even involves itself in such details as requesting particular people for key positions on the projects. The second organization, which may be a joint venture, is the "project" organization that actually does the work. It is usually set up explicitly for the purpose of accomplishing that particular set of tasks. The project organization formally controls the people who do the work; it recruits, hires, and assigns them to positions; it develops hierarchies and chains of command. People typically work for a project organization for one to five years. The third sort of organization involved in these oil projects is the "base" organization. Base organizations are the actual employers of the people working on the oil projects, and an employee is "mobilized" from such an organization to work on a project.

Responsibility for the employee is therefore divided up among these three organizations. The employee continues to be paid by the base organization – the project organization gives the money to the base organization which then pays the employee. Salary level is set by the base organization, and promotion is also largely controlled by the base organization. A person may work in a project position that is above or below his or her base organization title. Such discrepancies are usually short term, but the point is that though the project organization decides what work the employee will do, it does not decide what his or her salary will be or what kind of job the person will be sent out for the next time around.

At the same time, many things are controlled by the project organization rather than the base organization. A person working on a project may well be supervised by someone employed in a different base organization. In such a case the tasks that develop human capital are controlled neither by the individual who is interested in developing competence in order to increase his or her own wages and job opportunities nor by the organization that might benefit by developing the person's competence so that he or she would be a more valuable commodity to rent out.

There is also a problem about how information about the increasing competence of a person gets fed back to the base organization. Since the base is responsible for reviewing the employee's progress, for promoting him or her when that is appropriate, for setting wages, and for deciding what jobs the person should be recommended for on the next project, it is crucial that the base supervisors get information about employees currently working on projects. Formal review processes exist to take care of this problem, but it is unclear how effective they are. Employees and base organization bosses worry about losing touch with each other. How serious these problems are varies, of course, with the representation of the base in higher level positions on the project. If one's supervisor on the project is from the same base, then the situation is quite different than if one's supervisor comes from a foreign joint venture partner.

The client organization also plays a part since it is responsible for specifying what kinds of people can fill what kinds of positions. This means that the whole process of certification, of documenting that a person is indeed qualified for a particular position, is shaped by the requirements laid down by the client company.

This organization of project work leads to a lot of variation in the degree to which the person who can assign an employee to jobs that will develop his or her competence will be a person in the same base organization. Similarly there will be a lot of variation in whether the opportunity for future use of skills one is currently learning will lie in the same organization that one works for now. Consequently the interrelations between the base, the project, and the client organizations create variations in the degree to which one's career fate is under the control of the organization one is employed by, as contrasted to under the control of market forces and of one's own investment. (Of course investment is only partly under one's own control since there are market determinants of whether there are jobs that will develop one's competence.)

Such questions of control are especially salient because of the short lifespan of a project. People hired out to projects in effect change jobs at least every five years. Since landing a job on a new project is not automatic, qualifications are carefully reviewed each time a person is recommended for a position. Workers must also review their attachment to employers at the time when the client is deciding which bidder to give a contract to, since their employer may not win the contract.

Project work other than that covered by actual construction and fabrication contracts is primarily engineering work (approximately 50-60% of the engineering consulting hours are engineering work) and this means that base, project, and client organizations will all be especially concerned with the supply of engineering talent. I will therefore focus especially on engineering careers in project work, using managerial and clerical careers primarily as points of comparison. I have chosen these three groups because this permits me to compare technical (primarily engineering) with non-technical (managerial and clerical) careeers, as well as to compare the careers of men (most engineers and managers) with those of women (clerical workers). We know from other work on careers that sex is an important variable in career development, and that most women do not have careers.

Although I have also drawn on internal memoranda from some of the engineering companies and projects, and on general and specialized press accounts of oil activities, the data for this paper come primarily from interviews with thirty-three employees of engineering consulting companies working on several different oil projects in the Norwegian North Sea. Using an interviewing guide, we interviewed thirty-one of these people extensively about their own careers, as well as about project work in general. Of these thirty-one, seven were also interviewed more informally in the early stages of research and six of the seven were reinterviewed later. I was able to get resumés for twenty-six of these people. Two high-level administrators were interviewed only in the early stages and were asked about the nature of careers in project work rather than about their own career histories. Of the thirty-one people for whom I have career histories, nine were clerical workers, eight were administrative and managerial personnel (one not engaged in project work), and fourteen were engineers and related technical workers. A few of the clerical workers had some supervisory responsibilities, while two of the fourteen engineers currently had primarily managerial responsibilities and five others had varying amounts of supervisory responsibility. All of the engineers were male and all of the clerical workers were female; one of the eight managerial and administrative employees was female. The interviews ranged in length from an hour to about four hours, typically running about two hours.

While these data should illustrate the variety of the experiences of people working in engineering consulting firms in the offshore oil sector, they in no sense represent the structure of Norwegian careers in general. Nor are they intended to – the case was chosen as a strategic rather than a representative one because I believed that career development would be a focus of attention in this setting. But we should not forget that organizational configurations similar to those of project work occur in other areas, and that career development problems should appear in similar forms in these settings. For example, one could argue that the complex organizational structure of a university, with the central administration controlling some things, individual departments controlling other things, and faculty members heavily involved in professional labor markets, parallels the organizational configuration of a project in important ways. Joint ventures and project work are also not uncommon, and a significant proportion of engineers make their careers in consulting organizations. Though estimates are hard to find, something like 5-6% of American engineers and 7.6% of Norwegian engineers work for consulting companies, and so should have career problems somewhat similar to those described in this paper.[4]

Engineering Careers: Since engineering is the heart of the oil projects, and since career development programs and governmental policies about the transfer of know-how are concerned primarily with engineering rather than with management or clerical staff, I will discuss the control of engineers' careers first and then compare the experiences of managers and clerical workers with those of engineers. The information on which this discussion is based is summarized in Table 5.1.

In the oil projects engineers and managers have permanent positions, while clerical workers are sometimes hired with temporary contracts or rented from suppliers of temporary office help. In general the engineers we talked to thought that they

Table 5.1: Resources for Career Development Available to Engineers, Managers and Clerical Workers

Factors Facilitating Control	Engineers and Related Technical Workers (N=14)	Managers and Administrators (N=8)	Clerical Workers (N=9)
1. Jobs available?	YES	YES	NOT ALWAYS
a. Work done by temporaries	Never	Never	Sometimes
b. Could get other jobs	13/14 no difficulty; 1/14 unsure now but easy a year ago; several commented that market now tighter.	8/8 could easily get another job; one comment about difficulties for women, another about credibility of young workers.	4/9 quite optimistic; 3/9 quite pessimistic, but jobs available for those with experience or willing to be "only secretary"; 2/9 jobs hard to get.
c. Applied for job and was turned down	10/14 never turned down, asked to apply; 1/14 "maybe, not sure"; 1/14 turned down for site job early in career; 2/14 turned down for jobs outside field or when just out of school.	7/8 never turned down; 1/8 turned down because of scheduling problem.	3/9 never turned down; 3/9 turned down; 3/9 never tried to get other jobs.

	OFTEN	YES	NO
2. Access to information about jobs?			
a. Location of current job provides access	Extent of access varied with discipline, position and seniority.	Generally well located.	Poorly located unless in personnel.
b. Contacts with others in 4 groups of organizations (client, joint venture partner, other domestic companies, own base organization)	Average engineer had extensive contact with people in 3.0 of groups asked about.	Average manager had extensive contact with people in 3.6 of groups asked about.	Average clerical worker had extensive contact with people in 2.2 of groups asked about; 3/9 commented that contacts were mainly with other clerical workers.
c. How would find new job	2/14 read papers for general information; 6/14 newspaper ads (1/14 would *not* use ads); 12/14 use contacts; 1/14 call interesting companies; 1/14 others call him; 1/14 would not look for job.	4/8 read papers for general information; 4/8 newspaper ads; 4/8 use contacts; 2/8 call firms directly; 2/8 others call him/her; 1/8 "no problem."	6/9 newspaper ads; 5/9 use contacts; 2/9 send letter (source of information about job unspecified).

Factors Facilitating Control	Engineers and Related Technical Workers (N=14)	Managers and Administrators (N=8)	Clerical Workers (N=9)
3. Job ladder?	YES	YES	SHORT
a. Past promotions	14/14 described promotions or major increases in responsibility as well as changes in rank and increases in pay.	8/8 described promotions; 1/8 said some of moves were sideways.	9/9 described promotions, but many added that these were changes in rank with no change in job; 1/9 described change that was more responsibility with no more credit.
b. Expectation about promotion	1/14 definite expectation; 12/14 indefinite but optimistic; 1/14 just promoted.	1/8 definite expectation; 3/8 unsure but optimistic; 2/8 just promoted: 1/8 not asked (leaving base).	2/9 definite expectation; 3/9 unsure; 4/9 no promotion expected.
4. Training and education available?	YES	YES	NO
a. Classes paid for by company	11/14 had taken class; 2/14 had not taken class (1 just out of school: 1 in company with no career development program); 1/14 no information.	8/8 had taken class.	2/9 course of 1-2 days; 3/9 longer class; 3/9 complained about not having courses or not being reimbursed.

b. Employee has plans for future, is optimistic about getting desired experience	13/14 have plans, optimistic about getting desired experience; 1/14 no plans.	7/8 have plans, expect to get desired experience; 1/8 in new field, ties to other jobs unclear.	8/9 short-range plans (3/9 wanted to learn word processing, 1/9 did not want supervisory job); 1/9 no plans, no chance of training.
5. Collection of information about employee?	YES	YES	NO
a. Relevance of previous experience	14/14 able to say how education, earlier work experience relevant; 1/14 military experience useful.	2/8 clear skill useful in offshore work; 5/8 military experience important; most uncertain or vague about why were qualified for first offshore job.	6/9 good at English; 9/9 general clerical skills; 1/9 maybe experience in engineering office; 1/9 no resumé when applied; many said no special reason were hired.
b. Contact with their career advisor in base organization	2/14 good contact, 9/14 little contact, 3/14 no contact.	7/8 good contact; 1/8 little contact (new field, ties unclear).	3/9 good contact (2/9 not extensive); 2/9 infrequent contact; 4/9 no contact or otherwise unsatisfactory.
c. Mentions of people important to career	3/14 people very important, detailed answer; 7/14 less detail; 2/14 stressed self-reliance; 2/14 no one important to career.	4/8 people very important, detailed answer; 3/8 less detail; 1/8 not asked.	7/9 mentioned someone could talk to; 1/9 stressed self-reliance; 6/9 complained about not having anyone to discuss career plans with.

Factors Facilitating Control	Engineers and Related Technical Workers (N=14)	Managers and Administrators (N=8)	Clerical Workers (N=9)
d. Special arrangements	Professional meetings.	Documented deputizing, frequent meetings.	1/9 mentioned need to fill base organization boss in on changes in experience; 1/9 mentioned special attention she had given to getting written recommendations from earlier jobs.
6. Dissemination of information about employee? (See also 2a, 2b, 5a-5d above)	YES	YES	NO
a. Project boss from same base organization	In 13/20 jobs project boss was not from same base organization as employee.	In 8/13 jobs project boss was not from same base organization as employee; 6/8 employees were supervised during part of project by boss from own base; 2/8 employees worked in section under client control.	In 7/14 jobs project boss was not from same base organization as employee.

would have no trouble getting jobs. They were not much worried about what they would do when their jobs on the current project ended and when we asked whether they thought it would be hard to find jobs with other organizations if for some reason they decided to leave their current base organizations, they all said that it would be easy. Some commented that jobs were tighter than a few years ago and said that this was because engineers from adjacent industries (like ship-building) were entering the offshore market as the recession hit their own industries. Still, no engineer thought he would have any trouble finding a job. And because these people are the core of project work, in the sense that much of the work is engineering work and bidders compete largely on the basis of the quality of their engineering staffs, engineers are employed on permanent contracts by their base organizations and, if anything, organizations centrally involved in the project organizations worry that they have to rent too many engineers from other less involved organizations and wish that they could "own" more of the engineers themselves.

This perceived abundance of jobs means that to some degree organizations are competing for engineering talent and this suggests that engineers will have more control over their own careers, unless organizations band together to set conditions of employment. Engineering consulting organizations are aware of these problems. Some of the rules for project work – such as the rule that a person who changes bases loses his or her project position – seem to be attempts to stem competition between organizations and to decrease the returns to individual engineers for "playing the market." Agreements between organizations about how to divide up responsibility for staffing engineering disciplines could also decrease the competition between organizations since a person would have to make his career in some specific organization if he wished to rise in a particular discipline.

One of the distinguishing features of project work is that employees are well situated to get information about jobs. They come into continual contact with people employed by other companies, and many of these people will be getting information from their parent companies about future projects since they will be spending part of their time doing conceptual studies or preparing bids. In addition, those working on projects learn about employment opportunities in client companies, vendor organizations, regulatory agencies, and the base organizations that send people to work on the projects.

Engineers are mostly well situated to get information about prospective positions. Except in those cases in which a discipline is staffed entirely from one base and works in isolation, engineers come into daily contact with peers from other organizations. They must meet with people from the client to get approval for their work throughout the project. They have to meet with vendors about equipment that is being purchased for the platforms. They have to coordinate their work with engineers in other disciplines.

But obviously some engineers are better placed to get information about jobs than others. The more senior the engineer, the more likely he is to be part of the team planning bids for future projects. Senior engineers will therefore have more information about jobs than younger engineers. Some disciplines work more in isolation, others must coordinate their work with other disciplines. An engineer working on a mud system will probably be more isolated than one working on instrumentation. Project engineers, whose job is to troubleshoot and to coordinate the work of various discipline engineers working on a particular area of the platform, will come into contact with the discipline engineers and also with employees of the client and site organizations. And there are some disciplines, like quality assurance, that are lower status and awkwardly located organizationally and whose engineers must seek out contacts in order to get their jobs done.

Since engineering jobs are ordered in ladders it is pretty clear to most engineers what jobs they are qualified for or will be qualified for in a few years. Jobs within a discipline on a large project may involve two or three ranks. One can move up to being a group leader and then perhaps to being a discipline supervisor and, if one is very good and very lucky, the engineering manager. But there are also other avenues of mobility, and the steps in these careers are less clear. A discipline leader could go into project engineer positions, and gain interdisciplinary experience, rather than continuing up the ranks of the discipline itself. Or he could try to get a job in a related discipline, and how difficult this is depends on the particular specialty. In general, specialties that require contact with other disciplines are ones from which one can transfer because one will already have some familiarity with the other disciplines from coordinating one's work with them. For the main-line disciplines [such as instrumentation, electrical, mechanical, or structural (or civil) engineering], the educational requirements are fairly clear, and this facilitates career planning. But there are other lines, especially those that have developed recently, for which educational requirements and career paths are ill-defined. Among these (in Norway) are quality assurance, loss prevention, and drafting.

When career paths are clear, people talk easily and coherently about their career plans. They can talk about wanting to learn some particular skill that will be useful in their line of work because it is clear to them what kind of work they are likely to be doing. Or they can talk about classes that might be useful because such classes have a predictable relation to the work itself. Or they can talk about wanting to get some interdisciplinary experience and have some sense of what kinds of jobs that experience might make them competent to perform. And while few of the engineers had any definite idea of when they could expect their next promotions, they did feel that they had progressed satisfactorily ("nothing out of the ordinary, just the regular increases in pay and responsibility") and would continue to do so. Such expectations provide a measuring stick against which progress can be compared and evaluated as either satisfactory or unsatisfactory. Career trajectories also make grievance procedures possible because one can say what is a "normal" career and complain if one is being denied appropriate promotions.

While I would normally expect clear career sequences to increase the control of the employee at the expense of the employer, in the case of project work both the control of the individual and of the engineering consulting organization are increased at the expense of the client. Since the base earns money by renting out its engineers, both engineers and base organizations want to push engineers up the pay scale and to argue that the requirements for the next higher rank have been met.

Engineers thought that three kinds of experience (besides their previous education) were relevant for advancement in their careers. Most engineers had taken short courses in new techniques and subspecialties and expected to do so in the future. Some of them also had taught such courses. If they had not already had it, engineers wanted to get site experience since this would allow them to get important feedback about their designs. And all but one of the engineers had some ideas about what kind of work they would like to do in the future either for interest or to increase their competence.

Besides asking what they wanted in the way of experience, we also asked whether engineers thought they could get such experience. Since the budgets include money for courses, engineers thought that they would be able to get the training they wanted. (There were three exceptions, a person who thought that his base would be unlikely to invest in him since he was leaving the offshore business entirely, a person whose base had no career development program, and an engineer working in a relatively low-status discipline who had been denied permission to take an extra day or two on a trip to confer with previous associates about how they were doing things.)

Our informants also thought that they would be able to get the jobs they thought would help them learn new skills. The exception here was the coveted site job, since this is allocated by the client. The interests of the base organization and the engineer usually coincide in questions of training so that the base, though it may not have perfect control over training opportunities on a project, will do what it can to provide classes and on-the-job training. But the base organization does not get to choose which people to send to the site, only which people to nominate.

Family responsibilities also limit the opportunities for further education or training that involve a change in location. Less encumbered people (those without children or spouses) are more able to pick up and move to a site for awhile or to allocate evening hours to classes. But men are in general more able than women to persuade a spouse to take a disproportionate share of the responsibility at home, so this limitation applies most severely to people in female-dominated occupations rather than in fields like engineering.

By and large, then, engineers did not feel that they had to fight to get the training that would make advancement possible. Most engineers felt that they had to take the initiative to ask for courses (though colleagues and professional associations did circulate announcements for courses), but that permission and funding would be granted. In some cases, engineers did specifically mention that their superiors had suggested the courses. This means that their experience is one of possibility rather than thwarted ambitions.

But engineering consulting organizations did more than just pay for engineers to take courses. They also invested heavily in on-the-job training. When the oil projects first started, Norwegian engineering firms sometimes had trouble placing their engineers on the projects. Only engineers with offshore experience could get jobs, but an engineer could not get offshore experience if he could not get hired. By offering to pay the wages of engineers during a probationary period of several months, some engineering companies were able to secure project positions for their employees. In other cases engineers were temporarily placed in positions somewhat below their qualifications so that they could learn the routines of project work. Base organizations made up the difference between the wage an experienced engineer could command in other markets and the wage he could get as a novice in the offshore market. Engineers were aware of these investments and talked about their bases "having plans" for them. When no appropriate project position was available or when plans to place him on a project fell through, an engineer would be employed in the base until a suitable project position could be found.

We must still ask whether anyone pays any attention to whether an engineer does his work well. Does anyone notice what kind of educational background he has, or whether he has had site experience? Some indication of whether such information is collected and attended to comes from our question about what it was that made the engineer attractive to his first offshore employer. People mentioned that their employers were impressed with their experience, indicating that the experience could be described in categories that were meaningful to employers, and that they had relevant training, indicating that training is sufficiently standardized so that one can say whether it is relevant and adequate. Engineering job descriptions seem to be precise enough and engineering tasks sufficiently distinctive that when an engineer describes past experience, another engineer can get some sense of what he is qualified to do. One engineering manager described asking applicants how they would do some specific task. References were also taken seriously and our informants talked about the problem of knowing someone who knew the reference so that they could assess the reliability of the information.

But problems were reported. The main complaint was that information was not being collected by those who had to make decisions about the engineer's career. While the project boss might know how the engineer was performing, his base boss would not necessarily have this information. When a subordinate and a superior come from the same base, this problem is less important since information about performance and growth can be collected in the course of the work.

It is clear, then, that information about the competence and experience of engineers is being collected. Their bosses on the project notice how they are doing, and people who have to read their resumés and interview them take this information seriously. There is enough agreement on the classification system for experience and education so that people do not complain that they are not given adequate credit for the work they have done. People do not very often complain that they are underpaid, assigned jobs beneath their qualifications, or denied promotions.

We must still ask how this information is disseminated since information channels will help structure the opportunities available to engineers. Since project work brings people together for one to five years and then disperses them, information about any given individual is likely to be available in dozens of companies throughout Norway and, especially for higher level personnel, in the vendors, engineering contractors, and oil companies of the U.S., England, France, and other countries. Thus far we have noted that engineers feel that information does not easily get transmitted back to their bases. It may be that if information flows more easily to other organizations, engineers will feel that their opportunities are greater there because their achievements will be recognized without them having to toot their own horns.

Engineers did say that they could always get jobs in organizations where their professional colleagues were located. This suggests that in project work the base organization may have little information advantage over other potential employers. Since the boss and co-workers are likely to come from other organizations, those other organizations are likely to have information about competence and performance. But any mechanisms that either make it more likely for boss and co-workers to be located in the same organization (such as interorganizational agreements about the staffing of particular disciplines) or provide for periodic collection of information by the base organization (such as annual salary reviews or periodic discussions of career development with a base organization supervisor) shift the information balance in favor of the base again. Of course the base starts with an information advantage since it had to collect some information in recruiting the engineer and has some information about career history from that point to the present. But the size of the information advantage of the current employer is considerably smaller in project work than in other situations.

While information about any given engineer is likely to be widely dispersed, the information that any given superior has about his subordinates will change over the course of the project. At the outset we would expect project managers to have more information about subordinates from their own bases and less about subordinates from other companies. Over the life of the project such inequalities would decrease. But information inequalities at the start of a project may mean that a superior will give the most critical tasks to people from his own base organization because he knows their interpersonal and technical qualifications. (He may also believe that he will be rewarded for acting in the interests of his base and developing the talents of its employees by assigning them challenging work.) Base organizations that control key project positions may therefore be in a position to *use* whatever information they do have about their own employees. This suggests that the *effects* of the dispersion of information will vary with control over resources like jobs and training opportunities. Without such control, information is of little use.

Overall, then, because of their centrality in project work and because of the special character of projects, engineers in project work have more control over their careers than we would expect in other professions or work settings. There are a lot of jobs available and the engineer has information about them. His career is organized into a ladder and this makes it easy for him to negotiate with employers about how much credit he should get for past experience and for his educational attainments. Further training is easy to get since base organizations provide time and money for courses and help engineers get jobs that will develop their talents. The exception here is that site jobs are controlled by the client who has no particular interest in helping some specific engineer. Because there is a common culture and because there is money to be made off good engineers, information about ability and experience can be and is collected, and engineers are therefore able to get certification for what they have done and learned. Experience is rewarded.[5] The only real problem is that the information is not always fed back to the base organization, and this means that pains must be taken to keep the base organization informed or the engineer will follow the information flow and go where he has the best reputation.

Managerial and Administrative Careers: Managers and administrators in oil projects are in an intermediate situation compared with engineers and secretaries. Their career lines and qualifications are less clear than those of engineers, but, unlike clerical workers, their experiences and abilities are taken seriously and considerable organizational resources are used for the career development of managers. Kanter (1977) and Pfeffer (1977) have suggested that ambiguity about qualifications coupled with a need for trust forces managers to select colleagues and successors who are like themselves and who have reputable (though perhaps irrelevant) educational credentials. I will argue that information problems are indeed serious, but that managers solve them by intensive information collection and by relying on contacts that are tried and true.

Managers express confidence that jobs exist, and they are more likely than other employees to know about these jobs since they are usually in on the planning sessions in which bid documents are prepared and jobs on future projects are divided up among an organization's employees. Even if his or her own organization does not win the contract, this information is useful since it enables the manager to guess what positions will have to be filled by the successful bidder.

While the career ladders of managers are not very well established, it is clear that what qualifies a manager to be a manager is managerial (including military) experience and particular educational credentials. When we asked managers what experience they would like to get, they talked about learning to manage systems, about wanting to prepare for international assignments by going to see how things were done elsewhere. Some of the younger managers also spoke of needing more time in the kinds of jobs they currently had so that they would be credible candidates for such jobs in the future. Several of them commented that clients and joint venture partners were skeptical that a young person could truly be "experienced."

What is really distinctive about managerial positions, though, is the way in which information about managers is collected and disseminated. Since there is a lot of ambiguity in managers' job descriptions it should be relatively difficult for anyone to say what a given manager is qualified to do. One should be able to say that the manager does his or her current job well or badly but not so easily whether that qualifies him or her for a different position. Because it would be so hard to judge whether an answer was right, an employer cannot test a potential manager the way one tests an engineering applicant by asking how he or she would handle some particular problem.

But managers make up for this ambiguity in several ways. First, they are very self-conscious about personnel questions and compensate for the inadequacies of their "tests" by collecting and evaluating more information. They watch each other to evaluate abilities, effort, and performance. They also train each other by assigning tasks to more junior managers and then watching to see how these subordinates perform. Since such assignments are usually made when the superior is going to be out of town, the tasks are ones that the superior routinely does so he or she will be able to compare the subordinate's performance and techniques with his or her own. This paired comparison provides more information than a test in which there is no comparison point, and the fact that the task is being done in the superior's name means that the superior will pay close attention to the subordinate's performance.

Further, because this deputizing is documented – for example, there may be an authorization specifying which responsibilities the subordinate has assumed in the boss's absence – it also serves the function of decreasing ambiguity for outsiders about the extent to which a subordinate is qualified for higher positions. The documented deputizing tells that the boss trusts the subordinate, which tasks the subordinate has performed, and which job he or she is being groomed for.

More than in engineering or clerical careers, social and professional circles are important. Kanter (1977) asserts that one of the main requirements for managers is that they be trustworthy. This requirement and the ambiguity about experience and ability would help explain the importance of connections in managerial careers. The managers we interviewed told of meetings of professional associations, planning sessions to solve staffing problems for future projects, and informal committees (with star-studded rosters) to solve critical personnel problems. In explaining their own qualifications for jobs, managers often told us that "so-and-so knew that I could do this sort of job since I had worked with him in the past, and he recommended me for this position." While others sometimes had difficulty telling us who helped them with their careers, managers and administrators gave detailed answers, suggesting that personal recommendations and contacts are crucial resources.

Earlier I argued that information shortages may lead supervisors to give choice assignments to people from their own base companies at the start of a project. We would expect to find the same phenomenon exaggerated in managerial and administrative careers. Since qualifications are more ambiguous and performance is harder to assess, we would expect that it would take longer to accumulate adequate information about managers and administrators. This would explain why managerial career assistance comes from collegial relations of longer duration while engineering career assistance can come from more recent collegial relations, why managers take such pains to preserve their contacts, and why we find top level managers being drawn from a common pool in one or two engineering companies and shipyards.

Though I have stressed the importance of personal connections in managerial careers, I do not want to underemphasize their importance in other careers. The difference is one of degree only. The greater the importance of trust and the more ambiguous the information, the greater the importance of personal connections. Because information about ability and training is clearer in engineering careers, connections are somewhat less important there.

Control over managerial careers is dependent, then, on the careful collection and dissemination of information. More than in engineering, this is an individual effort, though much of the work can be done as part of a manager's official duties. Jobs are not so clearly related to one another as in engineering, so managers individually and collectively must construct connections and argue that particular experience qualifies one for certain jobs. But this is what is involved in constructing the personnel policy of an organization or project anyway. We should not be surprised, though, that a considerable amount of the work on personnel policy serves the collective self-interest of managers.

Clerical Careers: Men and women arrive at their jobs in different ways, their qualifications for these jobs are different, the work they do is different, and the care with which they and their colleagues train and test them and keep track of their achievements is also different. And this all holds despite organization-wide policies about career development. Since almost all of the women who do project work are clerical workers, we can talk about these differences between men's and women's careers by discussing the differences between the career paths of clerical workers, on the one hand, and managers and (especially) engineers, on the other.

Clerical workers are considerably less certain than either managers or engineers that there are jobs for them should they decide to leave their present positions, and they are also less confident that their bases will be able to find something for them to do when the current project ends. Managers and engineers did not mention the possibility of redundancy, but clerical workers did. How the future looked varied with the age and nationality of the clerical worker. Older women thought that they would have trouble finding work, and foreigners employed by Norwegian companies specifically to work in the offshore business felt that their prospects were especially bleak.

But even when there are jobs, clerical workers (except perhaps those employed in personnel departments) are not well placed to know about them. Clerical workers do not have professional meetings at which they can gather information about openings, though at least one base organization with a large clerical staff is starting to have meetings with clerical workers to discuss plans when major projects run down. Clerical workers seemed aware of their relatively poor information. They were much more likely than managers and engineers to say that if they were looking for another job they would check the want ads in the newspaper. Engineers and managers talked about checking the want ads just to see what was available, to keep up on the field.

Secretarial and other clerical careers involve short ladders with relatively few opportunities for further training and advancement. Clerical workers often said that they did not expect any further promotions because there was no higher level in secretarial work. The split between secretarial and other career lines, which is crucial to the definition of clerical work as "women's work" and to the low wages paid for this work (Oppenheimer, 1973), depends on the existence of clear qualifications or clear recruitment paths for other careers. In publishing, where recruitment paths are poorly established and qualifications ambiguous, clerical workers become editors nearly as often as do sales personnel (Caplette, 1982). It may be clear that secretaries lack the technical training to be promoted into engineering positions, but it is less clear why they are not promoted into administrative and managerial positions given the continuity in the tasks and the historical pattern of training managers by having them apprentice as clerical workers (Lockwood, 1958).

We also asked about experience or training they would like to get. Several clerical workers mentioned wanting to get experience with word processing and hoped that word processing would lead to a career in computer work. Such hopes seem unrealistic. Glenn and Feldberg (1977) provide evidence that computerization leads to a deskilling of clerical work rather than to increased opportunities for clerical workers. Further, career paths in computer science are becoming better defined and usually involve formal training; one does not hear computer specialists reporting that they started out as word processors. If people are going to get into a new career through experience in a related field rather than through formal training, they need to come into contact with people who can give them rudimentary training and certify that they qualify for the new career. A minimum requirement, then, would be that word processors have frequent contact with computer specialists. But word processing was not done in the computer room, so clerical workers did not even have regular contact with computer people.

In talking about classes, clerical workers painted a much less rosy picture than other workers. Several mentioned that the secretarial budget at the base did not provide as much money for courses as did the budgets of other sections. Courses either were not arranged or were overbooked.

A good command of English is an important qualification for clerical personnel working in the offshore business. Ironically enough, foreign clerical workers, hired specifically because they were English speakers, found that they could advance no further unless they learned Norwegian. And while workers could learn English during work hours, there were no similar provisions for learning Norwegian and no promise that this relatively heavy investment in company-specific capital would actually lead to advancement. Education in general, and language training in particular, does not fit into any training sequence or lead to any advancement in a secretarial career. This is largely because secretarial careers are not organized into a progression of jobs requiring more and more skill.

Clerical jobs, like managerial ones, vary a good deal in the actual tasks that they involve. Our informants told us that though being a secretary often involves more than being *just* a secretary since duties vary from one boss to another, it is hard to get credit for the work one has done. With only a few exceptions, the clerical workers felt that their backgrounds made little difference and that even if they had had jobs that involved a lot of responsibility they could not claim credit for their experience. While administrators and managers adjust to the ambiguity in job content by carefully collecting information about their peers' backgrounds and abilities, no one pays this much attention to clerical workers. Not only was there no system of documented deputizing (secretaries do this without documentation or even acknowledgement), but in addition bosses often claimed responsibility for the work that secretaries had done.[6] Women felt that they could not go to other employers and say what they had actually been doing because there was no reason for prospective employers to believe that they had done all that. As confirmation of this, we were told about an administrator who had his secretary type letters and do filing and failed to see that many secretaries *wrote* their bosses' letters. Secretaries believed that this administrator did not give them adequate credit for their work when discussing with them what jobs they might be qualified for. Several clerical workers also reported that their home office supervisor did not believe that there was any advantage to having more than about five years of secretarial experience.[7] Information about the development of clerical workers is neither collected nor disseminated.[8]

What all this suggests is that there are some careers that no one controls. While base organizations may be interested in boosting the salaries of engineers and managers that they "own," they have quite a different view of the careers of clerical workers. Clerical workers are not the ones they make money off. Clerical workers have a support function and are provided as a service to the project in much the same way that the building and canteen are. Just as an engineering consulting company does not provide a luxurious work site or a four-star restaurant, it will similarly not try to upgrade its secretarial staff so that it can supply the executive secretaries rather than the receptionists on the next project. When organizations try to stem competition by dividing up responsibility for the leadership and staffing of various disciplines, they do not worry about competing with each other for the best secretaries. No organization wants to organize clerical careers, and this means that no one provides the resources that would enable clerical workers to develop and control their own careers.

Conclusion

The organizations and individuals involved in projects have partially conflicting interests in career development. From the point of view of the base organization, professional employees are simultaneously its labor force, its product, and its capital. This creates an internal conflict in strategies for the use of the labor power. If labor is only labor, one might want to get the most work for the lowest price – to exploit it. If labor is a product, one wants to advertise and sell it. But when it is also capital equipment one wants to retain it. From the perspective of the base organization, then, the problem is to keep good personnel firmly attached while expanding their competence (and therefore increasing both the amount for which they can be "rented out" and the ability of the base organization to staff large projects). From the point of view of the client and project organizations, the problem is to get competent workers at acceptable wages and to generate sufficient loyalty to a project so that the project interest in continuity will not be completely sacrificed either to the base organization's or the individual's interest in career development. From the individual's point of view the problem is to fashion his or her work situation and career trajectory so that he or she develops in a satisfactory way, retains some control over his or her own fate, and has an acceptable day-to-day experience.

What we see, then, is a competitive struggle among organizations and between organizations and individuals for control over careers. Some features of project work create unusual opportunities for individual control. Because project work brings employees into contact with people from many different organizations, word about an individual's qualifications and experience gets spread around and individuals receive information about available positions. Both of these can facilitate building careers across organizations. Because projects are of limited duration and because key personnel leave before a project ends, employees must change jobs and will often have a chance to move up over the life of a project. Both of these encourage career planning.

Organizational policies shift control from individuals to organizations. To encourage stability in attachments to base organizations, base organizations and project organizations often formally agree that a person moving from one base to another loses his or her project position. Under this rule inter-company mobility cannot be used as a strategy to raise one's position or salary unless one is willing to forfeit one's job on the present project. Such policies presumably not only decrease moves between base companies but also reduce jockeying for status on projects. They do this by raising the transaction costs of moving. In addition, base organizations usually control the application process (rather than applying directly, one agrees to have one's name submitted), and the project organization formally controls appointment to positions on the project and promotions within it.

Even in matters where individuals have considerable leeway, organizational influences can be found. For example, foreign oil companies had to be convinced that Norwegian shipyard experience was relevant to oil project engineering. Engineering consulting companies were instrumental in negotiating the definition of "relevant experience"; individuals could not easily manage this for themselves. Though resumé writing seems, superficially, to be a matter under individual control, when employees must be able to prove that they have really had some kind of experience in order for their base organizations to place them, resumé writing comes under organizational control. Experience is only relevant when it can be summarized on a resumé and organizations control the "trail of paper" that backs up the line on the resumé.

Ironically enough, insofar as what individuals want most is career development, the main strategy that a base organization should adopt to retain control over key employees is also one that makes these employees progressively more independent.[9] If an organization tries to stimulate loyalty by offering to help people develop their abilities and document their experiences it is also making them more independent as their resumés become more solid and as organizational certification becomes less relevant. Good high-level employees will not need their base organizations to back their claims to competence; clients and other engineering organizations will already know about them.

This suggests that control over careers is not at all zero sum. The quantity of control is not fixed. Rather, when any one group has more control other groups have more control as well. The competitive struggle for control seems to be good for all parties involved not because it decreases the price of labor (the price of labor does not decrease in the short run, especially not when governmental policies encourage the use of local labor) but because it increases the supply of human capital. Employers institute policies to develop and retain their workers, but in attempting to control employee careers they also provide the resources that allow workers to control their own careers.

But this also tells us what makes for more or less control. When we examine the case of engineers, the group with the most control, and compare their situation with the situations of other groups, we see that the resources that permit engineers control over their own career development are largely resources created by organizations attempting to control these same careers. This tells us that we would expect *control over career development to be greatest in those groups which are most central to the mission of an organization and most important in giving it an edge over competitors.*[10]

When an organization is interested in developing the abilities of a group of people and in retaining them as these skills increase, it will create hierarchies, job descriptions, and training programs; it will pay attention to educational qualifications and experience; and it will collect and disseminate information about these people. But these are the very factors that enable people to control careers themselves. When there are career ladders individuals can measure their progress. When information has been collected, individuals can see that it gets passed to those *they* want to have it. When there are training programs, employees can get the training and then use their skills wherever they see fit.

Groups of employees more peripheral to the mission of the

organization or less important to its competitive advantage will still benefit from these organizational policies. When an organization decides that engineers should have annual career discussions with their supervisors, it will usually institute this as an organizational policy applying to all employees. If not, other groups can appeal on grounds of equity and get the policy extended to them. But this may mean that they get watered-down benefits either because the organization explicitly grants them a diluted benefit or because the benefit was designed to meet the needs of the core group and therefore does not really serve the interests of peripheral groups. Career development discussions do not do much for secretaries unless career ladders are changed. Rights to be reimbursed for additional schooling do not give much advantage when extra education does not qualify one for a better job.

When career development is not taken care of through organizational policy, it is sometimes managed in alternative ways. Career planning may be an unintended consequence of some other feature of the organization such as task assignment. When the interests of some group are not well met by the organizational policies on career development, this group may take care of career development collectively (though not exactly as an organizational function). For example, managers in carrying out their jobs of organizing and overseeing often have occasion to collect information on the abilities and experience of their colleagues and to disseminate information about themselves. Unions may also arrange for career development of their members (though the method is different than that used by managers).

But this is not to say that career development problems are always taken care of. Those who are neither central to an organization (so that the organization is not interested in controlling their careers) nor assigned tasks that allow them to arrange their own career development may in rare cases be situated at a point in the organization where information about jobs or about employees is collected or may, as a result of participation in some *ad hoc* committee, have contact with people who have such information. This will give them one of the resources necessary for career development. But while access to this one resource may make them relatively advantaged compared with others in the same line of work, they will not really have much control. When the organization is not interested in developing a person's career (or not interested in the careers of a whole group), and when the person is not in a category that can collectively provide for career development, then he or she will find it difficult to control his or her own career. A career that no organization or collectivity wants to control is usually a career that does not grow.

The resources for career development have to be created. Important questions, then, are who creates resources, when, and for whom.

Organizations create career development resources for key employees when they are worried about losing them. They create such resources not because they want to increase employee control over career development but because they wish to offer incentives to these key employees. Two things should be noted about the organizational provision of career development resources. First, the resulting inequality between various categories of workers in opportunities for career development is not due to organizational planning. The organization probably does not care one way or the other about such inequality. Rather, inequality in career development chances is the *by-product* of policies (offering incentives to key people) that do serve organizational needs. Secondly, we should note that when *employer organizations* create resources for career development they create *more* of them than do other bodies. While employers create career ladders, training and evaluation programs, and information systems, employees acting in concert (either formally, e.g. in unions, or informally, e.g. in meetings of managers) are usually only able to provide a few career development resources.

In this study we have seen that, in the North Sea situation, engineers are relatively advantaged. Because they are the bread and butter of engineering consulting companies and the basis for competition for contracts, the organizations try to help engineers develop. But this in turn means that engineers themselves have a good deal of control over their outcomes. Engineering consulting companies probably care less about their managerial and administrative personnel than about their engineers. But since managers and administrators are the ones responsible for many organizational policies, they can look out for their own interests. Clerical workers are neither crucial to the organizational interest nor able to arrange policies that will benefit themselves. If stratification in organizations is the combined result of organizations pursuing their interests and well-placed individuals designing policies to benefit their own groups, those who are neither central to the organization nor able to design policy will come out on the bottom of the heap.

NOTES

[*] I would like to thank Howard Becker, Tom Colbjørnsen, Arlene Daniels, Mark Granovetter, Per Heum, Christopher Jencks, Mary Jo Neitz, Svend Otto Remøe, Arthur Stinchcombe, and Christopher Winship for helpful comments on an earlier draft.

[1] See Okun (1980) for a general discussion, and Somers and Tsuda (1966), Taira (1970), and Cole (1979) for discussions of how job security for some depends on insecurity for others in Japanese firms.

[2] See March and March (1978) for a discussion of the implications of sampling variation for career development.

[3] See Mostacci-Calzavara (1982) and Shack-Marquez and Berg (1982) for evidence on class, racial, and ethnic variations in income returns for finding jobs through contacts. It is interesting to note here that in the publishing industry where men and women both occupy important positions, women still get information about jobs from women and men from men (Caplette, 1982).

[4] The estimate for the United States is a guess based on information about electrical and electronic engineers. Among electrical and electronic engineers, 5.7% work in consulting (Institute of Electrical and Electronic Engineers, Inc., 1975:B-4). The employer list included 35 categories. Only three of these (electronic computing equipment, electric companies and systems, and the Federal Government) employed a higher proportion of electrical and electronic engineers than were employed in consulting. Among students graduating with a B.A. in engineering, about 35% are electrical and electronic engineers (Engineering Management Commission of Engineers Joint Council, 1977:16). I have no reason to believe that electrical and electronic engineers are any more or less likely to be employed as consultants than other engineers. The estimate for Norway comes from Holm (1980:55).

[5] According to Holm (1980:60), engineers in the oil sector receive more career rewards for experience than engineers in any other industry.

[6] Charlton (1983) suggests that personal secretaries and their bosses have joint tasks – "our work" – but that the boss gets to claim credit for the pair's accomplishments.

7 Among clerical workers one finds both an internalization of expectations about achievement (so that clerical workers will say that they are getting "good experience") and small signs of dissatisfaction with those expectations (one clerical worker reported that she had "more experience than qualifications" and many others reported dissatisfaction with what the career development and career advice programs really offered them). We should be careful to notice both sides of this ambivalence rather than taking reports of satisfaction at face value. Blauner (1964) found similar evidence of acceptance of the work role among female textile workers; they did not even complain about stretch outs.

8 This failure to collect information should create some problems for the organization as well as for the secretary. Without this information about clerical workers' experience and abilities, it should be difficult to arrange a "good fit" between a secretary and boss. But if a secretary's job is to "fit" any boss, the flexibility required of her may solve the organization's problem.

9 According to Holm (1980:43), 35% of Norwegian firms report using career development opportunities as an inducement in recruiting engineering personnel. An important issue in the literature on human capital is who should pay for investments in general human capital (Becker, 1975:16-37 discusses investments in general vs. firm-specific capital). Economists generally argue that individuals themselves will pay to learn skills that can be used outside the firm. Most of the skills that engineers are learning are usable outside the firm, at the very least in the other companies involved in offshore oil. In this case, it seems that employers offer to pay for the investment but then adopt interorganizational policies to make it costly for an employee to use the investment elsewhere.

10 My point here is similar to that made by Davis and Moore (1945) about rewards being allocated on the basis of functional importance except that I am adding two further conditions: (1) that a category of employees be important to an organization's competition with other organizations, and (2) that there be other employment opportunities for the employees in the category.

CHAPTER 6

DELAYS IN GOVERNMENT APPROVALS IN NORWEGIAN OFFSHORE DEVELOPMENT

Arthur L. Stinchcombe

The Regulatory Task in Norwegian Oil Exploitation

The oil and gas on the Norwegian continental shelf belongs to the Norwegian state, and because Norway is democratic, to the Norwegian people. The job of regulating oil exploitation is therefore not one of putting limits on others' exploitation of "their own" resources, but rather one of *maximizing the return to the landowner*. Because the landowner is a democratic state, the maximization is not only maximization of money return but also imposing *the society's evaluation* of the various outcomes. The activity as a whole must be managed so as to satisfy many values, such as the safety of workers, employment creation, Norwegian control of the economic fate of the country as a whole, long run conservation of resources, protection of fishing and marine life, as well as returning profits to the state. (For a list of the objectives of Norwegian concessions policy, see *Stortingsmelding*, 1979-80:39-43, where the values above are all mentioned.)

To put it another way, the job of regulating the Norwegian oil industry is that of *wise administration of petroleum resources and activities*, rather than "regulation" as it is ordinarily conceived. The state should leave discretion about oil matters in private hands only if public purposes are better achieved by private decision. The liberties of the citizenry are not invaded if any given decision is taken by the government rather than by an oil company. All that is required by the rights of citizens is that, within reasonable limits, the government should not promise the oil companies one thing to get their consent or to induce investment, then deliver something else. We can only expect "honest commercial dealings" between partners with partly opposed interests in the bargaining between the private oil companies and the Norwegian state. If the government then takes all further oil activity for itself, rather than using oil companies, it is nothing more than the owner of an ore body or a forest deciding to exploit it himself.

But this means that the regulatory framework for the oil business is different from other sorts of regulation. A monograph on the legal status of exploitation permits (Arvid Frihagen, 1979) starts in the first paragraph by saying that a proposed law allowing the oil authorities "to set more detailed conditions on the various permits, sanctionings, and approvals given under the new law" merely legalizes the *de facto* discretion that they have previously used. While a particular permit or approval gives the rights specified therein to the concessionaire, the concessions' terms and conditions are not fixed by law. This is reflected in the fact that earlier concessions have quite different terms than the later ones. The terms are supposed to be used to achieve Norwegian political ends, not to recognize the rights of oil companies.

The procedure in all the organs of state control, the Royal Ministry of Oil and Energy, its subsidiary technical organ, the Oil Directorate, and the state-owned oil companies, Statoil and Hydro, is therefore more of the nature of decision-making than of administration of regulations. When a plan for field development is submitted, the question to be asked is, "Does this plan maximize long run money returns to the state (or maximize safety, or employment of Norwegians, or sales by Norwegian firms)?" rather than "Does this conform to the regulations?" In order to answer the maximization question, one has to ask what alternatives are possible, and to judge these in the light of landowner returns (or safety, employment, sales), rather than to consider only the project submitted for conformity to regulations. The problem of the government then is more similar to the procurement of a weapons system than to an ordinary regulatory "approval."

What the operating oil company has to do then is to convince the Ministry, the Oil Directorate, and Statoil (which is generally a co-owner) that a given plan is the best that can reasonably be achieved. There is some *a priori* presumption that the private operator or the private oil companies in the owner group will favor proposals which maximize returns to the oil companies rather than to the state, will skimp on safety whenever it is expensive (perhaps especially in Norway where the financial liability for occupational deaths and accidents is ridiculously low), and will hire the most experienced labor (most often not Norwegian) and buy goods and services from the lowest bidder, who might well not be Norwegian. (In *Stortingsmelding*, 1979-80, previously cited, the government simultaneously recommends that contracts be entered into on a purely business basis, and that Norwegian contractors win 75% of the bids. See p. 62, paragraph 4.4.2 for the 75% figure, and p. 46, paragraph 3.3.2, point e, for buying Norwegian goods as a criterion for giving concessions.) Since the partners' interests conflict, and it is the private partners that make the proposals while the state responds, suspicion that the proposals do not maximize the landowner's interest tends to govern the negotiations.

The government regulatory bodies (and Statoil, which has been a partner in all the fields since the first with a large enough participation so that it has effective veto power) have two main responses to this situation. One is to insist on being in on all meetings of the owner group or of the operator project team from the earliest stages, seeing all the data and the interpretations made from them, and getting a chance to comment on all preliminary plans. This enables them to participate in decisions, rather than to approve or disapprove of the companies' decisions, though it is of course the power of disapproval that gives the state bargaining leverage in these early meetings. The other is to require the operator to develop alternative plans, then (if it can) to convince the Ministry and the Directorate that the plan chosen is the right one. The requirements for documentation are then similar to what the requirements are supposed to be for the Environmental Protection Agency in the U.S., developing the "next best" alternative and comparing the consequences of the chosen plan with the next best alternative. What makes this documentation requirement burdensome then is not the quantities of documents which interpret X rays of each weld (which the building contractor has to submit to the operator), but rather that the operating company can fully expect that the document it submits may well be used against its interests. The Ministry and the Directorate require the operating company to provide them with the administrative and engineering work required to challenge their own decisions.

Democracy by Delay

One of the main problems of a pluralistic democracy is to balance the mild interests of majorities against the intense interests of minorities. A good example in Norway is the hydro-electric development of the Alta river basin in Northern Norway, which will tend to disorganize the patterns of herd management for the Lapps' reindeer. The Lapps, or at least some of them, were strongly opposed to the development because it threatened their culture. The rest of the society were somewhat benefitted by an adequate supply of electricity without the pollution and danger from nuclear or fossil fuel electricity generation. It is perhaps characteristic of Norwegian politics that the government, although it had a parliamentary majority in favor of development, postponed the development for a year for further study of the question, and in particular for hearings and studies of the preservation of Lapp interests.

The project was approved again after the year's delay, by the same majority (the Labor Party, which constituted a minority government, together with the Right Party which has a classical liberal-capitalist ideology). To put it a bit contentiously, the Lapps by their intensity of interest got a year's delay instead of getting influence on the final outcome. A very similar delay even with a parliamentary majority was used in the decision to do exploratory drilling North of 62° Latitude. The fishermen of Northern Norway were strongly opposed to the drilling start, and it was passed by the same coalition of the Labor Party and the Right Party.

A second main problem of democracy is starting projects which have their own dynamics, which then commit the polity to a policy which, at some time in the future, they might not choose. An American example is that a free market in energy sources made the U.S. dependent on the petroleum exporting countries, which people might not have chosen if they had known that cheap energy meant dependence. An example in Norway is the policy of giving concessions for the exploration for oil. The first such concessions were given without explicitly giving the Norwegian government the right to delay field development, so if anything was found one had to expect that it would be developed immediately. This meant that Norwegian society was committed to whatever level of development was implied by the finds of reservoirs, rather than some level chosen by themselves.

One strategy for controlling the consequences of such projects with their own dynamics is to delay the start. For example, the concessions for exploration were explicitly used as a means of controlling the size of petroleum development on the Norwegian shelf. In the white paper on petroleum policy cited previously (*Stortingsmelding*, 1979-80), it was urged that the right to delay development, written into the most recent concessions, be used instead of delay of exploration to control the amount of activity and amount of production. But members of the regulatory bodies who participated in writing the white paper acknowledge that the oil companies are willing to take up exploration concessions under the condition of potential delay of development "because they think maybe it won't be delayed after all." The general point is that whenever minorities are being given the right to organize an institution which will have its own dynamics and create its own pressures, delay in starting the institution is a means of majority control.

Delay can therefore be a means of recognizing the seriousness of opposition of minorities, or of recognizing long run interests of the majority that are undermined by giving a minority the right to start up an institution. But delays can furthermore be simply a time to figure out what the interests of the clumsier party in a bargain really are. An oil company has a relatively simple set of utilities, steady profits and low risks, and it is relatively clear who within the company has the right to decide what policy will maximize the utility. A country has a complex utility function with many objectives, and it is not clear who should decide it, and in particular it is not clear that some engineers or economists in the Ministry or the Directorate should choose policies to maximize the public good. Consequently the state tends to be a clumsy bargaining partner, not knowing what it wants nor who should decide what it wants. Consequently the state tends to be well served if basic policy choices are made with all due deliberation, while the oil companies' interests are served by decisive businesslike behavior in which fewer values are taken into account.

An example was the decision about marketing gas from the Frigg field, which is roughly half on the British side, half on the Norwegian side (it is managed by the French state oil company, ELF, which works through a Norwegian subsidiary). The British half was developed immediately, because British policy provides that all gas in the North Sea be landed in Britain and sold to the gas monopoly. The Norwegian policy is that gas should be landed in Norway *unless* it can be shown that it benefits Norway to land it elsewhere. So ELF had to consider all the possible markets for Norwegian Frigg gas (England, the continent, liquified and shipped to the U.S., Sweden after landing in Norway, a Norwegian petrochemical complex based on gas at Karmøy) before the Norwegian government would approve a plan. The Norwegian approval came about a year after the British one. The choice turned out to be to sell the Norwegian half of the gas also to Great Britain, but proposals are still being made to construct pipelines to alternative markets so that the monopoly position of the British buyer cannot be used against Norwegian interests. An oil company might have made this decision in a much smaller time had it been acting alone, because some of the alternatives were only viable if criteria other than profits were used in the evaluation. The delay then was simply a device to carry out a more complex evaluation job.

Besides acknowledging minorities, delaying the creation of uncontrollable institutions, and giving time for clumsy bargainers, delays can also have the function of preserving the right to change one's mind. For example, after meetings on a given problem in which the partners have come to an agreement, it is American practice to write up the agreement after the meeting and to send copies of what was understood to be the conclusion to all the parties. Then if the agreement has been misunderstood, it can be clarified, and if there is no objection it is understood that the interested party has the right to go ahead and plan on the basis of the written version. The Norwegian authorities object to this practice, and will not initial such memoranda or the plans based on such meetings. That is, they will not give piecemeal approval in written form, though they will comment on things they find unsatisfactory during the planning phase. It seems that their objection is that written approvals make the decision final, so if objections to that decision develop later, the documents stand in the way of the authorities changing their minds.

British regulatory practice in the oil industry has much the same effect as the American "memoranda of understanding," but by a different device. Authority to approve plans is delegated (with a few exceptions) by the British Ministry to a group of approved private certifying organizations (among them Det norske Veritas). These private organizations develop rules and standards for approving plans. But the crucial point for creating certainty on the part of the operator is that these organizations will initial partial plans as they are approved, and those initials can be appealed to by the operator if the certifying organization later changes its mind. Because the certifying organization can be replaced by another one, they are interested in giving their approvals in a way that facilitates the work of the operator.

In contrast to American and British practice, then, the Norwegian refusal to give an approval does not mean that the work cannot go ahead, but only that it may have to be undone and done over later. In a sense then these delayed approvals are not delays at all, but merely ways of redistributing risks and uncertainties. When the Norwegian Petroleum Directorate was new and inexperienced, it is easily understandable that they might want to say, in effect, "As far as we can see now, you can go ahead, but we may learn more later and then have objections." What makes the continuation of this policy more understandable, even though presumably the Petroleum Directorate has enough experience now, is that the authorities consider themselves to be policy makers administering a national resource, rather than facilitators of private activities. Like their partners the oil companies, they want to reserve the right to change their minds if necessary to maximize returns.

Perhaps the most dramatic case of changed opinion was the evaluation of the one-platform solution for the Statfjord B construction. When in Summer 1976 the oil companies were thinking of a two-platform solution, the Minister of Industry sent a stiff letter to Mobil, the operator, saying that "the recommendation of two platforms was not in agreement with the plans the Government and the *Storting* have dealt with, and furthermore in disagreement with the development plans the Ministry has approved. The Ministry urged the owner group to carry out the work as soon as possible in accordance with the development plans as approved" (Moe, et al., 1980:205. The (presumably English) letter is summarized in Norwegian and I have translated the summary back into English. The date of the letter is 21 June 1976). Less than six months later (11 Nov. 1976) the Norwegian Petroleum Directorate wrote a letter informing Mobil that: "The Norwegian Petroleum Directorate has therefore come to the conclusion that there ought to be built a separate residential platform connected to Statfjord B." (Moe, et al, 1980:206. The source translates the English letter, and I have translated back).

These two letters are not quite as contradictory as they sound, since the first was opposing a plan with two production platforms, each with residential quarters, while the second was proposing to separate the residential quarters from production, and was based on a safety regulation issued about three weeks after the first letter was sent. But there is clearly an embarrassment involved in having given written approval, including even a letter from the Minister, to a plan, and then changing your mind. It made good sense to learn about evaluating the total risks in the intervening period, and once this was learned it was clear that a fire or other production disaster could be a lot more damaging if it also endangered the living quarters. The final result was a platform with living quarters and production and drilling together, but with maximum separation of the functions and special isolating walls and structures.

To put it another way, the delays in a case like this really allow the government *to set the agenda* for decision. A parliament which does not control its own agenda is not a real parliament, but rather an advisory body for the King. Similarly, to force the Norwegian authorities to make a decision on safety questions when they were not ready to make it would take the decision out of their hands. Delays in approvals then can put the control of the agenda back in the hands of the approving authorities. An operating oil company may then decide (and may have to decide) to take the risk of going ahead before the relevant item comes up on the agenda. But this then does not delay construction, but merely increases the operator's risks.

When are Delays Seen as Delays?

A striking feature of our interviews on delays in approvals is that most of the people, both from the government and from the oil companies, did not see the time used in negotiating a solution as a delay. Even in the relatively clear case of a difference of a year between British and Norwegian authorities in approving a marketing plan for Frigg gas, both the authorities and the operator regarded the time as that necessary to get the decision made, not as a delay which could have been avoided. That is, decision time and decision work has to be adjusted to the decision task, and just as one would not call the construction of a platform delayed because one could build it on land in half the time, so also one does not call a complicated Norwegian marketing approval delayed just because a simpler British one can be done quicker.

But if one calculated the present value of the income and expenditure stream from a project, assuming a ten percent time discount rate, then *at the point of the discovery* the Norwegian half of the field was worth 10 percent less than the British half, due to the year delay in development. (As it turned out the Norwegians collected their share of the returns from the rapid British approval, because of the way the unitization agreement worked.)

The formal economic question is, then, whether the added

refinement of the decision by taking a year was worth 10 percent discount of the current value of the find. The question of administrative reform is one of whether a more rational, and particularly quicker, approval process would pay for itself if one compared the costs of the reform to what we seem to be losing from slow decisions, roughly 10 percent of the current value of all the Norwegian oil resources, which could be obtained if the rapid British system were introduced.

This formal economic reasoning is not used in the perception of approvals delays: the purpose of this section is to suggest why the time for decision making by the government is not seen as a delay, is not entered into the sensitivity analyses which show delays to be the most crucial factor in profitability after oil prices in the Moe rapport (Moe, et al, 1980:108-111), and otherwise not really analyzed by decision makers.

We will deal with the perception of delay under five headings: (1) *Delay as a Positive Utility*, as a means for controlling the pace of development, (2) *Rate of Return versus Present Value*, with the usual business practice of calculating rates of return on investments resulting in not calculating the costs of decision time, (3) *Legitimate Representation and Delay*, for the quantity of decision work is increased by taking account of more interests, which increases the time a decision is expected to take, which then is not seen as an unreasonable delay, (4) *Firm Schedules and Perception of Delay*, for schedules are set only late in the decision process, so there are no schedules to violate and hence no perceived delays at early stages, and (5) *Earlier Requests for Approvals*: signals to authorities that an approval will be required and requests can be submitted earlier, so that the approval comes when it is needed and no costs of delay are incurred.

(1) Delay as a Positive Utility: If the *Storting* deliberately delays exploration permits in order to even out development and to conserve resources into the next century, they must have, at some level of activity, a *positive utility* for delays. This means that the discount rate of 10 percent we used above in the present value analysis should be, in some cases, an *earnings* rate instead. A development approved next year rather than this year will not burden this year's Norwegian economy, which has been having an

unemployment rate of about 1 percent and has strong demand for skilled workers. And the extra year of oil production after the turn of the century when the reservoir is nearly drained may be more valuable to the government of that time than a year of earlier returns five years from now – gas and oil may be scarcer by that time, or the prices may be higher, or the Norwegian need for taxes and royalties may be greater.

There are two keys to the trouble with the usual methods of setting the discount rate for present value calculation: (a) from a social point of view the *expenditures* can have a positive utility as well as the *returns*, but only when there is unemployment or employment in less productive activities – that is, if jobs created soon must go to foreigners, because there are no Norwegians free and qualified to fill them, while jobs created later go to Norwegians, then later *expenditures* are better, even if this means the returns also come later, (b) the uses of money coming into the Norwegian state coffers now do not necessarily return the 10 percent rate they would if they came into the coffers of an oil company. While Kuwait or Saudi Arabia may invest abroad at 10 percent if they cannot invest the returns usefully at home, such a policy may not be politically possible in Norway. In Norway the extra early returns might well go into higher agricultural subsidies. So the discount rate that is sensible for a government (or for a society) may be considerably less than that used for private business purposes. Rather than alter the calculations, however, the government simply does not calculate the costs of delays, so there is little pressure to increase returns by pushing decisions through rapidly. (I should note, however, that when a strike of production workers threatens the *current* returns to the state of about 100 million Kr. per day, this easy attitude toward postponing returns does not exist.)

(2) Rate of Return versus Present Value: Most businessmen do not start to calculate whether an investment is worthwhile until they must borrow money (or take money out of profits) for expenditures. At that point the present value method of calculation gives the same results as the rate of return method. But a delay *before investment* has very different implications under the two methods. If time only starts to run when the investment is

made, as is typically the case with rate of return calculations, then no delays that occur before expenditures really count. Construction delays lower profitability, but decision delays before construction start do not. Since long delays in the approvals process come in the early negotiations about the division of the benefits, and in the early conceptual stages of the design, the only expenditures are for the time of a few top executives and high level engineers.

But if the practice of rate of return calculations encourages underevaluation of the costs of delays in decisions, such as those caused in the early stages by the approvals process in Norway, the crucial psychological fact is that one does not start calculating returns *or* present value until the decision is mostly made. Until one knows what one is going to build, one cannot calculate either costs or output. Consequently one has no estimate of what is being lost in a decision delay until that delay is over and one has decided what to build. By that time the number is of only historical interest.

An inspection of the cost figures in the Moe committee report (1980:*passim*) indicates that much of the increase in costs between the first estimate and the completed platform comes from deciding to build more complicated structures (or more structures) than were anticipated at the very beginning. This means that any calculation of the cost of decision delay would have been overestimated at an early stage, because, as it turned out, the projects were not nearly as profitable as the original sketch plans involved in the judgment of commerciality would imply.

Part of the reason they were not as profitable is that other objectives, such as increased safety or reservoir conservation, were taken into account in the decision process. This means that the decision process *was productive of other utilities*, which would not otherwise have been achieved. Thus the cost of the delay in present value of the income stream has to be balanced against the returns of the delay, namely a decision that is better for other objectives. Until those other utilities are incorporated into the plan, their value cannot be calculated. Since these other values are not usually assessed in money terms, it is hard to calculate their value in any case.

The general point here is that costs are only real to decision makers when they can be calculated. Both because of the rate of return method by which the value of projects is calculated (with the start at the time of expenditures) and because the costs and benefits of the decision delay can only be calculated once the decision is known, delays during early planning and negotiations are not seen as costly.

(3) Legitimate Representation and Delay: Suppose an oil company sends a contract for design engineering work to a Norwegian supplier, and it contains a clause that says the contractor will be liable for all losses that they cause. The supplier then might have to pay the full value of the platform in case they caused a serious accident, in some cases up to 10 billion Kroner. But even the oil company cannot insure for that much, let alone a small Norwegian firm. If the oil company then says, "If you want the business, sign the contract within a week," it is clearly coercive. Consulting insurance companies, drafting a new contract, and negotiating about the changes, will clearly take more than a week. We recognize in this case that refusing to delay prevents the contractor from representing his own interests.

The general situation of the Norwegian state and the oil companies is a bilateral veto, so that both parties have to agree before either one can act. That is, the relation is rather similar to the relations of a selected contractor and an oil company as described above. Since it takes more time to *change an offer by the other party* than to *accept* a "final" offer, any limitation on negotiating time is also a limitation on the right to represent one's own side in the negotiations. The purpose of many of the delays in approvals is exactly to change the offer by the oil company, rather than a failure to accept on time.

If an oil company recognizes the right of Norway to choose a market for its gas in order to maximize its own advantage (and perhaps an oil company like ELF, owned by the French government, may recognize such rights of states more easily), then if it takes a year to see to it that the interest is represented, this year is not seen as a delay. If on the other hand an oil company expects to make the profits from pipelines that transport the oil and gas from a field it has developed, and then the landing permit is delayed in order to gain a large interest in the pipeline for Statoil, it may be seen as a delay. The time may in fact be seen as a delay by both sides, because the state may not see that the oil company has any legitimate interest in monopolizing a profitable enterprise transporting oil and gas that belong to the Norwegian state, while the oil company may not see why profits created by its exploration and development activity should go to the state.

That is, decision delays caused by the failure of one of the parties to agree to the solution that is on the table may not be seen as delays when everyone believes they have a right to disagree, and when the delay is related to reasonable purposes that party is supposed to represent. Often parliaments use long time periods to create the bills they finally pass, for example in hearings in which interested people have a chance to testify, or in negotiations among parliamentary groups about the content of the law, and so on. The actual decision by voting then may take only a few minutes, *provided* the representation has been effectively carried out beforehand. Similarly the formal approval, comparable to the parliamentary vote, for the pipelines from Ekofisk only took a few days, while the negotiations on the division of ownership between the Phillips group and the Ministry took considerable time. Delays for representation of interests are needed to build a compromise. Since the decision work in building a compromise is being done continuously, if trying to reach a compromise is legitimate, then the time is not a delay.

(4) Firm Schedules and Perception of Delays: Just as one cannot spend money on a project until one has decided what to build, so one does not schedule activities in a project until one has decided what activities are needed to build it. But if at a very early planning stage one never expected to be done with the decision by June, then July is not a delay. Schedules are simultaneously plans and expectations. Until the expectations have been set up, until schedules have been drawn, one cannot fall short of them. But schedules get set up late in the decision process, so one does not have standards to judge delays before that time.

An exception which illustrates the generalization arose in the case of the approval of the Statfjord B platform design, which is also one of the few approval delays that have been explicitly identified by the oil company as delays (Medley, 1979). The expectation of the schedule for approval was set because Mobil proposed a design that had, in all essentials, been approved for the Statfjord A platform. Thus Mobil saw the negotiations as being all completed except for the final approval, and had set up a schedule of engineering work and construction with that in mind. Since the schedule existed, the time lapse was seen as a delay.

(5) Earlier Requests for Approvals: If an oil company knows that negotiating a conceptual design approval in Norway takes a year (I suppose this is about the average for recent cases), then one can start talking about design with the authorities already when the decision on whether the field is commercial is being made. Commerciality depends on what design is required, and in the Norwegian situation this decision depends on negotiation with the Norwegian Petroleum Directorate and the Ministry. So consultation with the government improves the decision on commerciality from the oil company's point of view, and also starts the process of getting approval for the general design of the structures for the field. In some such cases then it does not cost anything, and may even have advantages, to signal to the government that an approval will be needed up to a year before the point the signal would be given in Britain. This is obviously especially true when there are inherent delays in the information collecting phase of the design process.

For example, the Ekofisk field was found in a kind of rock which holds a lot of petroleum (high porosity) but which is usually hard to exploit because oil and gas do not travel long distances through the rock easily (low permeability). Some of the oil companies in the owner group thought the field would not be commercial, because very expensive wells would only drain small areas of reservoir rock, because the oil and gas could not travel long distances to the well. The way Phillips, the operator, advocated testing this was to produce a few exploratory wells at a high rate. If the rock had low permeability, then these wells would soon give out, and one would know that the reservoir was not commercial. If they did not give out even at a high rate of production, then that must mean the permeability was high enough to make the field commercial. This however required some considerable time in the information collecting activity of exploiting the exploratory wells.

But then the design of the field installation could be negotiated with the government as more and more information came in. Even though the authorities were very inexperienced, since Ekofisk was the first field, the negotiations on design never really delayed construction.

In contrast the Danish authorities had not been in on the design phase of the Ekofisk pipeline to Emden, so there was an approval delay until, finally, it was agreed to cover the portion of the pipe that runs through the Danish sector. Because there was no normally expectable information collecting or construction which occupied the time after the approval was applied for in Denmark, there were true costs to the delay and the delay was psychologically real.

Overall, then, most of the intervals of time used to negotiate approval with the Norwegian government are not seen as delays. The government does not press decisions through rapidly, partly because the *Storting* wants delays to even out the work. The costs of delays are not calculated because they come before any big investments are made. The parties whose interests are represented during the long negotiations are seen as legitimate participants in the decisions, so the time they use is seen as necessary. There is no schedule for the decision at the early stages, so executives cannot be late because no one has told them when to be finished. And delays in approvals do not delay construction if they are applied for far in advance.

Approval as a Political Process

The Royal Norwegian Ministry of Petroleum and Energy and the Norwegian Petroleum Directorate have had to make up regulations corresponding to multiple poorly defined goals, while state competence was growing and the policy of state intervention was gaining ground. They have preserved their freedom to make up or change regulations by refusing to say specifically what is acceptable, and refusing to initial what they have orally agreed to. But this creative stance toward regulation has meant that they had to make up their minds for each decision about what the regulation should be.

Each decision is then legislation, rather than application of the law. This legislation is different from that in the *Storting* primarily because there is no clear way to defeat minorities. If there are clear laws and regulations, then it is easy to satisfy the "rule of the bureaucrat's decision": "Never do anything against which a well-founded criticism can be leveled." When there are no regulations, the rule of the bureaucrat's decision is in effect a rule of unanimity within the Ministry or the Directorate. In a parliament, the members expect to be criticized, and the final majority vote makes it legitimate henceforth to ignore minority criticisms. But if in an administrative organization there is no way to defeat a minority, then the bureaucrat is exposed to the criticism of the minority until the minority is satisfied. And this leads to what is in effect a unanimity rule among people recognized as sources of legitimate criticism, including at least all high officials of the Ministry or the Directorate itself.

The procedure in the Norwegian Petroleum Directorate reflects this effective unanimity rule. For each major project requiring a series of reviews there will exist a committee of representatives from the various relevant subsections of the Petroleum Directorate. One of the members of this committee will be appointed as coordinator of communications with the operator. The membership of the committee is rather informally defined, and may shift from time to time. The chair also shifts, especially as the project moves through the stages of exploratory drilling and evaluation, marine installations design and construction, drilling of production wells, and production. The subsections in the Norwegian Petroleum Directorate more or less correspond to these stages of field development. The reason all subsections have to be represented at all major decision points, and hence on the committees throughout the project, is that stages are interdependent, and a given construction decision, for example, limits the possible well drilling plans and thus the possible exploitation plans for the reservoir. But at any one time the chair or coordinator of the committee is likely to be in the subsection which corresponds to the stage of development of the work.

The coordinator then first of all manages the paper flow and the scheduling of meetings. He first refers a proposal from the operating oil company to the representatives of the various sections. These representatives (making use, if necessary, of other people in their section) then make comments on the plans, which only circulate within the Directorate. On some points they may also consult the Ministry or authorities in other jurisdictions. Discussions continue, and at some point a letter of reply is drafted. This is also circulated for comments, and a meeting of the committee, perhaps with the addition of the chiefs of the subsections, may take place before the final decision. There is however no formal way to bring the proceedings to an end. The committee members do not have a vote, there is no organ which formally takes the decision by formally incorporating their opinions, there is no formal schedule for deciding. When the head of the Norwegian Petroleum Directorate and the coordinator for the project sign the letter of reply to the operating oil company, we know that the decision has been made. Up to that time one keeps discussing until people manage to come to an agreement.

When the Directorate develops new regulations, a similar "formally endless" process happens. For example, in the development of guidelines for risk analysis by the operating oil company of the preliminary platform conceptual design, the Directorate's publication of the preliminary guidelines took place about 18 months after the beginning of the development process. What set the process going was dissatisfaction among some of the people involved in the negotiations about the safety features of the design of the Statfjord B platform. They believed that the Directorate had not known what they wanted, so they and Mobil had talked past each other during the negotiations. Two or three people informally kicked the idea around, wrote notes to each other about what was needed in the way of risk analysis at the early stage of planning a platform, and started discussions. Obviously a complete risk analysis could only be done after the design had been worked out, by which time the engineering design money would have been spent and would be practically speaking too late to change the main features. Some of these notes were circulated to others in the Directorate.

A working group was set up having two people from the Directorate and one from Det norske Veritas. The working group also had an advisory committee which included an academic technical person, a director of an institute for technical and applied scientific research, and a specialist in explosions and fires. The working group surveyed what was done in industries with comparable problems, including nuclear power plants, liquified natural gas plants, chemical plants, and the like. This was summarized in a confidential document for discussion within the Directorate. They then drafted a confidential document on the strategy they might follow and the philosophy of risk management behind it.

The next stage was to draft a document for public commentary, on what they thought such a set of guidelines ought to contain, and why. In that document they also suggested some numbers that might go into such a guideline. For example, they suggested that the design analysis should analyze what happens to the main bearing structure, the getaway paths, and the shelters and evacuation areas, in all major accidents which have an expected frequency greater than once every 10,000 years of platform life. This is grounded philosophically in the idea that the disaster risk level should be set at one death per 100 million person years of work on the platform, in order to keep the overall risk level, including ordinary industrial accidents as well as disasters, under ten deaths per 100 million person-working-years. By some approximations in the intermediate calculations, such as maximum disaster death rates, this requires that all accidents with a probability of occurrence more than once every 10,000 years have to be kept from being disasters by the design of the platform. Hence the Directorate ought to require the designers to show that most of the people on the platform will be safe in all accidents more frequent than this. (Incidentally, this seems to me a very intelligent way to approach the problem.)

A number of other numerical criteria were proposed for acceptance criteria, such as that in any "design accident" (one that is frequent enough so that one has to design so that it will not be a disaster) the getaway paths should be usable for an hour after the start of the accident, and that housing, shelter areas, and evacuation areas had to be shown to be safe for four hours.

This preliminary document was then sent out for commentary to all operators in Norway, was presented by a Norwegian delegation to the safety and design people in the home offices of the operating companies in the U.S. and France, and was sent to companies who had explicitly faced the problem themselves, such as the ICI chemical company.

The commentary on the document was summarized in another confidential document circulated in the Directorate. This was used, along with responses to it from within the Directorate, in drafting the preliminary guidelines which were published.

The next stage is to follow the usual procedure for all new regulations, by calling the interested parties (around 50 or so) for hearings on the proposal, consideration within the Directorate of the comments so elicited, and a decision within the Directorate which will have three possible outcomes: (a) revise and issue as guidelines, (b) do more work, revise, and circulate for comments again, or (c) scrap and start all over.

This is a description of a particularly difficult regulatory task which had not been accomplished effectively elsewhere in the world, and a particularly creative solution. The adoption of regulations on the size of furnishings of quarters by taking over almost wholesale the regulations for merchant ships from another part of the government must have been much simpler (though very costly for companies that had built quarters to U.S. standard). The pattern of multiple rounds to get comments from other bureaucrats before risking reaction from outside is probably typical of all government bureaucracies.

The potentially endless repetition of cycles of comment, revise, is characteristic of procedure under unanimity rules. The fact that it comes to a tentative close in Norway after only 18 months is probably related to the fact that the Norwegian Petroleum Directorate had about 250 total employees at the time, including typists and engineers fresh out of engineering school. The small number of relevant critics within the Directorate probably makes unanimity procedures work better.

It is usual in such unanimity structures that informal norms put pressure on the last objector to be quiet after a while, and people who are *always* difficult to get consent from get informally shunted aside, accidentally left off committees, promoted to a staff position whose consent is not required, given a research task on an innocuous subject, or otherwise dealt with. We did not have any chance to investigate these informal equivalents of voting someone down.

If the Norwegian Petroleum Directorate had set up specific regulations in every area, so that any official in the Directorate could say what the Directorate thought, then such internal politics on regulatory policy would not take place between the application and the approval for a particular project. But since the regulation is, in important cases, really legislation, we have to ask for each decision what the policy making procedure actually used looks like. The procedure used in important matters in Norwegian oil regulation might better be described as "crystalization of a decision" than "decision making." The crystalization involves adding on each layer of molecules from the various commentaries until the structure of the decision is complete. Such crystalization goes faster when a general consensus building process has previously taken place, as for example in the development of the risk analysis guidelines. But at any rate the announced general policy that a reply should go out to the operating oil company within four weeks (or one operator's summary of its experience that they usually had a reply in three weeks) does not mean that the negotiations for an approved plan usually take three weeks. It merely means that the Norwegian Petroleum Directorate has a political system which can produce a tentative legislation as a basis for the next round of negotiations in about three or four weeks. Compared with other legislatures, of course, this is not a bad performance record at all.

Disputes about Delays

The general Norwegian regulatory position is that simultaneous drilling and production, or simultaneous construction and drilling, are only permitted when it can be shown that they do not produce an unacceptable level of danger. The permits for simultaneous operations have great importance for the profitability of a platform in its early years.

For example, the Statfjord A platform has two legs that can be used for drilling operations, which will in the long run also therefore have well heads through which production of oil and gas is carried out. A drilling program with 42 wells, 21 in each leg, will take several years to complete. If one must use each leg only for one function at a time, so that one produces the wells only in the first leg while drilling another well in the second, and then switches, this will double the time needed to drill all 42 wells because only one leg is used for drilling. During the time of the drilling there will be only half of the wells already drilled in production, so the production is only half. Since during this time (in 1980) the interest on the value of the whole platform, roughly a yearly cost of a billion crowns, or 200 million dollars, has to be paid out and one gets in return only half of the total drilling capacity and half of the total production, the profitability of the platform is drastically reduced for this period. But this pressure for simultaneous drilling and production runs up against safety problems.

After the construction is complete, the main uncertainty on the platform is in drilling operations. One reason is that until the layers of rock underground are well mapped (i.e. until after several wells have been drilled) there are substantial risks of unexpectedly hitting high pressure pockets of gas, with nothing but drilling mud holding the gas down in the well. Another main reason is that many tons of drill train, casings, and the like, have to be lifted in and out of the hole and to be uncoupled and recoupled, and even a well trained crew that is familiar with the equipment sometimes has accidents in so many repeated lifts, uncouplings, and couplings. A third reason applies specifically to drilling from platforms, that the drill holes are near to each other near the top (they are normally far apart on land), so that one can drill into another drill hole which has high pressure gas and oil coming up through it. The danger from tricks of nature underground, high pressure pockets, decreases as one knows the field better with more wells, and danger from human error on the drilling floor decreases with more experience and with those small improvements in equipment and procedure that skilled workers introduce over time, so that drilling becomes safer over time on a given platform or in a given field.

But what these two arguments taken together mean is that the longer one delays approval of simultaneous drilling and production, the longer the platform functions at half productivity, but also the safer the operation can be when it is started. The time point at which simultaneous drilling and production is approved, then, is the point at which one says implicitly that the added safety available from further delays is not worth the cost of having the platform work at half capacity. While neither Mobil in applying for permission for simultaneous drilling and production in both legs, nor the Norwegian Petroleum Directorate in giving approval, are able to calculate specifically what this tradeoff between safety and profitability is, and they do not argue that "a human life is only worth X crowns," the delay of approval while more information comes in is a decision about that tradeoff, and the approval at a given point in times fixes the tradeoff.

Similarly if one starts drilling while there are still hundreds of construction workers on the platform, a blowout during drilling would endanger more people than it would if delayed. During the construction phase Norway has tolerated a death rate of over one per 1,000 person-years of work (Norges Teknisk-Naturvitenskapelige Forskingråd, 1980:93), while the tentative standards of the Directorate for the drilling and production period are that they cannot tolerate more than one death per 10 million person-years of work (Norwegian Petroleum Directorate, 1979:15). But it is clear that the already dangerous work of construction is rendered even more dangerous by drilling while construction is still going on. Further these first wells are the most dangerous, for the reasons specified above. Construction usually winds down gradually, so that the time point for approval of the drilling start is also implicitly a tradeoff between safety and risk to more construction workers and profitability.

More generally, whenever a real cost of some kind, such as risk level to human life, is a declining function of the time delayed before an approval is given, and profitability is also a declining function of the time delay, then the choice of the time point of approval is necessarily a choice of the money price one puts on the real cost, in this case the money price of increased safety. Perhaps naturally the safety authorities take a different view of what this money price should be than do the oil companies, though of course neither can formulate their disagreement in these terms and survive in a humane political system like Norway's. A Danish minister of health and welfare got into serious trouble in the media for suggesting such a calculation for expensive life-main-tenance in hospitals, and she is not an international capitalist oil company.

In these cases the authorities may choose deliberately to cause a delay because that delay itself is a choice of a resolution of the different interests of the oil company and the state. That is, a dispute about the price of safety can, in such a case, get translated into a dispute about how long to delay, at least partly because it is politically impossible to conduct a dispute on the real question openly.

A second way in which disputes about other things can become disputes about delays comes from reversing the reasoning we outlined above about representation of interests. If the government wants to coerce information out of an oil company for their own purposes (e.g., they want geological information so that they can evaluate their own seismic studies in nearby areas which they hope to exploit with Statoil ownership), or if they want a half interest in a pipeline, the authorities can simply refuse to issue a landing permit for the oil and gas until the information or the half interest in the pipeline is forthcoming. Our point above was that representation of interests could be seen as legitimate, and hence not be seen as a delay. But representing interests that the oil companies do not see as legitimate can also often be done effectively by delays – delays in this case are seen as coercion. Delay as a method of coercion then resolves disputes about how much information the government gets or about how much interest in the pipeline it gets, but the dispute about how long the delay should be is a part of the dispute about those other questions.

Conclusions

Because approvals by the Norwegian oil authorities are really policy making rather than application of regulations, the analysis of administrative delays is really the analysis of delays in policy making. It is the agility of the joint decision making mechanisms built up on the interface between oil companies and the Norwegian state that we have had to analyze, rather than "red tape." Political systems are rarely evaluated for speediness, for productivity of decisions per person-hour, for fitting the complexity of decision work to the complexity of the problem. We have had to move uncertainly and cautiously in this analysis, because available organizational theory does not tell us very much about the time used for several parties to come to an agreement, and such negotiations are the real substance of Norwegian oil regulation.

The first question we asked was what functions the delays might have in a democratic political system. The government in Norway has used delays to acknowledge the seriousness of minority opposition to development and oil projects. They have also delayed opening up areas for exploratory drilling, and have written into exploration permits the government right to delay field development, to keep within the capacity of the Norwegian economy. They delayed longer than the British in making a marketing decision for their gas because they wanted more study of alternatives and wanted the alternatives evaluated by more criteria than the British did. Being clumsier in bargaining because of their complex interests, delay enabled them to bargain more effectively. The authorities use delays in putting approvals in writing in order to preserve the right to change their minds. Thus delays often serve political purposes and result in policies more favorable to the government. These positive functions of delays may help explain their existence.

Then we explored five reasons why delays may not be considered delays, why lack of consciousness of the costs of the delay may help explain why the delays are there. These were that governments for whom delays have positive functions may simply not try very hard to reduce them, may not think about ways to move more speedily, that people may not start to calculate the costs of delays until they are paying interest on an investment, that people regard the time necessary to modify a decision so it will be acceptable to a legitimate party to the negotiations as necessary decision making time, that schedules are not developed until late in a decision making process so time used when there is no schedule is not seen as a delay, and that people adapt to potential delays by requesting an approval sooner. Thus there are good reasons that the functions sometimes served by delays should remain latent.

Because the regulatory authorities in Norway are fitting decisions to a complex reality which is different in each oil field, they are really making legislation rather than applying regulations. Hence we can ask how long the legislative process takes. The formal procedure in the Norwegian Petroleum Directorate is to keep discussing until an agreement emerges between the various officials in the Directorate, and to keep negotiating with the oil companies until an agreement emerges between the authorities and the companies. The development of efficient structures with committees and coordinators for each major decision, and the long term discussion to come to a general understanding in the Directorate on such general questions as the approach to risk analysis, increases the agility of the Directorate for making policy quickly. But quick policy making is still not nearly as fast as "a prompt and speedy trial" might be in cases where one is merely applying regulations.

Finally we have pointed to some cases where the choice of an amount of delay is a resolution of another conflict of interest between the government and the oil companies. Safety of simultaneous activities generally increases with longer delays in approval of these activities, but at a decreasing rate, while longer delays lower productivity. So the choice of a delay is a choice of how much power to use to coerce desirable behavior in minimizing accidents, in giving information, or in dividing returns.

Because delays in approvals in the early stages of field development are costly, it is wise to analyze the causes of these delays to see if they can be reduced. But the main finding of this paper is that delays in approvals in the oil business in Norway are often necessary time for making rational decisions. One should not sacrifice too much rationality of public policy in order to hurry things along.

CHAPTER 7

THREE ORIGINS OF RED TAPE

Arthur L. Stinchcombe

In a study of administrative causes of delays in construction projects in Norway (Stinchcombe, 1979), I noticed that in the schedule ("network diagrams") for the projects much time was allocated to getting government approvals or to approving bid documents, to evaluating bids and letting contracts, and that contractors complained about the amounts of documentation and time required for these approvals. (On the planned delays for approvals, see Bent, 1979; on actual delays see Moe et al., 1980: pp. 108-11, 205-206, and Medley, 1979; on documentation Usterud, 1976, and Tovshus, 1976.) The literature on "red tape" in the United States and elsewhere suggests that delays in getting administrative decisions are seen as a problem in a wide variety of administrative settings (Gouldner, 1952; Sharp, 1952), and that a relatively simple reconsideration of procedures can cut governmental reporting requirements for approvals in half, and also cut the documentation the applicant has to submit about in half (Gregg and Diegelman, 1979).

Some recent work by Barry Schwartz on the causes of waiting in queues bears directly on the question of what theory we might use to account for delays (Schwartz, 1975, 1978a, 1978b; see also Zeruvabel, 1976). But much of the theory is generalizable only with difficulty to deal with such things as a year-long delay in approving a design for an oil platform because the Ministry did not think it was safe enough (Moe et al., 1980:205-206). The literature on work flow in industrial organizations sometimes has very illuminating analogies to what one imagines might produce work flow problems in making administrative decisions (Huge, 1979). But people do not stand in lines before various bureaucratic stations with the same patience that partially finished parts in a machine shop do, and yet delays of a year or more are more common in disputes about environmental impact of a project than they are in passing through a sequence of stations to register for classes in a university. In a previous study about a long delayed driver's license in Venezuela I have commented on the structural factors that determined the Latin American experience "that all branches of the government, characterized by long hierarchies and rule-bound behavior, do not give a damn whether they do their jobs or not" (Stinchcombe, 1974:11). But this account had nothing to do with standing in a series of queues, nor with disagreements about policy, but rather with people starting work late and quitting early. Delays in the court system in the United States are often apparently due to short working days and long vacations of judges.

These difficulties in generalization suggested that there were several distinct phenomena going on, several distinct ways in which red tape arises. This essay proposes that there are three main distinct ways in which red tape originates: (1) multiple queues, (2) bureaucratic rewards incongruent with bureaucratic purpose, and (3) policy uncertainty.

Multiple queues are problems with the work flow that originate whenever a system involving sequential processing of a case at several bureaucratic stations develops queues before each station (on sequential processing in general, see Thompson, 1967:54-65). The more routine the administrative process, the more likely it is that most red tape will be due to work flow problems. A relatively pure case happens in the sequence of stations they used to have to give physical examinations for draftees, in which a busload of potential draftees would come in together, and if one's name began with "S" one tended to stand in line at each step of the physical in a queue which had almost everyone else on the bus in it. That is, the queue was not only at the first station, but a backlog of unfinished work accumulated before each station and delayed the draftee many times over. When the busload was finished, all queues would be completely empty until the next busload came in, at which time people would wait again in the queue before each station. If one person did the whole examination, as is usual in private practice, one might stand in only one queue (physicians also typically keep one waiting again after one is undressed, but this is not really necessary).

By bureaucratic rewards incongruent with bureaucratic purpose, I mean that the bureaucrat does not pay any cost for lengthening the regulation manual, nor for requiring more information than he or she can ever use, nor for taking his or her time in processing an application. Non-competitive service rendering organizations, such as clinics operated by public authorities, do not lose clients by requiring them to wait a long time – there is no other place to get a driver's license or to get free medical care (see Schwartz, 1975:24-30). If a bureaucrat instead gets rewarded for mending political fences, and if the fences are in Caracas while the license issuing office is in the East of Venezuela, the Traffic Inspector is likely to be in Caracas rather than issuing driver's licenses. The trick of bureaucratic motivation is to make the rewards of the bureaucrat an increasing function of how well he or she does the job, in the cases at hand issuing licenses or treating public patients. Clearly much red tape has its origin in the fact that bureaucrats, unlike salesmen, are not paid commissions if they manage to satisfy a customer. After the sale is firm, for example in deliveries, the commercial worker, like the bureaucrat, gets no rewards for satisfying the customer, so we all wait for deliveries as for bureaucrats.

Finally policy uncertainty causes delays because making a policy decision takes time and attention, while following a routine does not. All of us have at some time decided to accept an unsatisfactory outcome of a bureaucratic process when the functionary tells us that if we appeal, that is if we insist on having policy made for our case in particular, we will not get the approval for at least three months. Many environmental organizations hope to impose nearly infinite delays on projects they do not like, by finding one after another thing wrong with the environmental impact statement. This is an example of a general phenomenon, that the capacity not to agree until one is satisfied is a source of bargaining power, or more simply of power. When several parties to a controversial decision have some degree of power to delay a decision, uncertainty about what the policy is causes delays.

A fine case is the extra year it took the Norwegians the approve development plans for the Frigg gas field (which lies partly in the Norwegian sector and partly in the British sector of the North Sea) after the British approval was given and construction had started on the British side. The reason for the difference was that the British marketing policy was clearly articulated beforehand: all gas found on the British shelf was to be landed in Britain and sold to the gas monopoly. The Norwegian law required that whatever marketing strategy was adopted be shown to be in the Norwegian best interest against all reasonable alternatives. It took a year for ELF Acquitaine, the oil company operating the field, to show that it was in the Norwegian best interest to sell the gas to the British gas monopoly.

Since, as we will argue, red tape is heterogeneously caused by at least three distinct classes of causes, the remedy has to be shaped to the cause. Shaping the work flow so that there are smaller backlogs at each station, or treating the whole of a given case at a single station, are the appropriate remedies for delays caused by sequential queues. Shaping the reward system of bureaucrats, so they are punished for creating troubles for their clients and rewarded for civil and expeditious treatment, is the remedy for red tape caused by bureaucratic rewards incongruent with bureaucratic purpose. And creating more agile negotiating and decision-making apparatus, or deciding on policy in advance, are remedies appropriate for delay caused by policy uncertainty.

Clarifying policy will not speed the sorting of the mails at the nodes of the mail system at Christmastime, nor will it get the Traffic Inspector of San Felix in Venezuela back on the job. Making rewards depend on speed of decision in cases of true policy disagreement creates an administration unresponsive to policy goals, and resolves policy disputes without debate. The main type of reward for speed in overqueued work flows is the bribe to see that one's own case gets special treatment, but this tends to disorganize the system as a whole so that everybody gets worse treatment – bribing the mailman in order to get one's money order found and delivered may get service, but does not solve the problem of delay in the French mail system (Sharp, 1952:408-409). Rationalizing the work flow presupposes that the people at each station care whether the clients stand in queue before them for too long a time. Heterogeneous ailments require heterogeneous treatments.

In the following sections I will elaborate the distinctiveness of the origins of the three kinds of red tape. I will argue that the subordinate causes of multiple queues red tape are the causes, respectively, of breaking up the processing of a case into separate stages, of arranging those stages in series, thus creating several queues, and of not controlling the backlog at each stage. The subordinate causes of bureaucratic rewards incongruent with bureaucratic purpose are causes of the rigidity of civil service reward systems, and the causes of inadequate measurement and feedback of client inconvenience. The subordinate causes of red tape due to policy uncertainty are the causes of conflicts over tradeoffs between objectives which have to be worked out in a lot of detailed situations, and the causes of shifts over time in the policy the government wants to apply to the cases.

How Many Queues Do You Stand In?

Consider the average queue at the checkout stand in a super-market. There are perhaps on the average of three people in front of one on a weekday, five on Saturday, and each of them takes an average of actual checking out of four minutes on weekdays, seven minutes on Saturday. So one waits in the queue an average of 12 minutes on a weekday and an average of 35 minutes on a Saturday, and then spends four and seven minutes respectively being checked out. The general point is that one spends three or five times as long in the queue as in being served.

Now suppose to save one minute of checkout time, the store divides up the checkout work into three parts, groceries, produce, and meats, for example. Then in a non-computerized checkout system, the checkers can memorize a larger share of the prices, and so check faster. On weekdays one stands in a line of nine people (three checkers' queues under the old system), each of whom takes a minute for groceries, so one waits nine minutes. But what happens next depends on whether one goes directly to produce and then to meat with no delay. In that case the customer saves three minutes waiting time and one minute checking time due to increased efficiency. Similarly on Saturday the customer saves five minutes waiting and one minute checking.

But obviously what is more likely is that one will *enter a new queue* for the produce, then *still another queue* for the meat. We might even suppose that these queues will be just as long as the first queue, nine people on weekdays. In such a case the customer will wait for 9x3 or 27 minutes on weekdays, save a minute on checkout, and be out in 30 minutes instead of 16. On Saturday such a multiplication of queues might cause the customer to wait for as much as 90 minutes in the three queues, save a minute on checkout, so he or she is out in 96 minutes rather than 42.

The reason a supermarket would not do this is that, when faced with a prospect of doubling their shopping time, customers would choose another supermarket. But note that, provided the store has floor space for all the queues, the supermarket saves wages by making the customers wait longer. Just as manufacturing plants have "work-in-progress" inventories which spend most of their time as "backlog" for each machine rather than being worked on, so our supermarket with division of checkout labor is simply putting more *people* into the work-in-progress inventory (on sequential queues of goods in manufacturing causing delays, see Huge, 1979). But as our analysis showed, it is only because *each work station* has its queue or backlog of work that the delay is multiplied. If the divided labor is locked into sequence with no gaps, then the time in the queue does not increase, for the three checkers function as one very fast checker.

This then brings up the question of the minimum time in the queue at each station, the minimum backlog of work needed to keep a work station busy. Here we can take a clue about where to start from the simple situation faced in industrial management with *strictly sequential* jobs on two machines. Huge gives the following table as an example of the time an assembly spent in backlog for a given work station, then time spent on assembly.

Table 7.1: Variations in Queue for an Assembly (in days)

Shop Order	Time in Production Queue time	Hands-on-time	Total
No. 1	22.5	2.5	25
No. 2	18.6	2.4	21
No. 3	20.7	2.3	23
No. 4	17.4	2.6	20
No. 5	24.7	2.3	27
Average	20.8	2.4	23.2

(Huge, 1979, p. 123)

What this table shows is that the previous work station was outputting the semi-finished assemblies an average of 20.8 days ahead of the time they went into "hands-on" assembly. Huge points out that if one took the shortest delay time, 17.4 days, and simply subtracted off 17 days work-in-process inventory from the backlog by running the two work stations in *somewhat* closer coordination, then this assembly process would never be delayed by lack of backlog.

Table 7.2: Consequences of Scheduling Work Stations More Closely
(subtract 17 days backlog)

Shop Order	Time in Production Queue time	Hands-on-time	Total
No. 1	5.5	2.5	8
No. 2	1.6	2.4	3
No. 3	3.7	2.3	6
No. 4	.4	2.6	3
No. 5	7.7	2.3	10
Average	3.8	2.4	6.2

(Computed here)

To be a bit more cautious, Huge recommends scheduling the production of the semi-finished parts for this machine or assembly station so that one *expected* to have an inventory of 7.7 days of work, so as to make sure that one would not calculate wrong when the previous work station was delayed on shop orders numbers 2 and 4. This would bring the average time in queue up to about 7.7 days, then adding 2.4 for hands-on production would give an average of 10.1 days in place of 23.2.

The general point is that, if the *previous* work station to the one we are examining is never in practice more than a week and a half (seven and a half working days) behind where we plan it to be, then there is no reason ever to have any more than a week and a half of backlog at our station as work-in-process inventory.

Now let us return to our supermarket with divided labor and customers as work-in-process inventory. If each customer divides the basket into groceries, meat, and produce, and sends a ten-year-old son with the produce, a nine-year-old daughter with the meat, and stands in the grocery line herself or himself, the total waiting time for the family will be the time in the longest queue of the three. This will on the average be over nine minutes on weekdays, because of the variation between the three queues. We have not given enough information above to calculate the average, but it might well be under the original 12 minutes, and the checking at the end of that line is now only a minute. So by *parallel processing of components* one can get both the advantages of division of labor and the advantages of avoiding sequential queues. The comparable solution in industry is parallel creation of subassemblies or modules, put together at the end. The delay time for changing a model on an assembly line then becomes a delay time on the longest subassembly plus the time for final assembling.

Thus there are three basic separable causes of multiple queues red tape: (a) the breaking up of the processing of a case into separate stages or work stations rather than treating the whole case at one work station, (b) arranging those work stations in series so that the case has to wait in several queues, and (c) not controlling the backlog at work stations by controlling admission to the processing system as a whole so as to minimize "inventories of cases in process." The causes and remedies of this type of red tape, then, are the causes and remedies (a) of breaking up cases into pieces, (b) of arranging those pieces in a series, and (c) of poor control over the accumulation of backlog at each station (or power to control admission to the beginning of the first queue).

(a) There seem in turn to be three subordinate causes of breaking up the processing of a case into work stations. The first is the usual cause of the fine division of labor, that it increases efficiency by allowing each station to become specialized in a particular operation, allowing greater efficiency. Our example of the checkout clerks being able to learn the day's prices for produce, meats, and groceries, but not being able to keep up with them all, is an example. A second cause is that one can use less skilled labor for divided tasks, so that one needs a mechanic to build a whole car, but can use immigrants fresh off the boat on the early assembly lines. The use of medically untrained people to do much of the medical examination of draftees is a case in point, for if any of the tasks require a physician, then if each case is treated as a whole at one station all require a physician.

A third, and perhaps the most pathological, is the unwillingness to delegate the authority for making the decisions to the people who do the tasks the case, so that after all the information is collected and all the relevant commentary and rules are looked up, the case has to go up the hierarchy until it reaches a person who can formally make the decision.

A good example is the process of getting a visa to work in Norway. The actual information needed is collected in two places, in the consulate abroad from the applicant, and in the firm in Norway that wants to do the employing (which has to explain why they cannot find a Norwegian to do the job). The employer actually usually has the information on the applicant but the law requires that one pretend it must be collected abroad. However, the firm does not have *authorization* to say that there are no qualified people available in Norway. This has to be certified by the local section of the police dealing with foreigners, basing themselves on information from the labor department. And the consulate abroad does not have authorization to issue the visas, but instead they have to be issued in Oslo. The result is that the consulate abroad and the firm never get into communication, and obtaining the visa takes several months.

The ultimate cause of such procedural red tape may well be that no Norwegian bureaucrat's career depends on whether he gives good service to foreigners who want jobs in Norway (when

Norwegian employers are desperate for skilled workers, as some-times happens in the oil industry, the process can be speeded up quite a bit). But the direct cause of delay is the lush growth of stages of authority, which causes the breaking up of a single case into stages of information collection and decision approval.

The corresponding remedies are to weigh the loss of efficiency for the client in the multiple queues along with the gain in efficiency of work from breaking up the processing of cases into pieces; to redesign the stages so that they are more tightly locked together so one gets the efficiency without the multiple queues; to hire or train more skilled workers so that they can handle all the work in a given case, and to delegate authority to the people who collect the information or who first review the case, so that there is only one queue in front of the caseworker.

(b) Two subordinate causes seem to account for tying the stages together into a sequence, producing a sequence of queues. The first is technical dependence of one stage on the others, so that the stages cannot be done at the same time but must be done sequentially. Actually this "cause" is really a whole series of heterogeneous causes, ranging from the fact that if the client himself or herself has to be present at the work station (as when draftees are being physically examined) one cannot have him or her simultaneously present in two places, to the fact that the assessment of the physical strength of a structure has to be made *before* one knows whether it will stand up when impaired by x percent by the heat from a fire.

Decisions are very often dependent on information collected at previous stages, so the filling out of a series of forms in the appropriate sequence ensures that all the relevant sub-decisions are in order before the final approval is given. In one case (Usterud, 1976) 14 documents were required by an oil company from a contractor for reimbursement of purchases made on the oil company's behalf, of which six had to have had approval before the charge would be paid. The required six approvals are, of course, refusals to delegate authority, which we have discussed above. But the other eight documents in the sequence are to make sure appropriate information reaches the oil company at the appropriate times, long before the final approval for the charge is made, because oil company decisions depend on the predicted arrival of the machine on order. (For a view from a disgruntled contractor, cf. O. Semb, 1976.)

The other cause of organizing decisions in sequence is that it makes the flow of decisions correspond to the hierarchy of decision, so that no document has to jump levels and no document is referred by a person at one level to a person at a lower level for decision (which would imply subordination of the superior to the inferior). If one has to put useless steps into the work flow to keep low level employees from having access to high level employees, or to put a high status decision maker in between two peers, one of whom has the information on the case and the other of whom has responsibility or expertise for making that sort of decision, then the client will have to wait for his case to go through the extra steps. Many sequential steps are part of the ritual of hierarchy.

(c) Three causes seem to account for managers not controlling the accumulation of backlogs at multiple queues in the process. The first is simply that they have not been taught to think about it, not being in the habit of reading industrial engineering journals or the articles on industry in *Harvard Business Review* (Huge, 1979). The pressures from clients who are mistreated are generally for special treatment of their own case, so that much of what a manager does is not to manage the system as a whole, but to see to it that cases which he or she has flagged get priority treatment at each work station.

The second is that civil servants resist measurement of the amount of time a case has been on their desk. If data on when each civil servant got a case, and when he or she released it to the next step in the sequence, were obtained and analyzed, then rewards could be given for prompt treatment and punishments could be given for delay. This redistributes power from the civil servant to his or her manager. Measuring times of cases in each civil servant's queue is greeted with much the same attitude as the time study engineer with the stopwatch is greeted with on the shop floor (Burawoy, 1979:180-183).

The third subordinate cause of managerial inattention is that the devices for controlling the queue before the first station require political power and authority, and not every manager is in a position to say, "I'm sorry, we won't be able to start on your case until April." But when the case has disappeared into the bowels of his or her organization, it is "in the nature of the work" that it does not appear again until the latter part of April (Huggins, 1973). In a democracy the management of a queue may require substantial resources. It has been alleged that the work that goes into answering complaints and giving information about the queue for new telephones in Norway costs as much as the interest on the capital investment required to eliminate the queue would cost. People in a democracy have a right to complain, and if one keeps them in a queue one has to pay the costs of dealing with the complaints.

The remedies for cases accumulating in the backlogs of multiple queues are then work flow studies to differentiate "hands-on" time from queue time and to reduce queue time, measurement of time lags at specific work stations, and authority to manage the queue.

Physicians and Civil Servants Do Not Wait for Clients, Clients Wait for Them

When Kafka portrays the endless mystery of the bureaucracy, the setting is vague as well, but one gets no impression that the idealized victim of red tape might write his Congressman. The correspondence of Congressmen in the United States is full of letters asking them to be "expeditors" for someone caught in a tangle of red tape, for the Congressman is a main channel by which the reward of an agency or a civil servant can be made, at least theoretically, a function of the irritation the agency or civil servant has caused a client. Authoritarian regimes, or bureaucracies formed under the Hapsburg Empire (even if by Kafka's time their clients were theoretically citizens) have very reduced channels for making a civil servant's career prospects a positive function of the promptness of service his or her clients receive.

While salespeople on a commission hover offensively over one as soon as one enters a used car lot, it takes a concentrated and high status clientele (such as the state civil servants who dealt with the LEAA [Gregg and Diegelman, 1979]) to get overall reduction in the amount of documentation and time that red tape occupies. Similarly when there is an undersupply of physicians, or when the physician is salaried by an emergency room rather than fee for service, one waits until the physician is ready, and the physician never waits for the client. The lower the status of the client, the less the client can make the server's reward depend on prompt service, and the longer the client waits (Schwartz, 1975, and especially 1978a; also Powell, 1978).

Perhaps the most indicative case illustrating this principle is Schwartz's analysis of waiting times for getting a reply from an academic journal (Schwartz, 1975). There is, of course, a very different reward for the editor in finding papers to accept, and arranging to get the final copy in time to get the issue out on time, than for rejecting papers on time. So the correspondence about rejections takes a lot longer than the correspondence about acceptances. That is, decisions that do not reward the editor (rejections) take longer than decisions that do (acceptances). For book publishers Powell indicates that, since an author of low status is probably not going to be published anyway, there are well established ways that editors preempt queues to put high status authors at the top, sometimes to the point of not even letting anyone else into the queue – in that case of course, the low status author does not wait very long, for all the good it does him or her (Powell, 1978).

The general problem is to make the reward of a civil servant a decreasing function of the amount of delay, extra useless form filing, runaround, and general irritation they cause clients. Clearly the first requirement is that civil servants' rewards be made dependent on some sort of performance measurement, rather than political party services, scores on civil service examinations, or currying favor with their supervisors. But this in turn depends on effective measurement of the delays or useless paperwork that are the responsibility of particular people, which depends in *its* turn on being able to identify responsibilities for delays and paperwork and collecting information on them. There are two broad classes of causes of lack of motivation to save clients' time: (a) rigidities in the reward system so that it cannot be made dependent on satisfying clients, and (b) inadequacies in the performance measurement system so that the punishments cannot be allocated to the person responsible for the most client trouble.

(a) Perhaps the purest case of rigidities in the reward system is the administrative system for parts of the work that have been subcontracted out, because then the rewards are fixed by contract. Bent (1979) estimates that in construction projects subcontracting (rather than direct hire by the oil company of workers in all the different crafts) adds from 10 to 20 percent extra to the total time required (Bent, 1979:Fig. 6, no page number), and that it adds 25 percent extra to the space required per workers because the work cannot be as closely coordinated (Bent, 1979:Fig. 18, no page number). Thus in this case the added delay and the added difficulty of motivating people to stay out of each other's way has a physical measurement. And this is in spite of the fact that one describes the work better, and further in advance, if one is going to use subcontracting than if one can rely on authoritative communication to workers when one changes one's mind later on. With better early information one might anticipate faster performance through subcontracts. The reason for greater difficulties in coordination is that the subcontractor's reward does not depend on how much trouble it makes for other subcontractors, so it does not make the workers' rewards depend on coordination of schedules and keeping out of others' way. This results in the organizational advice that if two activities have to be coordinated, they should be packaged together into the same subcontract (Tovshus, 1976).

The general causes of rigidity of reward systems in the civil service are civil service regulations. While it is normal that larger organizations have more formalization of all aspects of their functioning, the rigidity of the specifications about how civil servants' rewards are to be determined undoubtedly has its origin in the suspicion that otherwise they will line their pockets, or in the suspicion that politicians will make the rewards dependent on political loyalty if they are not made rigid. Once the systems are rigidified, of course, trade union pressures tend to prevent introducing "arbitrary" judgment of performance into the career fates of their members. When it is difficult to measure performance, all attempts to make rewards dependent on performance require "arbitrary" judgment.

(b) But perhaps a deeper problem is that unlike the used car lot, the government does not normally have a good measure of whether the service to the client was satisfactory. One cannot make reward, even informal reward, depend on performances that cannot be observed. There is remarkably little in the way of effort to get information fed back to the people causing the waiting (or the useless documentation) about how much it is costing the client. I was for example shocked (because it had never occurred to me it was possible) to see a sign at the University of Arizona Hospital telling clients that if they have not been called within a half an hour, they should check back with the desk. This is such a simple device to create a minor inconvenience in the lives of the clerks (and I suppose, through the clerks, in the lives of the nurses and physicians) if people have to wait too long, thus making costs to the bureaucrat increase with delay for the client. Even such measuring devices for client inconvenience, the proportion waiting more than half an hour, are uncommon, let alone devices to bring the delay to the attention of the bureaucrats who should solve the problem.

Similarly, requiring people to initial and date a routing slip when a case has to pass a series of stations provides the bureaucrats' superiors with easily accessible records of sources of delays. Requiring a memo to be attached to the routing slip if there were more than a couple of day's delays, explaining why it took so long, would increase the costs of forgetting to process a case, and also provide diagnostic information about serious causes of delays, delays not due to inattention. The key here is the institution of simple measuring devices that will locate delays and pin them on a responsible person.

Information demands by agencies grow because the agency that requires the information does not have to pay for its collection. In general, cost accountants within firms do not require a lot of information they do not plan to use, because they have to pay for it. If they might sometime use some extra information, they will wait until that time and commission a special study to collect it (see Stinchcombe, 1974:23-29, especially 25). In the case described by Gregg and Diegelman (1979) cutting in half the information requirements involved complaint by powerful state officials, and while it is not quite clear from the account, it is probable that the requests for funds (averaging several hundreds of pages) were filled out by people whose salaries ultimately came from the granting agency. That is, there was an unusual amount of feedback on the costs of the requirements to the agency that created the requirements. The costs of, for example, environmental impact statements paid by companies exploiting natural resources are not paid by the administrators of the National Environmental Policy Act, let alone by the environmental groups who challenge their inadequacy in court. Some of these information requirements are, however, sufficiently routinized that they only have to be typed again for each submission – these are commonly referred to as "boilerplate" in the survey research business, and roughly half of a survey research proposal consists of such redundant information.

To make rewards of a civil servant a negative function of red tape, one needs a measure of the red tape generated by the civil servant, and the rewards of civil servants cannot be rigidly fixed. The causes of rigidity and of poor measurement of red tape are therefore the causes of delays and paperwork.

Policymaking Time as Delay

The third origin of delay and excessive information requirements is policy uncertainty. Some bureaucrats are too timid to take decisions, and there are structural sources of timidity. The rule for keeping your nose clean in a bureaucracy might be formulated as: "Never take a decision against which anyone (anyone who has to be listened to) can offer any reasonable-sounding objection." Where such a rule is formalized, as in the court system, very long delays may be caused by continuances, rationalized by a wide variety of reasonable-sounding objections to going ahead and deciding.

But it is not only bureaucrats who act this way; such delays are very common in legislatures. In fact the provisions for making sure one has heard all sides and that all relevant interests have had a chance to have their influence are generally more extensive in legislatures than in bureaucracies.

An especially clear case is the delay of the development of the Alta river basin in Norway, which will disrupt reindeer herding patterns of Lapps. The government had a clear parliamentary majority for going ahead, consisting of the (ruling) Labor Party and the opposition Right Party, with the various center parties and the far left party supporting the Lapps. But when the Lapps carried out a vigorous demonstration against the project, the government postponed the decision for a year to consider it further. The same proposition was passed with the same majority a year later. The year delay was out of respect for the rights of all interested parties, and particularly of the Lapps, to represent their points of view fully and effectively.

In general, then, there will be delays in administrative matters whenever formal or informal legislation has to be passed between the submission of the application and the decision on the case. Or to put it another way, the more uncertain it is under the existing policies and regulations what the outcome of a decision will be, in general, the longer the decision will take, and the more decision-work it will create in the form of creating information, soliciting opinions, negotiating, and the like.

Probably two main causes produce policy uncertainty in a given area: (a) conflicts between objectives, where detailed tradeoffs have to be worked out in a multitude of particular cases, as with environmental protection or affirmative action in the United States, and (b) a shifting situation confronting the government over time, as with the regulation of the oil resources in the North Sea for the Norwegian government.

(a) Both environmental protection and affirmative action have turned out to be regulations of the procedure by which decisions are made. The idea behind the procedures is that the authorities who decide these matters have to be able to show that they have considered the values of minimizing damage to the environment, or of abolishing discrimination in the labor market, while making decisions whose main purpose is exploitation of resources or effective hiring. While one might not expect the recruitment process in an engineering school to produce as many female or black candidates for an opening as one would expect in a sociology department, one wants the appointing authorities in *both* cases to be able to show that they have considered carefully the tradeoffs between the fastest methods to find an acceptable candidate, and the methods which equalize chances between the races and between the sexes. Similarly while the concrete problems of environmental damage from disposing of nuclear wastes are very different from those of disposing of hot gases and particles from a coal fired generator, we want electric utilities to be able to show that they have considered our costs in living with radiation and with smoke when deciding on how to build the plant.

In particular, in order to distribute power to the representatives of different interests in such dispersed decisions, it is often explicitly provided that they shall have time to collect evidence, challenge conclusions, or appeal decisions to the courts. It is an empty right to have your interests considered, if you have no control over how adequately they have to be considered before the decision is taken. The right to call a delay in decision making is therefore a necessary part of every grant of powers to affect a decision. Clearly the grants of powers to environmentalists to delay decisions until a court decides that the environmental impact statement is adequate has been a central source of delay in many American government and industrial projects (Taylor, 1984: Appendix E). But clearly also if the level of incompetence and one-sidedness of the environmental impact statements provided in the first years after the Environmental Protection Act had been tolerated with no right to delay projects, environmental considerations would still be of small weight in our policy making.

Thus delays in situations where tradeoffs have to be worked out in a variety of different concrete circumstances have two sorts of subordinate causes. The first is the elaboration of procedures required to show that everything has been considered in every decision, and been considered sufficiently well that we can have confidence in the resulting tradeoff. The stretching out of university recruitment by an extra two or three months, and in particular the necessity for reviewing thoroughly the materials of absolutely hopeless cases, are clear examples of this elaboration.

The second subordinate cause is that in order to distribute the right for an interest to be considered in a decision, one has to distribute the right to delay that decision until that interest is in fact considered. Such interests then do indeed make use of the right to delay decisions. The growth of documentation to show that one has followed the elaborated procedure, and to answer the objections of those who have petitioned for a delay until they are satisfied, has the same two sorts of causes.

(b) But the policy uniqueness of cases can come from shifting policy as well as from distinctiveness of the cases. The Norwegian government quite deliberately set out to have a shifting policy over time for regulating their oil fields. They knew they could not very well develop the first fields, because they had no oil engineering experience, no experienced companies, no petroleum curricula in their engineering or business administration schools. But because they were both Norwegian nationalists and socialists, they wanted to end up, several decades hence, being able to run their own oil fields under Norwegian governmental ownership. Consequently they wanted to have a different ownership structure in each field, to have a different weight of American and British versus Norwegian expertise and supply contracts in each, to have a different division of the profits between multi-national capitalism, the Norwegian state, and the Norwegian people as time went on. To put it another way, except in trivial matters the Norwegian government did not want to have regulations, but instead wanted to make policy on a case-by-case basis. And that in turn meant that they wanted to make policy in each case, *between* the time the oil company submitted a proposal, and the time they settled on what the oil company was going to do.

Perhaps the clearest case of this involves also the tradeoff between safety and expense in the Statfjord field, which is managed by Mobil for an owner group in which the Norwegian state oil company has an effective veto (Moe et al., 1980:205-206). The first platform (Statfjord A) was designed and approved and under construction when the second design (Statfjord B) was submitted to the Norwegian Petroleum Directorate for approval. The design was in most respects similar to the design for Statfjord A, and in particular the safety features were very similar. But the Norwegian government decided that this was not after all safe enough, that having the residential quarters on the same platform with drilling and production meant that risks in drilling and production would also threaten all the crews, and not only the crews working in the immediate area.

It took approximately a year, and a great many engineering hours, to come to an agreement about how off-duty workers were to be protected from the effects of a catastrophic accident in the drilling and production end, and the costs of the platform that was approved were very much higher (besides Moe, see Medley, 1979). While part of the complication came from trying to work out tradeoffs between the two objectives of safety and engineering "reasonableness," much of the delay was due to the fact that the Norwegian government was changing its mind about what standards ought to be applied. In fact it was several years later (February, 1979) before the Petroleum Directorate issued its first "regulations" on safety, the "Preliminary Guidelines" for safety evaluation of platform design (Norwegian Petroleum Directorate, 1979). Even these do not specify clearly the safety tradeoffs. They only specify the materials required to be submitted for consideration in policy-making on the particular design proposal.

The result of this situation of systematically shifting policy is that the Petroleum Directorate (and the Royal Ministry of Oil and Energy) are not really regulatory authorities, but rather co-participants in the decision process. They and the oil companies come to an agreement on policy for each field, or in this case for each platform within the field. Formally speaking this process involves legislation in the *Storting*, in which the field development plan for each field is approved. But this formal legislation is the tip of the iceberg, and most of the mass of making of the new policy for each field is below the parliamentary surface, in the Ministry and the Oil Directorate.

The case we mentioned earlier of the gas field that stretched over into the British sector, in which it took the Norwegians a year longer to approve the plans than it did for the British, shows the procedural side of this policy making delay. For it is formally required that the oil company show, *to the satisfaction of the Norwegian government*, that their marketing plan is the one most advantageous to the Norwegians. If a government has not made up its mind what is most advantageous beforehand (as the British had), then requiring a year of study and consideration to make up one's mind about several billions of dollars is not an unreasonable allowance.

What the Norwegians have done, more or less gradually, is to speed up their own procedures inside the Oil Directorate for making policy in a hurry, by appointing "expediters" for each major case that has to be decided, by setting themselves goals of the time it should take, and otherwise by trying to organize themselves as an efficient "legislature." Agile policy making structures, with the courage and competence to balance interests and the political standing to make their decisions on new policy stick, are required to decrease red tape caused by policy uncertainty.

Conclusion

Delay in getting a decision, or "red tape," is not a variable that has been defined so as to be a "clinical entity," a disease with a single cause and a single remedy. Similarly to say that endless forms and information requirements are features of "bureaucracy" collapses the analysis into a single cause, which only covers the variety of cases because the cause is so vaguely described. In this essay I have tried to specify three broad classes of causes of "red tape," of excessive delay in getting a decision out of a bureaucracy and of excessive requirements of documentation, *"la paperas-serie."*

In general I have concentrated on the non-pathological causes, because I believe that the ordinary democratic process ought to be able to handle pathologies. While it may be the case that timid bureaucrats sometimes delay a decision because they do not want to say no and hence to give the client a chance to object, I do not believe the mass of waiting for bureaucrats can be analyzed by appeal to such special pathological causes. I have considered red tape to be a normal product of common features of bureaucracy.

But I have also specified three rather distinct causes, which vary from one situation to another and from one bureaucracy to another. Insofar as red tape has the three distinct causal origins I have suggested, it will require different remedies. Learning to make policy more rapidly is perhaps just what the Norwegian Petroleum Directorate should do to reduce decision delays, but it will not reduce our standing in multiple lines when we get a physical for Selective Service.

The three origins I have suggested are the arrangement of the decision work into stages, and the accumulation of a queue of unfinished work before each of the stages; the rigidity of rewards of civil servants and the lack of measurement of delays caused to clients, resulting in a bureaucrat's rewards not being negatively affected by his or her causing a client's delay; and policy uncertainty, causing the delays of legislating to be inserted between application for a decision and issuance of the decision.

Generally speaking the remedies for the multiple queues delays is industrial engineering, either by consolidating serial treatment so one waits in only one queue, or by reducing the intermediate inventories of "work in process." Delays caused by bureaucratic rewards not being in congruence with bureaucratic purpose can be improved first of all by measuring client delays as a routine administrative procedure, and secondly by making rewards and punishments – even slight punishments such as having the client come back up to the desk every half hour – dependent on avoiding client delays. Delays caused by making policy between the application for a decision and its issuance ultimately require political remedies, figuring out how to make policy beforehand for the bulk of the cases so that the decision can be an application of a regulation rather than an occasion for legislation, or creating agile and effective negotiations and policy-making structures.

Similarly, of course, research on red tape should have as its first stage a diagnosis of which general kind of cause is operating, because in one case one should study work flows, in another one should study feedback from performance to reward, and in another still one should study the sources of policy uncertainty.

At a more fundamental level, perhaps, delays are always caused by relative indifference to the convenience of the person or organization delayed. Used car lots competing with the lot across the street do not put clients in multiple queues, make sure salesmen (if not repairmen in their shops) are rewarded for satisfying clients, and make policy ahead of time on what deal they will make "just especially for you." That is, they avoid all the causes of delays, because if they do not the client will go across the street. Increasing the delays that environmentalists can cause for development projects means increasing the relative weight of environmental over developmental considerations, as well as delaying the developers, but it does reflect downgrading the rights of developers to expeditious treatment. The multiple queues in the physical examination line are merely the first of a series of long queues for the draftee, all in an atmosphere of massive contempt for his welfare. We arrange for Congressmen's and Congresswomen's rewards to decline if they do not serve their constituents, showing that we can arrange bureaucratic rewards congruent with bureaucratic purpose as well, if we choose. The ultimate cause of all three immediate causes of bureaucratic delay and paperwork is political indifference to people waiting.

BIBLIOGRAPHY

Aagaard, P.M., and C.P.Besse
1973 "A review of the offshore environment – 25 years of progress."
     Journal of Petroleum Technology 25 (December):1355-1360.

Ager-Hanssen, Henrik
n.d. "North Sea cost escalation." Paper delivered in Houston.

Alchian, Armen and Harold Demsetz
1972 "Production, information costs, and economic organization."
     American Economic Review 62 No. 5 (December):777-795.

Allman, Eric and Michael Stonebreaker
1982 "Observations on the evolution of a software system." Computer 15
     (June):31.

Barlaup, Asbjørn (ed.)
1976 Det Norske Veritas, 1864-1964. Oslo: Det norske Veritas.

Barnard, Chester I.
1946 "Functions and pathology of status systems in formal organiza-
     tions." Pp. 46-83 in William F. Whyte, ed., Industry and Society.
     New York; London: McGraw-Hill.

Becker, Gary S.
1975 Human Capital. Second Edition. Chicago: University of Chicago
     Press.

Becker, Gary S. and George J. Stigler
1974 "Law enforcement, malfeasance, and compensation of enforcers."
     Journal of Legal Studies 3 No. 1 (January):1-18.

Bent, Jamie
1979 "Cost and planning engineering for North Sea projects." Stavanger,
     Norway: Norwegian Association of Cost and Planning Engineers,
     Transactions of their first annual meeting, April 3.

Blau, Peter
1955 The Dynamics of Bureaucracy. Chicago: University of Chicago
1963 Press.

Blaug, Mark
1974 "The empirical status of human capital theory: a slightly jaundiced survey." Journal of Economic Literature 14 (January):827-855.

Blauner, Robert
1964 Alienation and Freedom. Chicago: University of Chicago Press.

Borch, Karl
1976 "The monster in Loch Ness." Journal of Risk and Insurance 43 (September):521-525.

Brooks, Frederic P.
1975 The Mythical Man-Month: Essays on Software Engineering. Reading, MA: Addison-Wesley Publishing Co.

Burawoy, Michael
1979 Manufacturing Consent: Changes in the Labor Process under Monopoly Capitalism. Chicago: University of Chicago Press.
1980 "The politics production and the production of politics: a comparative analysis of piecework machine shops in the United States and Hungary." Political Power and Social Theory 1:261-300.

Caplette, Michele
1982 "Women in book publishing: a qualified success story." Pp. 148-174 in Lewis A. Coser, Charles Kadushin, and Walter W. Powell, Books: The Culture and Commerce of Publishing. New York: Basic Books.

Charlton, Joy C.
1983 "Secretaries and bosses: the social organization of office work." Unpublished Ph.D. dissertation. Northwestern University.

Coase, R. H.
1937 "The nature of the firm." Economica 4:386-405.

Cohen, Linda
1979 "Innovation and atomic energy: nuclear power regulation, 1966 to the present." Law and Contemporary Problems 43 No. 1:67-96.

Cole, Robert
1979 Work, Mobility, and Participation: A Comparative Study of American and Japanese Industry. Berkeley: University of California Press.

Commons, John R.
1924 Legal Foundations of Capitalism. New York: Macmillan.

Cooper, Bryan, and T.F. Gaskell
1976 The Adventure of North Sea Oil. London: Heinemann.

Coulam, Robert
1977 Illusions of Choice: The F-111 and the Problems of Weapon Acquisition Reform. Princeton, N.J.: Princeton University Press.

Dahl, Robert A. and Charles E. Lindblom
1976 Politics, Economics, and Welfare: Planning and
c1953 Politico-Economic Systems Resolved into Basic Social Processes. New York: Harper.

Davis, Kingsley, and Wilbert E. Moore
1945 "Some principles of stratification." American Sociological Review 10 (April):242-249.

Det norske Veritas
1977 Consequences Analysis of Arrangement of Drilling and Production Platforms with Living Quarters. Report #54-26-15-A.
1978 Risk of Blow-Out Accidents of the Norwegian Continental Shelf: An Investigation Carried Out for the Royal Ministry of Petroleum and Energy.

Donovan, L. J., and J. J. Owen III
1977 "A method to estimate the pollution risk and cost of OCS oil transportation." Journal of Petroleum Technology 29 (June):639-648.

Elvik, Halvor
n.d.   Dagbladet. Oslo.

Engineering Management Commission of Engineers Joint Council
1977 The Placement of Engineering and Technology Graduates. New York.

Fjeld, Svein
1978 "Reliability of offshore structures." Journal of Petroleum Technology 30 (October):1486-1496.

Frihagen, Arvid
1979 Vilkår ved Utvinningstillatelser. Bergen: Universitetsforlaget.

Gebelein, C. A., C.E. Pearson, and M. Silbergh
1978 "Assessing political risk of oil investment ventures." Journal of Petroleum Technology 30 (May): 725-730.

Glenn, Evelyn Nakano and Roslyn L. Feldberg
1977 "Degraded and deskilled: the proletarianization of clerical work." Social Problems 25 (October):52-64.

Gouldner, Alvin W.
1952 "Red tape as a social problem." Pp. 410-418 in R. K. Merton and others, Reader in Bureaucracy. Glencoe, Illinois; New York: The Free Press.

Granick, David
1954 Management of the Industrial Firm in the USSR. New York: Columbia University Press.

1967 Soviet Metal Fabricating and Economic Development. Madison: University of Wisconsin Press.

Granovetter, Mark
1973 "The strength of weak ties." American Journal of Sociology 78 No. 6:1360-1380.
1974 Getting a Job: A Study of Contacts and Careers. Cambridge: Harvard University Press.
1983 "Labor mobility, internal markets and job matching: a comparison of the sociological and economic approaches." Unpublished paper. State University of New York at Stony Brook.

Greene, Mark R.
1973 Risk and Insurance. Third Edition. Cincinnati: South-Western Publishing.

Gregg, James J. H. and Robert F. Diegelman
1979 "Red tape on trial: elements of a successful effort to cut burdensome federal reporting requirements." Public Administration Review 39 No. 2:171-176.

Heimer, Carol A.
1981 Reactive Risk and Rational Action: Managing Behavioral Risk in Insurance. Chicago: Unpublished Ph.D. dissertation. Published in revised form by University of California Press, 1985.
1980 Substitutes for Experience-Based Information: The Case of Offshore Oil Insurance in the North Sea. Discussion Paper No. 1/81 Bergen, Norway: Institute of Industrial Economics. Xeroxed publication. Reprinted in revised form as Chapter 3 of this volume.

Hesselmann, Christian
n.d.   The Norwegian Oil Risk Pool. Bergen, Norway: Vesta Hygea. Photocopy.

Holm, Tore
1982 "Virkninger for industrien av oljesektorens rekruttering av teknisk personell." Arbeidsrapport 45, Bergen, Norway: Industriøkonomisk Institutt.

Huge, Ernest C.
1979 "Managing manufacturing lead times." Harvard Business Review (September-October):116-123.

Huggins, W. H.
1973 "We need bottlenecks." Intellectual Digest 4:53-54.

Institute of Electrical and Electronic Engineers, Inc.
1975 JEEE 1975 U.S. Membership Salary, Fringe Benefits, and Opinion Survey. New York. Prepared by Hughes Associates, Inc.

Jaques, Elliott
1972 The Measurement of Responsibility: A Study of Work,
c1956 Payment, and Individual Capacity. New York: Wiley.

Kanter, Rosabeth Moss
1977 Men and Women of the Corporation. New York: Basic Books.

Kidder, Tracy.
1981 The Soul of a New Machine. New York: Avon.

Klein, Benjamin, Robert G. Crawford, and Armen A. Alchian.
1978 "Vertical integration, appropriable rents, and the competive contracting process." Journal of Law and Economics 21:297-326.

Kreiner, Kristian
1976 The Site Organization: A Study of Social Relationships on Construction Sites. Unpublished dissertation at the Technological University of Denmark.

Lindblom, Charles E.
1959 "The science of 'muddling through.'" Public Administration Review 19 (Spring):78-88.
1977 Politics and Markets: The World's Economic Systems. New York: Basic Books.

Lockwood, David
1958 The Blackcoated Worker: A Study in Class Consciousness. London: Allen and Unwin.

Lund, Morten
1978 "The insurance of fixed production installations in the North Sea – with special reference to insurances covering the construction period." Trans. by Nicolas Wilmot. Part 6 in Mads Krohn. Knut Kaasen, Morten Lund, John Rein, and Petter Chr. Sogn, Norwegian Petroleum Law. Oslo: Scandinavian Institute for Maritime Law.

Macaulay, Stewart
1963 "Non-contractual relations in business: a preliminary study." American Sociological Review 28 (February):55-66.
1966 Law and the Balance of Power: The Automobile Manufacturers and Their Dealers. New York: Russell Sage Foundation.

Mansfield, Edwin, John Rapoport, Anthony Romeo, Samuel Wagner, and George Beardsley
1977 "Social and private rates of return from industrial innovations." Quarterly Journal of Economics 91:221-240.

March, James C. and James G. March
1978 "Performance sampling in social matches." Administrative Science Quarterly 25 No. 3:434-453.

Marschak, Thomas, Thomas K. Blennan Jr., and Robert Summers
1967 Strategy for R & D: Studies in the Microeconomics of Development. Berlin; New York: Springer.

Medley, E. J.
1979a Interview, Teknisk Ukeblad, 126 aargang, nr. 22, for 18 May.
1979b Bergen Norsk Petroleums Forening, meeting. Bergen, 22 May 1979.

Miller, Ian H.
1978 "Bygging av forskjellige plattformtyper på land, ved land, til havs."
      NIF proceedings of a conference at Fagernes Hotell, 5-7 June 1978.

Mincer, Jacob
1974 Schooling, Experience, and Earnings. New York: National Bureau of
      Economic Research.

Moe, Johannes, et al.
1980 Kostnads Analysen: Norsk Kontinentalsokkel, Del I and II. (Cost
      Analysis: Norwegian Continental Shelf, Part I and II.) Oslo, Norway:
      Royal Ministry of Oil and Energy, 29 April.

Moses, F., and B. Stahl
1979 "Reliability analysis format for offshore structures. " Journal of Pe-
      troleum Technology 40 (March): 347-354.

Mostacci-Calzavera, Liviana
1982 "Social networks and access to job opportunities." Unpublished
      Ph.D. dissertation. University of Toronto.

Nelson, Richard R. and Sidney G. Winter
1982 An Evolutionary Theory of Economic Change. Cambridge, MA:
      Belknap Press of Harvard University Press.

Newhouse, John
1982a The Sporty Game. New York: Knopf.
1982b I "Betting the company." New Yorker (June 14):48-105.
1982c II "Turbulent." New Yorker (June 21):46-93.
1982d III "Big, bigger, jumbo." New Yorker (June 28):45-86.
1982e IV "A hole in the market." New Yorker (July 5):44-89.

Norges Teknisk-Naturvitenskapelige Forskningsråd
1980 "Risikovurdering." Rapport Nr. 26-27, Sikkerhet på sokkelen.
      Trondheim: Norges Teknisk-Naturvitenskaplige Forskningsråd.

NOROIL
1980a "Safety." NOROIL 7 (April):31-32.
1980b "Safety regulations." NOROIL 7 (April):33-35.

Norwegian Petroleum Directorate
1978 Regulations for Instrumentation, Recording and Processing of
      E(environmental)- and P(platform)-Data.
1979 Guidance for Evaluation of Platform Conceptual Design. No. 23.
      Stavanger, Norway: Norwegian Petroleum Directorate.

Okun, Arthur
1980 Prices and Quantities. Washington, D.C.: Brookings.

Oppenheimer, Valerie Kincade
1973 "Demographic influence on female employment and the status of women." Pp. 184-199 in Joan Huber (ed.), Changing Women in a Changing Society. Chicago: University of Chicago Press.

Oxford, Gilbert E.
1965 "Ratemaking, underwriting, and loss adjustment in marine insurance." Pp. 285-301 in John D. Long and Davis W. Gregg (eds.), Property and Liability Insurance Handbook. Homewood, IL: Richard D. Irwin.

Page, John S. and Jim G. Nation
1976 Estimator's Piping Man-Hour Manual. 3rd Ed. (Estimator's Man-Hour Library). Gulf and Western Publishing.

Parsons, Talcott
1962 "The professions and social structure." Pp. 34-49 in Essays in Social Theory. New York: Free Press.

Peck, Merton J. and Frederic M. Scherer
1962 The Weapons Acquisition Process: An Economic Analysis. Boston: Division of Research, Graduate School of Business Administration, Harvard University.

Pfeffer, Jeffrey
1977 "Towards an examination of stratification in organizations." Administrative Science Quarterly 20 No. 4:553-567.

Piore, Michael J.
1975 "Notes for a theory of labor market stratification." Pp. 125-150 in Richard C. Edwards, Michael Reich, and David M. Gordon (eds.), Labor Market Segmentation. Lexington, MA: Heath.

Powell, Walter W.
1978 "Publishers' decision-making: what criteria do they use in deciding which books to publish?" Social Research 45 No. 2:227-252.

Reiersen, Eivind
1978 Paper delivered at NIF Conference, Fagernes Hotell, 5-7 June 1978.

Reve, Torger and Egil Johansen
1982 "Oganizational buying in the offshore oil industry." Industrial Marketing Management 11 No. 4 (October):275-282.

Reve, Torger and Ray Levitt
1983 "Organization and governance in construction." Stanford, CA: Stanford University. Unpublished paper.

Rosenbaum, James
1981 "Careers in a corporate hierarchy." In Donald J. Treiman and Robert V. Robinson (eds.), Research in Social Stratification and Mobility. Greenwich, CT: JAI Press.

Ross, Stephen A.
1973 "The economic theory of agency: the principal's problem." American Economic Review 63 (May):134-139.

Schelling, Thomas C.
1960 The Strategy of Conflict. London: Oxford University Press.

Scherer, Frederic M.
1964 The Weapons Acquisition Process: Economic Incentives. Boston: Division of Research, Graduate School of Business Administration, Harvard University.

Schwartz, Barry
1975 Queueing and Waiting: Studies in the Social Organization of Access and Delay. Chicago: University of Chicago Press.
1978a "The social ecology of time barriers." Social Forces 56 No. 4 (June): 1203-1220.
1978b "Queues, priorities, and social process." Social Psychology 41 No. 1:3-12.

Selznick, Philip, Philippe Nonet, and Howard Vollmer
1969 Law, Society, and Industrial Justice. New York: Russell Sage Foundation.

Semb, O.
1976 "Leveranse av utstyr, "Case" – en presentasjon av en leveranse." NIF, Kontinentalsokkelen, Conference held at Gausdal Høyfjellshotell, 8-10 November 1976.

Shack-Marquez, Janice and Ivar Berg
1982 "Inside information and employer-employee matching processes." Fels Discussion Paper 159. School of Public and Urban Policy. University of Pennsylvania.

Sharp, Walter Rice
1952 "Procedural vices: *la paperasserie*." Pp. 407-410 in R. K. Merton and others, Reader in Bureaucracy. Glencoe, IL; New York: The Free Press. Reprinted from Sharp, The French Civil Service: Bureaucracy in Transition. New York: Macmillan, 1931, pp. 446-450.

Simon, Herbert
1957a "A formal theory of employment relation." Pp. 183-195 in Simon (1957b)
1976 Administrative Behavior. Third Edition. New York: Free Press.

Somers, G. and M. Tsuda
1966 "Job vacancies and structural changes in Japanese labor markets." In R. Ferber (ed.), The Measurement and Interpretation of Job Vacancies. New York: Columbia University Press.

St. Amant, L. S.
1972 "The petroleum industry as it affects marine and estuarine ecology." Journal of Petroleum Technology 25 (April):385-392.

Statoil
1982 Project Organization Guide. Stavanger, Norway: Statoil.

Stinchcombe, Arthur L.
1959 "Bureaucratic and craft administration of production." Administrative Science Quarterly 4 (September):108-187.
1974 Creating Efficient Industrial Administrations. New York: Academic Press.
1979 "Delays and project administration in the North Sea." Bergen, Norway: Institute of Industrial Economics. Xeroxed publication. Reprinted slightly revised as Chapter 1 in this volume.
1980 "Delays in government approvals in the Norwegian offshore development." Bergen, Norway: Institute of Industrial Economics. Xeroxed publication. Reprinted slightly revised as Chapter 6 in this volume.
1982 "The deep structures of moral categories, eighteenth century French stratification, and the revolution." Pp. 62-95 in Ino Rossi, (ed.), Structural Sociology. New York: Columbia University Press.
1983 Contracts as Hierarchical Documents. Stanford: Stanford Graduate School of Business. Unpublished. Reprinted slightly revised as Chapter 2 in this volume.
1984 "Authority and the management of engineering on large projects." Bergen: Institute of Industrial Economics. Xeroxed publication. Reprinted slightly revised as Chapter 4 of this volume.

Stockfisch, Jacob A.
1973 Plowshares into Swords: Managing the American Defense Establishment. New York: Mason & Lipscomb.

Stortingsmelding
1980 Stortingsmelding Nr. 53. (1979-80).

Storvik, Kåre
1976 Paper delivered at NIF, Kontinentalsokkelen conference, held at Gausdal Høyfjellshotel, 8-10 November 1976.

Summerskill, Michael
1979 Oil Rigs: Law and Insurance. London: Stevens and Sons.

Taira, Koji
1970 Economic Develoment and the Labor Market in Japan. New York: Columbia University Press.

Taylor, Serge
1984 Making Bureaucracies Think: The Environmental Impact Statement Strategy of Administrative Reform. Palo Alto: Stanford University Press.

Teece, David J.
1976 Vertical Integration and Divestiture in the U.S. Oil Industry. Stanford: Stanford Institute for Energy Research.

1981 Asset Revaluations and the Appropriability of Returns from Inventive Activity. Stanford Business Research Paper No. 425.

Thompson, James D.
1967 Organizations in Action. New York: McGraw-Hill.

Toong, Hoo-Min and Amar Gupta
1982 "Personal computers." Scientific American 247 No. 6 (December):86-107.

Tovshus, K.
1976 "Entreprenørens syn på entrepriseform og prosjektorganisasjon." NIF, Kontinentalsokkelen. Conference held at Gausdal Høyfjellshotell, 8-10 November 1976.

Tronstad, Leif
1979 "Insurance." Chapter in Description of Framework for the Petroleum Activity on the Shelf.

Tveit, Odd, Bjørn Myklatun, Torstein Bohler, and Odd Vesterhaug
1980 "Risk analysis of a typical North Sea petroleum production platform." Proceedings, Offshore Technology Conference:501-508.

Tversky, Amos, and Daniel Kahneman
1974 "Judgment under uncertainty: heuristics and biases." Science 185:1124-1131.

United Nations Conference on Trade and Development
1978 Marine Insurance: Legal and Documentary Aspects of the Marine Insurance Contract.

Usterud, O.
1976 "Administrative prosedyrer og rutiner i forbindelse med entreprenørens og byggherrens samarbeid i byggeperioden (entreprenørens syn.)" NIF, Kontinentalsokkelen, Conference held at Gausdal Høyfjellshotell, 8-10 November 1976.

Williamson, Oliver E.
1975 Markets and Hierarchies: Analysis and Antitrust Implications. New York: Free Press.
1979 "Transaction cost economics: the governance of contractual relations." Journal of Law and Economics 22 (October):233-261.

Wilmot, Nicolas
1975 The Contract of Marine Insurance in English and Norwegian Law. Bergen, Norway: Institutt for Privatrett.

Winter, William D.
1952 Marine Insurance. Third Edition. New York: McGraw Hill.

Zeruvabel, Eviatar
1976 "Timetables and scheduling: on the social organization of time." Sociological Inquiry 46:87-94.

INDEX